ColdFusion® 5:
A Beginner's Guide

Jeffry Houser

McGraw-Hill/Osborne

New York   Chicago   San Francisco
Lisbon   London   Madrid   Mexico City   Milan
New Delhi   San Juan   Seoul   Singapore   Sydney   Toronto

McGraw-Hill/Osborne
2600 Tenth Street
Berkeley, California 94710
U.S.A.

To arrange bulk purchase discounts for sales promotions, premiums, or fund-raisers, please contact Osborne/McGraw-Hill at the above address. For information on translations or book distributors outside the U.S.A., please see the International Contact Information page immediately following the index of this book.

ColdFusion® 5: A Beginner's Guide

1234567890 CUS CUS 01987654321

ISBN 0-07-219109-0

Publisher   Brandon A. Nordin
Vice President & Associate Publisher   Scott Rogers
Acquisitions Editor   Jim Schachterle
Project Editor   Elizabeth Seymour
Acquisitions Coordinator   Timothy Madrid
Technical Editor   Chris Faure
Copy Editor   Marcia Baker
Proofreader   Marian Selig
Indexer   Robert J. Richardson
Computer Designers   Tara A. Davis, John Patrus
Illustrator   Michael Mueller, Lyssa Wald
Series Design   Gary Corrigan
Cover Design   Greg Scott
Cover Illustration   Kevin Curry

This book was composed with Corel VENTURA™ Publisher.

Fresh out of college, I worked as one of the tech guys at a small advertising firm that specialized in business-to-business print advertising. As a member of the team that helped to ramp up the Web side of the business, I became close friends with many of the team members. When the company hit upon bad times, the project manager of our team was the first person to get the axe. The president of the company called me into his office after a morning meeting to reassure me that the company would recover. This one-on-one pow-wow lasted just long enough to prevent me from saying goodbye to my beloved coworker.
She was gone by the time I got out.

This book is to dedicated to Nicole

About the Author

Jeffry Houser has been working in web development for seven years. He graduated with a computer science degree from Central Connecticut State University in 1997. He accumulated a wide range of experience as the tech guy at a small advertising firm, and with numerous technologies including Lotus Notes, iCat, and ColdFusion, touching upon various aspects of the IT world including application and web development, server administration, and help desk support. Jeffry has achieved certification in both Lotus Notes and ColdFusion.

Jeffry started the company DotComIt in 2000. Its unique business model is designed to offer development help for developers. DotComIt works mainly with small web development firms that are lacking in technical skill, and with corporate IT departments.

In his spare time, Jeffry plays guitar as half of Connecticut's premiere original alternative folk rock duo, Far Cry Fly. You can check out Far Cry Fly on the Web at www.farcryfly.com. When not gigging or programming, he likes to play computer adventure games. His favorite series include Ultima, Monkey Island, and Space Quest.

Jeffry can be reached via e-mail at jeff@instant coldfusion.com. Check out the web site for this book at www.instantcoldfusion.com.

Contents

PART 3
Appendixes

Acknowledgments

First and foremost, I'd like to thank Jim, Tim, Elizabeth and all the folks at McGraw-Hill/Osborne for giving me the opportunity to write my second book. I also want to thank Chris, the technical editor of this book: You did a great job answering all those tough questions I kept throwing at you. I would take a muffin for you.

I want to send out an extra-special thanks to everyone who bought my first book, *Instant ColdFusion 5*. I appreciate the support. I want to thank the folks at Allaire and Macromedia for developing, and continuing to develop, the ColdFusion software. I want to thank everyone in the on-line community, especially Mike from HouseOfFusion, for maintaining the ever-important mailing lists.

I want to thank anyone I've ever had a chance to work with, including Stephenie, Laura, Valleri, Krista, Greg, Rick, Barry, Lou, Karl, Suzanne (who does everything), Jim, Aaron, Ed, Jed, Chris, Judy, Casey, and Kristen.

I want to thank my family and friends for keeping my stress level high and sanity low (or is that the other way around?): Karen, Kevin (KJ), Kevin (KH), Kristin, David, Mom, Dad, Tammi (for cracking the whip to get me to continue writing), Jude (and Tom), Angela (who has been calling this her book since before I started writing it), Jenni (and Luke), Lori (and Blaine), Tim (for teaching me power chords and because I forgot to thank him in the first book),

Shadow (digitaloverdose.org), and everyone who has ever bought any Far Cry Fly merchandise.

I want to thank Frito-Lay for making Doritos; Bachman for making Jax; Hostess for making cupcakes with cream filling; Snyder's for making Garlic Bread Nibbler pretzel things; and whoever thought of putting chocolate and peanut butter together. There wasn't a moment of writing when I didn't have one of these goodies in my mouth.

I also want to thank everyone I forgot to thank above, and finally, I want to thank you, the reader, for buying this book. I appreciate your continued support and hope you find the book to be a useful resource! Let me know what you think: www.instantcoldfusion.com.

Introduction

In my experience with web development, I have often had the opportunity to maintain pre-existing code. It has been my experience that many web developers are lacking in computer programming and database design concepts. The content of this book serves two purposes: to teach ColdFusion basics and to teach computer programming concepts. Each module is geared toward a specific programming concept and how to implement it in ColdFusion. This book is put together based on concepts that are taught in most introductory courses for first year computer science students in college, using ColdFusion as the language of choice.

Who Should Read This Book

This book was written on the assumption that you have a little knowledge of the Web and HTML, but no prior programming or ColdFusion experience. If you're a graphic designer who knows HTML and wants to start developing more complex web sites, then this book is for you. If you are a competent programmer who wants to learn how to program in ColdFusion, then this book is for you. If you are an experienced ColdFusion programmer, but want to learn programming concepts, then this book is for you. If you already know everything there is to know, then you must be rich and can buy this book just to support the author.

You should already have access to a functional ColdFusion server so that you can create HTML or CFML documents using a text editor.

How to Read This Book

This book was written to be read one module after the other, in succession. However, this is not necessary to your understanding of ColdFusion. If you want to jump to a specific topic, such as Conditional Logic, CFScript, or Database Design, please do so. Each module can stand alone, independent of all other modules. Modules will reference relevant topics in other modules as they come up.

The files that are referenced throughout the book can be downloaded from www.instantcoldfusion.com. When we mention the web site for this book, this is the site we are referring to. The files will also be available from the McGraw-Hill/Osborne site at www.osborne.com.

What This Book Covers

This book is divided into three parts: The Basics, Programming Concepts in ColdFusion, and Appendixes.

Part 1: The Basics

The first part gives you the ColdFusion basics that you need to develop your applications.

Module 1, "The Web and ColdFusion" gives you a short history of the Web, and introduces you to HTML.

Module 2, "All about Variables" introduces you to variables, and shows you how to create and use them in ColdFusion.

Module 3, "Database Design Theory" teaches you about database design, and shows you how to normalize your database.

Module 4, "Parameter Passing and Forms" shows you how to pass parameters in the URL. and introduces forms and form elements.

Module 5, "SQL: The Language of the Database" introduces Structured Query Language, and shows you how to use it to communicate with your database.

Module 6, "Getting Things Done in ColdFusion" teaches you about ColdFusion expressions, and talks some more about ColdFusion data types.

Part 2: Programming Concepts in ColdFusion

The second part goes over specific programming concepts and how you can apply them in ColdFusion.

Module 7, "ColdFusion's Application Framework" shows you how to set up the Application scope in ColdFusion, including persistent variables and the Application.cfm.

Module 8, "Making Decisions with ColdFusion" shows you how to make choices in ColdFusion about what code block to execute.

Module 9, "How to Loop in ColdFusion" demonstrates how to repeat specific sections of code.

Module 10, "Reusing Your Code" shows you how to modularize your code using includes and custom tags.

Module 11, "Handling Errors in ColdFusion" teaches you about error handling in ColdFusion.

Module 12, "CFScript" provides an introduction to, as well as an exhaustive reference to, ColdFusion's scripting language.

Module 13, "Lists" teaches you about lists and list processing.

Module 14, "Complex Variable Types" introduces structures and arrays, and shows you how to use them in ColdFusion.

Part 3: Appendixes

The final part contains appendixes to provide you with additional information.

Appendix A, "Answers to the Mastery Checks" provides all the answers to the Mastery Check questions that appear at the end of each module.

Appendix B, "What Is the Next Step?" points you in the direction of the next level in your ColdFusion educational process.

Appendix C, "Web References" is a list of web sites that you can turn to for more information.

Special Features

There are many special features in this book. All modules (chapters) are grouped together, which is ideal for individualized learning. Each module opens with a list of goals that it sets out to fulfill.

Modules include *Hints*, *Notes*, and *Tips*. These are short asides that relate to the topic on hand. *Ask the Expert* sections are in-depth explorations of related topics that take you beyond the normal text.

One or more *Projects* are located in each module, guiding you, step-by-step, through the creation of specific code. Annotated code listings are sprinkled throughout the text and projects to illustrate specific concepts and to emphasize portions of a template.

To quiz yourself along the way, simple *1-Minute Drills* are located throughout the text. A *Mastery Check* is included at the end of every chapter, providing a deeper analysis of what you have learned.

Part 1

The Basics

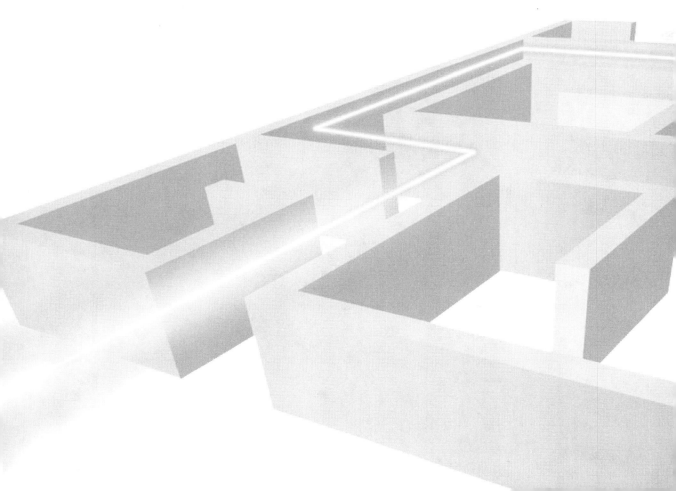

Module 1

The Web and ColdFusion

The Goals of This Module

- Introduce the Internet and the World Wide Web
- Introduce HTML, ColdFusion, and ColdFusion Markup Language
- Compare ColdFusion to other technologies
- Define a Coding Standard
- Teach you how to build your first web site

This module offers a brief history of the Internet and how the World Wide Web came into existence. We'll introduce HTML, which is the language of the Web, and explain what ColdFusion is and how it works. We'll go on to define a standard of coding and discuss the benefits of good documentation. We'll complete the module by creating a sample web site. Those readers experienced in web development might want to move on to Module 2. For those interested in the background material, we look to the time before the groundwork for the Internet was put into place.

A Short History of the Internet and Web

First let's examine how the Internet was created and by whom. Then you learn about the Web—from its humble beginnings to the powerhouse it is today.

Laying the Foundation for the Internet

In the 1960s, the government funded a research project called the Advanced Research Projects Agency Network (ARPANET). Most of the computer processing in the 1960s was done with punch cards. It took days to get results. ARPANET developed the idea of connecting computers together and, by the end of 1969, they could demonstrate the concept by connecting four nodes together in the ARPANET network across the United States.

The Internet grew from the research of Bob Khan and Vint Cerf in the 1970s. Building on the ARPANET research, they looked to define a standard way to transfer data between two computers. The research of Khan and Cerf led to the definition of the Transmission Control Protocol/Internet Protocol (TCP/IP). TCP/IP, as it's commonly known today, defined how packets of information could be passed from one computer to another before reaching their final destination. The paper that defined the TCP/IP protocol was published early in 1974.

Around the time the protocol research was being conducted, hardware-based networking standards were coming into existence. Ethernet came out of the Xerox PARC research team and IBM developed the Token Ring technology. Many companies were able to create their own local networks. With standards existing in the hardware and software markets, the Internet, as we know it, began to take shape. Years of further research, development, and testing occurred before this network of networks was ready to be unleashed on a wider scale in 1983. The National Science Foundation started a program in 1995 that would establish Internet access throughout the United States. The Internet began slowly, swallowing up local networks and making them global. The Internet was used for functions such as e-mail, file transfer protocol (ftp), and telnet. All this happened before the invention of the World Wide Web.

The World Wide Web

Tim Berners-Lee had an idea: He wanted to create a common place for sharing information, with the information grouped together in decentralized nodes, where any one node could be connected to any other node. Berners-Lee implemented this concept in the early 1990s and called it the World Wide Web. While the Internet has a tangible base in the collection of computers and the networking wires that connect those computers, the Web is the collection of information.

Berners-Lee coined the phrase "World Wide Web" based on a mathematical term. A *Web* is a space where anything can connect to anything else. He wanted

❓ Ask the Expert

Question: You mentioned Xerox PARC developed Ethernet. What is Xerox PARC? What other technologies came from Xerox PARC and how did they affect the computer industry?

Answer: Xerox PARC is a research facility sponsored by Xerox, the famous copier company. *PARC* stands for Palo Alto Research Center; its mission is to explore the architecture of information. In the 1970s, PARC created Ethernet technology, the graphical user interface (GUI), and object-oriented programming (OOP). Xerox didn't realize the potential for these concepts. Ethernet went with the researcher who developed it, Bob Metcalf, and he formed 3Com. Steve Jobs of Apple computers saw the GUI Interface and bought it up. If Xerox had understood these inventions, it would probably be at the head of the computer world today. You can find more information on Xerox PARC by pointing your web browser to http://www.parc.xerox.com.

to stress that each piece of information was a discrete unit that could be linked to anything. Berners-Lee created a hypertext editor for the NeXT system in 1991. He spent the next three years convincing people by creating clients and servers for other operating systems. (Mosaic, an early version of Netscape, was coded during this time.) Each year, the number of users on the Web increased tenfold.

In his original program, Berners-Lee defined the UDI, HTTP, and HTML protocols—standards in use today. A Universal Document Identifier (UDI) is now known as a Universal Resource Locator (URL). You use this identifier to locate and link to, the information you seek. Hypertext Transfer Protocol (HTTP) is the definition of how to send a page from its source—the server that contained it—to its destination, the browser. Hypertext Markup Language (HTML) is the language of the Web.

Berners-Lee eventually established an independent third-party group to foster standards on the Web. This group is the World Wide Web Consortium (W3C), which defined the standard tags that make up HTML, currently in its fourth rendition. You can find more information on the W3C at **w3.org**. Although HTML defines the layout of a page, you still need a program to translate your markups into the final page the user sees. These programs are called *web browsers*.

The Browser Wars

The two most commonly used web browsers on the market today are Microsoft Internet Explorer (IE) and Netscape Navigator. In the beginning, things were simpler for web developers and the companies that created the browsers. If you coded HTML to the standards, you had no problem with your page displaying in any of the existing browsers. As the market grew, Netscape and Microsoft broke away from the standards creating their own extensions of HTML.

Note

The third most popular browser is Opera, designed as a small and fast alternative to the major browsers. You can find information about Opera at www.opera.com.

The separation between Navigator and IE complicated the life of the average web developer because each browser branched in different directions. Whenever one company created a tag to perform one task, the competing company would create a different tag to perform the same task. What you wrote for one browser quickly became unreadable in the other. To complicate matters, the implementation of the HTML standards that each browser took started to vary, so even if you followed the written standards, your web page might not have appeared the same in each browser. This competitiveness did have a benefit, though: The Web evolved more quickly than it would have if the public had to wait for the W3C to move HTML forward.

It now seems the Microsoft browser, Internet Explorer, has continuously increased market share, while Netscape Navigator's usage statistics have steadily decreased. It looks as if the browser wars will soon be over, with Microsoft coming out on top. The problems web developers have in creating multibrowser code will become fewer.

American Online (AOL) recently bought Netscape. For a long time, AOL has included a version of Microsoft IE with its software. Some believe if AOL were to integrate Netscape into a new version of the AOL software, it could flip-flop the browser wars overnight. AOL, which recently merged with Time Warner, isn't expected to do this because it might be construed as anticompetitive behavior. With the recent AOL/Time Warner merger, the company has the opportunity not only to control the content that people see, but also the delivery of that content. This is the state of the Web today.

1-Minute Drill

● Who created the World Wide Web?

● What are the two most widely used browsers?

● Tim Berners-Lee created the World Wide Web.
● Microsoft Internet Explorer and Netscape Navigator are the two most widely used browsers.

A Simple HTML Primer

Without the Web, ColdFusion wouldn't exist. In this section, you learn about HTML, which is the language of the Web and how it works. Then you learn about general HTML basics that are used throughout this book.

The Origin of HTML

HTML is the acronym for Hypertext Markup Language. *HTML* is a language used to define the look and feel of a web document. People with no prior programming knowledge can use and easily understand HTML. HTML is *not* a programming language. Programming languages are the tools of information technology (IT) professionals, used to solve problems and automate tasks.

Note

The term "markup language" stems from the days before computers. A printer would have to format, or markup, this text before printing on a printing press.

Berners-Lee defined HTML when he released his first web programs in 1991. HTML is an implementation of Standard Generalized Markup Language (SGML), which is a language used to define other languages. SGML defines how data and documents interchange. HTML was later turned over to an independent standards group, the W3C, which still manages it today. HTML is currently in its fourth rendition.

Common Elements in an HTML Page

HTML is a tag-based language. A *tag* is a piece of text preceded by a greater than (>) sign and followed by a less than (<) sign. A sample tag is `<html>`. Most HTML tags have a start and an end tag. An end tag begins `</`, so the end tag to `<html>` is `</html>`. You place your text between the start and end tags. The HTML tag defines an HTML document.

Note

The Document Object Model (DOM) is a universal way to define how an HTML page can be accessed from a programming language. Covering the DOM is beyond the scope of this book.

An HTML document has two parts: the header and the body. As you might expect from the previous paragraph, the *header* is defined between `<head>` and `</head>` HTML tags, while the `body` is defined between `<body>` and `</body>`. The header usually contains a title for the document, using the `<title>` start and end tags. The body of an HTML document is more complex than the header because it contains the text of your document.

Note

The ColdFusion Markup Language (CFML) was designed as a tag-based language, so it would easily integrate with HTML. Understanding HTML is a good first step toward understanding CFML.

Let's begin by examining a sample HTML document. You can open SampleHTMLDocument.htm in your HTML editor of choice and follow along. The document is as follows (access it at SampleHTMLDocument.htm).

```
<html>
<head>
 <title>Sample HTML Document </title>
</head>
<body> ◄─────────────────── Start body tag
Some Sample HTML Document Text

</body> ◄──────── End body tag
</html>
```

The first thing you see in this document is an open HTML tag. Next, you see the head tag. Insert a title of the document using the title tag. After the title, insert the close title tag and following that, you insert the close head tag. Next comes the body of your document, which is enclosed between open and close body tags. In this document, you don't have a comprehensive body, only some simple text. As you move forward through this book, the body portions of the documents you create become more complex. End your HTML page with the end HTML tag. Before moving away from HTML to start discussing ColdFusion, let's first examine a few HTML tags we'll use exhaustively in this book.

Note that in HTML, a way exists to customize the behavior of a single tag. This customization is called an *attribute*. For example, an attribute to the body tag is bgcolor. *Bgcolor* defines the background color of the current HTML document. Attributes are listed after the tag name, but before the greater than (>)

sign that closes the tag. If you want to change the background color to red, you could use the background tag like this: `<body bgcolor=" #ff0000">`.

Basic HTML Tags

The Web is supposed to be a group of potentially unrelated units of information, or nodes, where any one node can link to another. With that said, understanding how to create links within HTML is vital. *Links* from one page to another are created using an anchor tag and its href attribute. The anchor tag is abbreviated to one letter: a. The *href attribute* defines where the link will go. The following page, SampleURLLink.htm, is an example of a link, which you can access on the web site InstantColdFusion.com.

```
<html>
<head>
 <title>Sample HTML Document </title>
</head>
<body>
<a href="http://www.instantcoldfusion.com">←———[ Link ]
 Instant ColdFusion
</a>

</body>
</html>
```

The first part of the anchor defines the link, which is linking to http://www. instantcoldfusion.com. Then you have some text. When displayed in a web browser, this is the text that's used as the link. Finally, you close off your link with the end anchor tag: `</a>`. You can see how the link appears in a web browser from the following screenshot.

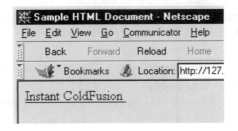

Two types of links exist: relative links and absolute links. *Relative links* link to other pages within the current web site, while *absolute links* go to a different web site. Our example uses a relative link. Relative links are set up the same way as absolute links, but the value of the href attribute is different. If you're linking to a file in the same directory, you only have to give the name of that directory. If you're linking to a file in a subdirectory, you need to type in the subdirectory, followed by a forward slash /, and followed by the filename, like this:

```
<a href="SubDirectory/MyFile.htm">
```

To link to a file that's a directory above your current directory, you have to add two dots and a slash before the filename, like this:

```
<a href="../MyFile.htm">
```

Many relative links are used throughout this book, so if you don't understand them now, you'll soon see them in action.

Before moving on to look at ColdFusion, you should see the HTML tables. *Tables* are a simple way to format display data and are used extensively throughout this book. You can think of an HTML table in the same way you'd think about a Microsoft Excel or a Lotus 1-2-3 spreadsheet. Data is presented in columns and rows.

To create a table, you need to look at three different HTML tags. The first is a *table tag,* which tells a browser when to start and end a table. Between the open and close table tags, you define each row with a table row (tr) tag. Finally, within the rows, you define each piece of data in the row using a table data (td) tag. Here's an example, which you can access on InstantColdFusion.com at SampleHTMLTable.htm.

```
<table>  ◄──────────── | Open table tag |
 <tr>
 <td>Insert your table data here</td>
 </tr>
</table>  ◄──────────── | Close table tag |
```

Hint

If your browser is showing a blank page, verify you aren't missing an end table tag. This is common in Netscape Navigator.

These five lines create a simple table. This table begins with the table tag, which tells the browser you're about to start a table. Following this, you use the tr tag to start a row. You only have one data cell within the row, specified between the td open and close tags. You can add additional rows and data cells to your table, as needed. When creating an HTML table, you want to make sure all your data lies within a table cell definition.

LinkPage.htm

Project 1-1: Creating a Page of HTML Links

The first project you'll do is create a page full of HTML links. Providing a page that links to other relevant pages is common on many sites and you can easily use it to demonstrate the use of HTML tables used throughout the book.

Step-by-Step

1. Create a blank document, using the HTML Editor of your choice. Notepad will work if you have nothing else.

2. Start your HTML page by adding the open and close HTML tags:

```
<html>

</html>
```

3. Add your HTML header to your page. Your resulting page should look like this:

```
<html>
  <head>
    <title>A Page of Links</title>
  </head>

</html>
```

4. Add the HTML body tags, as shown in the following:

```
<html>
  <head>
    <title>A Page of Links</title>
  </head>
  <body>

  </body>
</html>
```

5. Create your table header. The heading of your table is any other row in the table. The first row of your table is used for this heading and two columns are included in your table. Put the link in the first column and a description of the link in the second column. The code is as follows:

```
<html>
 <head>
   <title>A Page of Links</title>
 </head>
 <body>
   <table>
    <tr>
       <td>Link</td>
       <td>Description</td>
    </tr>
   </table>
 </body>
</html>
```

Your table starts out with the table tag. Following that, create your header row. The row is sandwiched between open and close tr tags. The columns are defined with the td tags and, when viewed through a browser, you can see the information between the td tags: Link and Description.

6. Your last step is to add a row or two of links to your table. You can easily copy your title row, remove the title headers, and add your anchor and description text to the first and second columns, respectively.

```
<html>
 <head>
   <title>A Page of Links</title>
 </head>
 <body>
   <table>
    <tr>
       <td>Link</td>
       <td>Description</td>
    </tr>
    <tr>
       <td>
        <a href="http://www.instantcoldfusion.com">
         Link
        </a>
       </td>
       <td>
        The web site for the book Instant ColdFusion
```

```
      </td>
    </tr>
    <tr>
      <td>
        <a href="http://www.optimizingcoldfusion.com">
         Link
        </a>
      </td>
      <td>
        The web site for the book Optimizing ColdFusion
      </td>
    </tr>
    <tr>
      <td>
        <a href="http://www.macromedia.com">Link</a>
      </td>
      <td>Macromedia's web site</td>
    </tr>

    </table>
  </body>
</html>
```

Project Summary

In the final step, you added three links on to your page. Your resulting page is as follows.

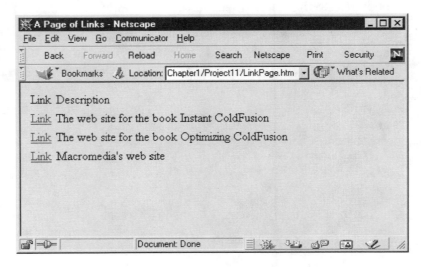

You can repeat Step 6 until you're out of web sites you want to link to. This is a simple implementation of some HTML tags. You build on these concepts as you progress deeper into the book. Now, let's look at what ColdFusion is and how it relates to you.

1-Minute Drill

- What is an HTML-formatting option similar to an Excel spreadsheet?
- What are the two parts of an HTML document?

An Introduction to ColdFusion

ColdFusion can be divided into two parts. The first is the ColdFusion application server and the second is ColdFusion Markup Language (CFML). First, let's examine the ColdFusion application server and see how it works, and then we'll compare ColdFusion to other web technologies. The remainder of this book is dedicated to understanding programming concepts with CFML within ColdFusion.

ColdFusion Application Server

Allaire Corporation was founded in 1995 by two brothers, J. J. and Jeremy Allaire. As the story goes, Jeremy was looking for a way to update the web site of a print publication regularly and easily. He didn't want to have to worry about knowing HTML or any other such technologies. He wanted a simple entry form. He asked his computer-programming brother J. J. for help in creating something that would simplify the task. After the project was complete, the two realized the potential of the technology they created and the first official release of ColdFusion followed shortly. In the year 2000, Allaire merged with Macromedia, the makers of graphic software for the Web.

At its heart, *ColdFusion* is a program used for database connectivity to the Web. ColdFusion is a server-side scripting language built to work in conjunction with a web server. Initially, all server-side programs—ColdFusion included—were called by the use of Common Gateway Interface (CGI). CGI isn't a

---

- Tables are an HTML-formatting option similar to an Excel spreadsheet.
- The header and the body are the two parts of an HTML document.

programming language, but a definition of how data can be transferred back and forth between the server and the client by using the HTTP protocol. CGI programs are server-side applications and they can be written in any programming language that can compile into machine code for the operating system on your web server. These programs are commonly written in Perl or C, but any compiled language will work. These programs take the data from the web client, process that data, and return information to the web browser.

ColdFusion was initially implemented as a CGI program. Over time, the program became too big to load into memory each time it was needed. This is where the server application programming interface (API) enters into the picture. The other way to implement a server-side language is to code it using the API of the web server. An API enables one programmer to extend the functionality of someone else's program. ColdFusion is implemented as a server API for most web servers and an interpreter is written to interface with the web server. Whenever the web server tries to serve up a page that includes specific ColdFusion directives, the interpreter executes the directive and returns the result of the code execution to the browser.

It's more resource-efficient to have the interpreter program constantly running, as opposed to loading a separate instance each time it's needed. You have the added benefit of having only one instance of the interpreter running, no matter how many users are on the site. This is a great benefit for the e-commerce sites that have many visitors on an hourly basis.

Ask the Expert

Question: You mentioned that ColdFusion is a server-side scripting language. Do other types of web languages exist? Are there other technologies to achieve dynamic functionality? How do these other technologies compare to ColdFusion?

Answer: A *server-side language* is a language that runs on the web server. *A client-side language* is one that runs in the web client, most commonly your web browser. Macromedia's ColdFusion or Microsoft's Active Server Pages (ASP) are two examples of server-side languages. JavaScript is the most common client-side language. Server-side languages give you more control over the server than client-side code and server-side programs often have access to file structure, data sources, and other server resources. Client-side languages won't have this server access, but they might offer you access to the client machine if it's needed. Client-side languages aren't a replacement for server-side languages, and vice versa. The trick is for a good developer to know which language to choose for the intended purpose.

How ColdFusion Stacks Up Against Other Technologies

You can examine quite a few web technologies that will allow you to achieve functionality similar to what you can achieve with ColdFusion. You could start by writing your own custom program using the CGI interface. CGI programs are commonly written in Perl but, as previously discussed, these can be written in any language you choose. Starting from scratch in this manner isn't an option used often today. ColdFusion is in its fifth rendition. Is it possible to replicate the functionality, robustness, and time-tested value of ColdFusion, starting from nothing? That's doubtful and there's no reason to reinvent the wheel. Additionally, ColdFusion programmers are numerous compared to the people who know a custom-built technology, so if you need additional help down the line, you'll have a better chance of finding it.

The most common competitor to ColdFusion is Microsoft Active Server Pages (ASP). Microsoft ASP is considered free because it's included with Microsoft's web server, Internet Information Server, as part of its server operating systems: Windows NT, Windows 2000, and Windows XP Professional. ASP isn't a cross-platform solution, however, because it only works on the Windows operating system (OS) with Microsoft's own web server: Internet Information Server. ColdFusion is a cross platform that works with different web servers, including Apache, Microsoft IIS, and Netscape Livewire, as well as platforms such as Windows and UNIX. ASP is hard for nonprogrammers to learn because its language is derived from Visual Basic. ASP is often tedious or complicated to perform simple tasks, such as database inserts, which ColdFusion can perform with a single tag.

PHP Hypertext Preprocessor (PHP) is an open-source competitor to both ASP and ColdFusion. As with ASP, PHP uses a scripting language instead of a tag-based language. PHP isn't a full-application server like ColdFusion and it doesn't have any of the advanced server functions, such as built-in verity indexing or server monitoring tools. Because no single company is behind PHP, it doesn't offer a support network you can rely on when things go bad.

CFML tag-based language is easy for many to understand and learn, and it complements HTML much better than a script-based language does. CFML tag-based languages also produce less code than their script-based counterparts. Less code means your application is easier and less costly to maintain and modify. In the past, people argued that ColdFusion isn't scalable and runs slower than either ASP or PHP but, with properly written code, this isn't the case. Macromedia tackled these past complaints head-on with the release of ColdFusion 5, which was specifically fine-tuned to improve performance. ColdFusion's ease of use, simplicity, and rapid development capability makes it the language of choice by many developers.

1-Minute Drill

● Name some technologies similar to ColdFusion.

● What is the name of the company that currently maintains ColdFusion?

The Software Development Lifecycle

If you want to put a broad definition on a *software program*, you might say it's a way to automate a task. That task can be anything from text manipulation to an operating system. Software programs are written in programming languages, such as C++, Perl, or CFML. Your web browser, operating system, and word processor are all examples of software programs. In the past, most software programs have been compiled programs to run on a particular operating system. These days, many web-based applications are designed to run in a browser.

Every software program goes through a development life cycle, starting in the product's conception and following through to retirement, where a product is no longer of use. Some different methodologies exist for the lifecycle of a software application, but many have these similar elements:

● **Requirements Phase** This phase defines what the client wants. In an ideal world, the end user creates the requirements for you. You often create it by interviewing the end user, examining some sample data and using old versions of the software, or evaluating complimentary software your new product is designed to run with. A good requirement might be "This application needs to be web based."

● Technologies similar to ColdFusion are Microsoft Active Server Pages and PHP.
● Macromedia is the company that currently maintains ColdFusion.

?Ask the Expert

Question: Is HTML a programming language? Is CFML?

Answer: HTML isn't a programming language. A *programming language* is a language designed to perform a list of separate instructions. Do you use HTML to perform a specific function? No, you don't. HTML is a markup language. A *markup language* is designed to describe how something looks, while a program language is designed to describe how something works. CFML, unlike HTML, is a programming language.

- **Specifications Phase**   While the requirements phase defines what the client wants, the specifications phase defines what you're going to give the client. This phase tells the client how you plan to meet their needs. Given the previous requirement, a specification might be "This application will be designed using Macromedia's ColdFusion 5 on a Windows 2000 OS, running Microsoft IIS web server." For web applications, this phase often includes the development of a site map and, perhaps, a quick mockup of the site, so the user can click through and view the functionality.

Hint

Sometimes the requirements and specification phases are lumped together into one. For small projects, you might be able to get away with that, but I've always had the best luck when I separate the two. Understanding the client's needs before trying to address them is a good idea.

- **Design and Implementation**   Now that you have an approved specification document, you need to turn that into software. When creating ColdFusion applications, I start with the database design. Then I will draw a map of the execution logic of the various pages, which is often based on the site map created in the specification phase. With the database design and a diagram of the execution flow, writing the code is easy. Most of this book focuses on this portion of the software development lifecycle.

- **Debugging and Testing**   Testing your application to find errors is important. During this phase, we also evaluate the code to make sure it fills the needs outlined in the requirements and specifications phases. In the Web, this often includes the act of surfing the newly created web site in different browsers and trying to cause errors by inserting invalid data.

● **Integration or Rollout** After you develop your application, you need to let people know this application is ready. In the non-web world, this step is complicated for enterprise class applications, often involving many months of installing software for the departments and users that need to use the application. With the Web, it's much easier. You simply need to notify people of the link where they can reach the new functionality.

● **Maintenance** While applications might take weeks or months to develop, they're often used for years or decades. The bulk of the software development life cycle is spent in the maintenance of the application. As people use the application, they think of ways to improve the existing functionality or of a new functionality to add. Major revisions often go through their own requirements and specification phases.

● **Retirement** All good things must come to an end. This saying also holds true for software applications. A time will come when the application no longer suits the needs of the company and it must be replaced with something more in line with the company's goals and aspirations. DOS is an example of a retired application that was replaced by Microsoft Windows 95.

The remainder of this book examines the design and implementation phases in detail. The first thing you need to know is what constitutes good coding habits. Following that, a coding standard used throughout this book is defined.

Developing a Coding Standard

You need to know about a few universal topics when you develop an application in any language. Let's look at some coding standards used throughout this book. Let's begin by examining a coding standard.

Why Have a Coding Standard?

You want to understand what a coding standard is and why you need one. A *coding standard,* in simple terms, is a routine way to name files and directories, and to format code. Let's examine some of the benefits of having a coding standard, and then you can learn to create your own.

One thing to remember when creating a coding standard is to keep it consistent. As described earlier in this module, the bulk of the time you spend on an application is in that application's maintenance. When you go back to examine your code, being able to sit down, and know what's happening and where it's happening is good. Standard file and directory naming conventions can help you do this. A *standard* can help you write, debug, and maintain applications more efficiently. If you have consistently used naming conventions and directory layouts for multiple applications, this also makes switching from application to application with an understanding of what's happening much easier.

Directory Structures

First, let's look at directory structures, including some important directories and subdirectories.

- **Root**   This isn't the same as the root directory of your hard disk drive. This is only the root directory of your web site. When a browser goes to your domain name, it points to this root directory. This directory isn't a named directory from the perspective of the browser and all other directories reside beneath this one as a subdirectory. In this directory, I like to store single HTML or CFML files that represent a single section of the site with one page. The root directory is also the prime place to store the home page.

- **Images**   The images directory contains all the images of the site.

- **Administration**   The administrative directory contains templates that allow the site owner or content creators to add or update data easily to the site. This directory is usually password protected in some manner. You learn about creating administrative templates in Module 5.

Hint

Naming the administrative directory something other than admin or administration isn't uncommon. Admin or Administration are directory names that can be easily guessed by someone trying to hack the site. Naming the directory something less descriptive, such as grapejuice, or giving it an obscure name makes the administrative section of your web site less prone to hacking.

- **Includes**   I like to use an include directory in our site. This directory contains all modular code samples. The concept of modularizing your web development code is discussed in Module 10.

- **Custom Tags** If you're using custom tags in your application, you might want to create a separate directory for them. You can also store them in the CustomTags directory of your ColdFusion installation or in the includes directory of your application. You learn about custom tags in Module 10.

- **Section Name** I like to create a directory for every section of the web site that includes more functionality than can fit into a single page.

Now that you've examined the directory structure, you also need to consider some naming conventions for the files that reside in the directories.

Types of Files in Your Web Site

This section looks at some of the different types of files created during your web site development:

- **Index** A custom that has been in the Web for a long time is to name your home page index. If no page is defined in your URL, many web servers are programmed to look for an index page. In the root directory, this page is the home page for your site. In sections directories, this page is usually the section home page.

Note

Some web servers are set up to look for default instead of index, but many are set up to look for both.

- **Includes** These are stored in the include directory and you learn about includes in Module 10.

- **Input** The input page is for entering data into a form. I name these templates after the type of data we're inputting and add the letter *i* to the end of the filename. If we create a user registration page on our web site, then I would name the page "registeri."

- **Update** The update page is for editing preexisting data. As with input pages, I name these templates after the type of data we're entering. I append the letter *u* to the end of the filename. For example, if the user were to go in and change her information, I would name the page "registeru."

- **Processing** This is the processing page for form elements. The input and update page types usually submit to this type of page. I would name these page types after the type of information being processed, with the letter *p* appended to the end of the name. Using the registration example, the name of the file would be "registerp."

- **Verification** All forms have at least two elements: an input page and a processing page. A third element is sometimes added between the two: a verification page. As with input, update, and processing, I would name the file after the type of data being edited. The letter appended to the end of this page is the letter *v*. To create a registration verification template, I would name the file "registrationv.cfm."

- **Delete** If we're deleting some form of data, we need a template to perform the delete statement.

Hint

Module 4 explains using an HTML form with ColdFusion.

The extensions of the pages in a web site have traditionally been .htm or .html. ColdFusion templates are given the extension of .cfm. Next, you want to learn some steps you can take to write your code, so it's easily readable and maintainable.

Writing Your Code

After you examine some standards you can use to create your files and directories, you still have one more issue to deal with. Once you find the page causing the problem, you need to open that page and read it easily. The first formatting tip when writing code is to indent all text between the start and the end tag. This makes following the logic path of the code easy.

The code in this book follows some standard naming conventions. All HTML and CFML tags are written in lowercase, such as the table tag. Tag attributes are written in lowercase, such as border or cellspacing, which are attributes to the table tag. ColdFusion variables are written in a mix of uppercase and lowercase, with the first letter capitalized and the remaining letters in lowercase. In places where the variable name is a compound word, the first letter of each word is capitalized, such as FirstName. Variable scopes are written in all lowercase. You learn about variables and their uses in Module 2.

One Minute Drill

● Name some different types of files we'll use.

● What are the first two steps in creating an application?

Structured query language (SQL) statements are all in uppercase. Database table names and columns use the variable syntax. Module 5 explores SQL in more depth.

Some coding standards have gained in popularity throughout the ColdFusion community. Historically, Allaire hasn't voiced a stance on development methodologies. Macromedia, which recently bought Allaire, hasn't released any official words on the subject. Fusebox is the most widely used ColdFusion methodology and Jeremy Allaire, Macromedia's Chief Technology Officer, was the keynote speaker at the 2001 Fusebox conference. Some believe this means Macromedia is endorsing Fusebox as the methodology of choice. I believe no single methodology will work well in every situation, so it's best to choose, or to create, a methodology that suits your needs best.

Note

You can find more information about Fusebox at www.fusebox.org. Information on another popular methodology, cfObjects, is located at www.cfobjects.com.

Index.htm;
LinkPage.htm

Project 1-2: Creating a Sample Web Site

This project to creates a sample web site. The simplest web site only contains a single page, like we created in Project 1-1. Here we are going to up the ante, and create a two-page web site. The first page will be an index page and the second page will be the page that includes the list of links we previously created.

● Update files, delete files, input files, processing files, and index files are the names of some different types of files we'll use.

● The requirements phase and the specifications phase are the first two steps in creating an application.

Step-by-Step

1. First, you want to create your home page. You can either get the files from the web site or create them as you go. Your home page file is Index.htm in the Project12 folder. Create a blank document in the HTML editor of your choice. Type your HTML header and the body of your document into your page. This should look similar to what you see in the following:

```
<html>

<head>
 <title>A Sample Home Page</title>
</head>

<body>

</body>
</html>
```

Start out with the open HTML tag. Then, you have the head and title. This page is titled A Sample Home Page. Those statements make up your HTML header. Next, you have the body of your page. You haven't yet added content to your home page, so the body portion only has an open and a close body tag before you end the template with a close HTML tag.

2. The next step is to add the content to your home page. You'll use a table to format the content. Your main table will have a single row and two columns. The following shows the modified code:

```
<html>

<head>
 <title>A Sample Home Page</title>
</head>

<body>

<table border="1">
 <tr>
   <td>

   </td>

   <td>Welcome to our Home Page</td>
 </tr>
</table>
```

A complete table

```
</body>
</html>
```

The first column contains the navigation of your site and the second column contains the content of the page. Because the content right now is sparse, I put in some text for our content column, which is a welcome message.

3. The final piece of your home page is to add in your navigation bar code in the first column of your table. Use a table inside a table to accomplish this. When a table is put inside another table, this is called a *nested table.* The following shows the updated code:

```
<html>

<head>
 <title>A Sample Home Page</title>
</head>

<body>

<table border="1">
 <tr>
   <td>

     <table>
     <tr>
      <td><a href="Index.htm">Home</a></td>
     </tr>

     <tr>
      <td><a href="LinkPage.htm">Links</a></td>
     </tr>
     </table>

   </td>

   <td>Welcome to our Home Page</td>
 </tr>
</table>

</body>
</html>
```

Navigation bar

The navigation bar for your small site has two links: one to the index page and one to a link page. Each link is stored in a table row of its own. You can see the resulting page in the following screenshot:

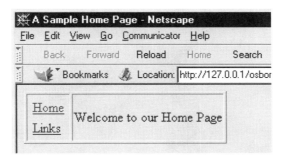

4. Next, you want to attack the second page of your web site, LinkPage.cfm, which is your link page. You want to set up your link page structure similar to your home page. Create a new blank document with your HTML editor of choice. You can copy the HTML head and body table from the previous example. Change the title in the HTML head and remove the welcome message from the second row of your main HTML table. The resulting page should look something like this:

```
<html>

<head>
 <title>A Page of Links</title>
</head>

<body>

<table border="1">
 <tr>
  <td>

    <table>
     <tr>
      <td><a href="Index.htm">Home</a></td>
     </tr>

     <tr>
      <td><a href="LinkPage.htm">Links</a></td>
     </tr>
```

```
     </table>

   </td>
   <td>

   </td>
  </tr>
</table>

</body>
</html>
```

5. Finally, you want to add the link portion to your newly created link page.

```
<html>

<head>
 <title>A Page of Links</title>
</head>

<body>


<table border="1">
 <tr>
  <td>

   <table>
    <tr>
     <td><a href="Index.htm">Home</a></td>
    </tr>

    <tr>
     <td><a href="LinkPage.htm">Links</a></td>
    </tr>
   </table>
```

```
  </td>
  <td>
   <table>
    <tr>
     <td>Link</td>
     <td>Description</td>
    </tr>
    <tr>
     <td>
      <a href="http://www.instantcoldfusion.com">
      Link
      </a>
     </td>
     <td>The Instant ColdFusion web site</td>
    </tr>
    <tr>
     <td>
      <a href="http://www.optimizingcoldfusion.com">
      Link
      </a>
     </td>
     <td>The Optimizing ColdFusion web site</td>
    </tr>
    <tr>
     <td>
      <a href="http://www.macromedia.com">
      Link
      </a>
     </td>
     <td>Macromedia's web site</td>
    </tr>
   </table>
  </td>
 </tr>
</table>

</body>
</html>
```

The contents of this page are borrowed from the previous example, which contains a table of links. You can see the results of our link page here.

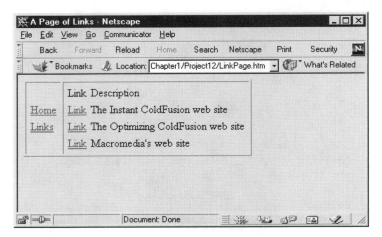

Project Summary

We'll use a similar page layout in most of the templates we create in this book, so you should understand what we created here and why. The table inside a table format works well for any but the most-complicated site layouts.

The Beauty of Good Documentation

Documentation may arguably be the most important part of your coding experience. No matter how solid your coding standards are, if you don't document the code as you go, maintaining your code will be difficult. And, without documentation, it will be almost impossible for someone else to maintain your code.

Hint

A difference exists between HTML comments and ColdFusion comments. HTML comments are placed between <!— and -->. CFML comments are placed between <!--- and --->. HTML comments have two dashes, where CFML comments have three. HTML comments will be streamed to the browser, but CFML comments won't.

Overall Documentation

At the top of every template, I like to include some documentation that defines the overall use of the page, the date it was created, and some other information. Here's an example:

```
<!---
Description: This is a Description of the Template

Entering: This is where we came from
Exiting: This is where we want to go

Dependencies: These are files that are needed for this
              template to run
Expecting: This is a list of variables we are
           expecting to be defined upon entry into
           this template

Modification History
Date        Modifier                Modification
************************************************************
09/15/2001  Jeff Houser, DotComIt Created
--->
```

I call this code a *documentation header* and put it at the top of every template. The information is enclosed in ColdFusion comment markers, which prevent it from being sent to the browser. This documentation begins with a description, which tells the reader the intended purpose of this template. Following that are two statements—entering and exiting—used to define the logic flow of the application. This tells you where you came from to get to this template and where you're going when you leave this template. These statements are most useful in form processing, which you learn about in Module 4.

Following the entering and exiting portion is a *dependency list,* which is a list of all ColdFusion templates referenced by the current template. You learn about code reuse in Module 10. The *expecting* section contains a list of variables expected to be previously defined when you execute this template. You learn about variables in Module 2 and passing variables between templates in Module 4.

The final piece of information included in your documentation header is a modification history. For the *modification history*, include the date the modification was created, the person and company that modified the template, and the type of modification performed. Enter the first modification as created to make note of which template was created and by whom.

Inline Documentation

In addition to the documentation header, you can include comments within the code to explain what's happening. These comments are called *inline documentation*. The use of these comments throughout the code is important to describe the logic of the application as it happens.

Inline documentation can be placed easily between the open and close CFML comment brackets, just as you did with your header documentation. The inline documentation is often shorter, only taking up a single line, and is interspersed throughout the code. The following would be a good example of inline documentation:

```
<!--- start a table here -->
<table>
  <tr><td></td></tr>
</table>
<!--- end the table here -->
```

Start the code segment with some documentation that says you're about to start a table. Then you have an HTML table, although a simple one. The table starts with a table tag, has one row with one cell, and then has an end table tag. Following this is another line of documentation, which states this is the end of your table.

1-Minute Drill

- How do you create an HTML comment?
- How do you create a CFML comment?

- <!-- Comment Here --> is how you create an HTML comment.
- <!--- Comment Here ---> is how you create a CFML comment.

Index.htm;
LinkPage.htm

Project 1-3: Adding Documentation to Your Web Site

Now that you've learned about the importance of documentation in your web site, you need to reexamine the code you created in Project 1-2. Take one page from your simple site, add a link page, and then add some documentation to it.

Step-by-Step

1. The first thing you want to add to your template is the documentation header. Your documented file is LinkPage.cfm and you can download it from InstantColdFusion.com. To create the file, open up the file you created in Project 1-2. Type in the documentation header, as shown below:

```
<!---
Description: A page of Links

Entering: N/A
Exiting: N/A

Dependencies: N/A
Expecting: N/A

Modification History
Date        Modifier              Modification
********************************************************
09/15/2001  Jeff Houser, DotComIt  Created
--->

<html>

<head>
 <title>A Page of Links</title>
</head>

<body>

<table border="1">
 <tr>
  <td>
    <table>
     <tr>
      <td><a href="Index.htm">Home</a></td>
     </tr>
```

```
   <tr>
    <td><a href="LinkPage.htm">Links</a></td>
   </tr>
  </table>
 </td>

<td>
 <table>
  <tr>
   <td>Link</td>
   <td>Description</td>
  </tr>

  <tr>
   <td>
    <a href="http://www.instantcoldfusion.com">
     Link
    </a>
   </td>
   <td>The Instant ColdFusion web site</td>
  </tr>
  <tr>
   <td>
    <a href="http://www.optimizingcoldfusion.com">
     Link
    </a>
   </td>
   <td>The Optimizing ColdFusion web site</td>
  </tr>
  <tr>
   <td>
    <a href="http://www.macromedia.com">
     Link
    </a>
   </td>
   <td>Macromedia's Web Site</td>
  </tr>

 </table>
 </td>
 </tr>
</table>

</body>
</html>
```

1

This page is described as a page of links. Because this is a standalone page, you needn't fill in anything for the entering or exiting portions of your header documentation. No dependencies exist and you aren't expecting anything to be defined when you enter this page. Put in N/A, for nonapplicable, for all these entries in your header. The modification history of the header includes my name, the company I work for, and the date the document was created. With the header safe, you can continue to the rest of the template.

2. Let's add some inline documentation to your template. You can see the completed code below:

```
<!---
Description: A page of Links

Entering: N/A
Exiting: N/A

Dependencies: N/A
Expecting: N/A

Modification History
Date        Modifier                 Modification
******************************************************
09/15/2001  Jeff Houser, DotComIt    Created
--->

<html>

<head>
 <title>A Page of Links</title>
</head>

<body>

<!--- Table for Page Layout --->
<table border="1">
 <tr>
  <!--- Start Navigation Bar --->
  <td>
   <table>
    <tr>
     <td><a href="Index.htm">Home</a></td>
    </tr>
```

```
   <tr>
    <td><a href="LinkPage.htm">Links</a></td>
   </tr>
  </table>
</td>
<!--- End Navigation Bar --->

<!--- start content of the page --->
<td>
 <table>
  <!--- Insert the Header row of table --->
  <tr>
   <td>Link</td>
   <td>Description</td>
  </tr>
  <!--- End Header row of table --->

  <!--- Start the contents of the table --->
  <tr>
   <td>
    <a href="http://www.instantcoldfusion.com">
    Link
    </a>
   </td>
   <td>The Instant ColdFusion website.</td>
  </tr>
  <tr>
   <td>
    <a href="http://www.optimizingcoldfusion.com">
    Link
    </a>
   </td>
   <td>The Optimizing ColdFusion website.</td>
  </tr>
  <tr>
   <td><a href="http://www.macromedia.com">Link</a>
   </td>
   <td>Macromedia's website</td>
  </tr>
  <!--- End the contents of the table --->

 </table>
</td>
 <!--- End content of the page --->
```

```
  </tr>
  </table>
  <!--- End Table for Page Layout --->

  </body>
  </html>
```

Start the table that defines the layout for your main page. You come to your first line of inline documentation and specify that you are to start the table for your page layout. Start your row and come to the first cell in the page layout. This cell contains the navigation bar, as is stated in the next comment. Then you display the navigation bar and finish off the table cell with a comment, declaring the end of the navigation bar

Next, move to the main content of this page and state that you're approaching that point with another comment. These comments clearly define the logical flow of the page. Move into your link table. First, you have the header row of the link table, and then you have the contents of your link table.

Project Summary

At this point, you should be able to see how the inline documentation helps to describe the flow of your template, opening and closing each specific section of the document. Comments are used more in-depth later in the book to define the ColdFusion processing. Good documentation practices are the mark of a good developer.

Module Summary

This chapter introduced you to some important background information about the Internet, the Web, and ColdFusion. You also learned about some basic HTML tags that will be used throughout the remainder of this book. You now have a solid foundation of knowledge, so you can move on to the next module and start to delve into some ColdFusion code.

✓ Mastery Check

1. The Internet grew out of research from a government-funded projected called _____.

2. The World Wide Web was created by Tim Berners-Lee based on the concept of many decentralized _____ of unrelated information being able to connect to each other.

3. HTML stands for:

   A. How To Make Links

   B. HyperText Magic Links

   C. Hypertext Markup Language

   D. Help Tim's Master Linage

4. Both HTML and CFML are _____-based languages.

5. Create an HTML page that links to Macromedia's Home Page.

6. What types of links can you make between documents (select two)?

   A. Absolute

   B. Full

   C. Relative

   D. Directory

   E. Master

7. The language of ColdFusion is called _____.

8. ColdFusion is an _____ server.

9. Two directories you might include in your web site are the _____ directory or the _____ directory.

10. The home page of a web site is called the _____ page.

11. Name some important documentation to put in your templates.

Module 2

All About Variables

The Goals of This Module

- Introduce variables
- Teach you how to create variables in ColdFusion using cfset and cfparam
- Discuss variable scopes
- Instruct you in outputting a variable's value using cfoutput

This module introduces you to variables, one of the most important concepts in programming, explains their uses, and shows you how to use them in ColdFusion.

A Variable Overview

We want to start by explaining what a variable is. Next, we will talk about two types of variables: simple and complex. Then, before moving on to specific ColdFusion code, you see the variable scopes available within ColdFusion.

What Is a Variable?

A *variable* is a place in memory used to store a value. ColdFusion variables exist in the memory of the server machine. Variables in programming languages are similar to variables in algebra. A variable is a name-value pair. This means you can use the variable's name to refer to the variable's value. While the variable name doesn't change, the variable value *can* change.

Variables can have multiple uses in any programming language. The value a variable contains can be defined either through user input or be created automatically within the program. Variables have many uses, some of which might be as temporary storage of user input (discussed in Module 4), for loop control (Module 9), or as a tool in error processing (Module 11).

Let's look at a real-world example where a variable is used. Open the word processor of your choice and type some text. Now, try to save the file. Your word processor will ask you for a filename before you can save the file to disk. The program is asking for your input, so it can create a variable. It creates an internal variable for the filename of your newly created file and uses the variable to name the file on disk. This is a variable created from user input.

Now, here's an example where a program might want to create a variable without user input: *FreeCell,* a popular card game available on most consumer Windows operating systems (OSs). When you launch FreeCell and start a new game, you can either select a new game to play or have the program select one randomly. If you have the computer pick a game randomly, the software must decide which game to pick. To do this, the software uses a variable. During the game play of this card game, the program probably also uses variables to keep track of the layout of the cards and what card is located at what position in the game.

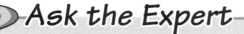 **Ask the Expert**

Question: You compare variables in programming languages to variables in algebra. How do I create a variable that will contain a consistent value throughout my application? Do programming languages support constants? Is there a way to accomplish that?

Answer: Most programming languages have something called a constant. *Constants* are name-value pairs, just like a variable. Unlike a variable, however, constants don't change their value throughout the execution of the program. Just like variables, constants in programming languages are similar to the constants in algebra. An example of a mathematical constant value would be gravity on the Earth. An example of a constant in ColdFusion might be a data source name. The ColdFusion language doesn't support constants. When the need arises for a constant, most developers create a variable in the request scope, discussed later in this module, and define it in the Application.cfm, discussed in Module 7.

When developing ColdFusion applications, variables have many uses. Whenever users type in something to a browser, such as a registration form, the information they input is turned into a variable when submitted to the server. Many web sites, such as Excite.com and Yahoo.com, let users customize their browsing experience. Each user's individual settings are put into variables and are used to build that user's customized page. Let's discuss the two main types of variables.

Simple vs. Complex Variables

Simple variables contain a single value. *Complex variables* are groups of simple variables and we will learn about them in Module 13.

A simple variable is a variable that contains a single piece of data. That data could be an *integer,* a number without a decimal, such as 1, 2, or 35. The data could be a *real number,* a number with a decimal value, such as 1.5, 6.9, or 365.0. A variable's data could also be a string, such as My String or TestString. A *string* contains any mix of alphanumeric characters. When writing code, a string is placed between quotes, while integers or real numbers aren't.

ColdFusion makes changing a variable from one type to another easy. ColdFusion is a *loosely typed language,* which means the ColdFusion interpreter automatically performs data conversions from one simple type to another simple type. Integers can turn into strings and strings can turn into real numbers, if necessary. If a string contains a valid number, then ColdFusion can turn a string back into its number value. When writing code, remember that these automatic conversions take time. Planning your code in advance can reduce the number of automatic conversions you need to make and could improve the efficiency of your application.

Variable Scopes

After discussing the different types of ColdFusion variables that exist, you'll learn about variable scopes. A *scope* defines the length of time the variable exists and how it's available for use. A list of all the ColdFusion scopes is shown in Table 2-1.

Scope Type	Prefix	How Created?	Availability	Comment
Local	variables	Using cfset or cfparam	Available during a single template's execution	Custom tags called by that template cannot access variables in this scope
Form Field	form	When an HTML form is submitted	Available during a single template's execution	We explore this scope in Module 4
URL Parameter	url	In the URL's query string	Available during the execution of the template called in the URL	Custom tags called by that template cannot access variables in this scope(URL variables are discussed in Module 4)
CGI Environment	cgi	By the server	Available by all templates	These values offer information about the browser's configuration and may change for each browser request
HTTP Cookies	cookies	Stored in the browser and can be created using the CFCOOKIE tag	Available during a single template's execution	These variables are stored on the user's machine

Table 2-1 ColdFusion Variable Scopes

Scope Type	Prefix	How Created?	Availability	Comment
Request	request	Using cfset or cfparam	Available during a single template's execution, including custom tags	
Server	server	Using cfset or cfparam	Available in all templates by all applications on a server	
Application	application	Defined using cfset or cfparam	Available during a template's execution; these variables persist between template executions	The CFAPPLICATION tag sets up some defaults for these variables (discussed in Module 7)
Session	session	Defined using cfset or cfparam	Available during a template's execution; these variables persist between template executions	The CFAPPLICATION tag sets up some defaults for these variables (discussed in Module 7)
Client	client	Defined using cfset or cfparam	Available during a template's execution; these variables persist between template executions	The CFAPPLICATION tag sets up some defaults for these variables (discussed in Module 7)
Caller	caller	Defined when calling a custom tag	Available in custom tags	Used in custom tags (discussed in Module 10)
Attributes	attributes	Defined when calling a custom tag	Available in custom tags	Used in custom tags (discussed in Module 10)
Query Result	QueryName	Defined using CFQUERY or the query functions	Available after the query is created	The scope prefix for this scope is user-defined
File	file	Created automatically after using the CFFILE tag with action = upload	Available during the template's execution after the CFFILE tag is used	These variables are created automatically and cannot be changed

Table 2-1   ColdFusion Variable Scopes (*continued*)

At this point, you probably have a number of questions about scopes. Each of these concepts is explored throughout the book and you will receive the background information you need. The scope focus in this module is the local variable scope. Many of the scopes are covered in future modules. The File and CGI are not covered in this book.

1-Minute Drill

● What is a variable?

● Name several types of variables in ColdFusion.

Variable Assignment in ColdFusion

Now that you know what variables are and some of their uses, we can learn how to create variables in ColdFusion. *Variable assignment* is the act of associating a value with a variable name. First, we examine two ColdFusion tags for this purpose: cfset and cfparam, which enable us to assign a value to a variable. Then, we'll learn conventions ColdFusion expects us to use when naming your variables. cfset is the simpler of the two variable assignment tags, so let's start there.

Using cfset

cfset is the primary means of variable assignment when writing CFML code. cfset takes the form:

```
<cfset VariableName = expression>
```

As with all tags, this one starts with a greater than (>) sign followed by the text cfset, followed by a space and the name of the variable. The variable name is similar to a tag attribute, except the name can be anything you want, whereas attributes are predefined. Some important variable naming conventions are discussed later in this module. An equal sign follows the variable name and a ColdFusion expression follows the equal sign. ColdFusion expressions are discussed in more detail in Module 6. At this point, you need to understand

---

● A variable is a name-value pair.
● Integers, real numbers, or strings are types of variables in ColdFusion.

that an expression can either be a string or number. When you use the value instead of a variable assigned to that value, this is called a *literal*. Here are some examples.

```
<cfset variables.ExampleString = "String Example">
<cfset variables.ExampleNumber = 1>
<cfset variables.ExampleNumber = 3>
```

As all your code should, this code begins with the documentation at the top. We state that the template is meant to be an example of cfset. With nothing else of note in the documentation header, we can move on to our cfset tags.

The first statement creates a string variable. The variable is named ExampleString and the value assigned to it is "String Example." Note that all the variables are prefixed with the word "variables"; thus, we're placing the variables in the local variable scope. The second cfset creates a variable called ExampleNumber with the value of 1. The third statement overwrites the ExampleNumber variable with a value of 3. You can't have two variables with the same variable name. The first value is completely forgotten. Let's look at the cfparam statement.

Note

A good practice is always to scope your variables. If a single variable name exists in multiple scopes, ColdFusion won't know which variable to reference and your application might produce errors.

Using cfparam

The cfparam tag is like the cfset tag on steroids. While both tags accomplish the same purpose, cfparam gives you more control. If a cfset tag is used to assign a value to an existent variable name, that value will be overwritten. You can use cfparam if you don't want to overwrite an existing variable. If the variable doesn't exist, however, you want to create it and set it to some default value. The format for the cfparam tag is this:

```
<cfparam name="VariableName" default="Value"
 type="data_type">
```

As always, the tag name comes first. The cfparam tag has three separate attributes: name, default, and type. The *name attribute* is the name of the variable you're defining. cfparam checks to see if the variable is defined. If the variable isn't defined, it creates the variable and assigns it a value specified in the *default attribute*. The *type attribute* can also detect whether the variable is of a specific type. If the variable isn't a specific type, then this tag will throw an error. Errors and error handling are discussed in Module 11.

Tip

cfparam is less efficient than cfset, so unless you have a specific reason for using cfparam, cfset is often the better choice.

Valid values for the type attribute of this tag are array, query, struct, binary, Boolean, date, numeric, string, UUID, a variable name, or any. Arrays, queries, and structures are complex data types, which are discussed in Module 14. Numeric, string, and Boolean are simple data types. *Boolean variables* are variables with a value of either 1 or 0 (True or False). ColdFusion stores Booleans internally as integers. Binary, UUID, and variablename are specialized versions of strings. If you assign the value of the type attribute to any, the tag won't check the type of the variable. This is the tag's default behavior. Here's an example.

```
<cfparam name="variables.ExampleString"
        default="String Example">
<cfparam name="variables.ExampleNumber" default="1">
<cfparam name="variables.ExampleString2"
        default="cfparam String Example">
```

The documentation header opens the template, stating we're using this page as examples of cfparam tags. When the first cfparam statement is executed, ColdFusion looks in memory and checks to see if the variable ExampleString exists. Because the variable does exist, you move on to the next statement. The next statement checks to see if the ExampleNumber variable exists. It doesn't, so we create it and assign it to a default value. The CFML interpreter moves on to the next statement. Here, the cfparam tag is looking for the variable ExampleString2, which doesn't exist. It creates the variable and assigns the default value "cfparam String Example" to it . We finish the example template with an end comment.

2

In real-world use, the main difference between cfparam and cfset is cfparam checks for a variable's existence before potentially overwriting a value. You can accomplish cfparam behavior by using some conditional logic and a ColdFusion function to test for the existence of a variable. You examine conditional logic in Module 8 and functions in Module 6, but the following is a sample of code that could be a replacement for a cfparam:

```
<cfif IsDefined("MyVariable")>
 <cfset MyVariable = "MyDefaultValue">
</cfif>
```

If you need to check for a variable's existence, cfparam makes your code more efficient to run and easier to read than the previous segment.

The previous example demonstrates the use of cfparam but, in this case, the cfset tag would have been a better choice because we know these variables didn't already exist. Let's step through some code that uses both cfparam and cfset.

```
<!-- some examples of cfset -->
<cfset variables.ExampleString = "String Example">
<cfset variables.ExampleNumber = 1>
<!-- end cfset examples -->

<!-- a few examples of cfparam -->
<cfparam name="variables.ExampleString"
         default="String Example">
<cfparam name="variables.ExampleNumber" default="1">
<cfparam name="variables.ExampleString2"
         default="cfparam String Example">
<!-- end cfparam examples -->
```

This template starts out with our documentation, and then combines some elements of our first two examples. First, the cfsets are executed, creating the variables ExampleString and ExampleNumber. Then we come to the first cfparam tag, which checks to see if the variable ExampleString exists. It does exist, so it moves on to the second line. The second cfparam tag checks to see if ExampleNumber exists. This is one we also created using a cfset. Since the variable already exists, we move on to the next line without performing any further processing. The final cfparam tag looks for the variable named ExampleString2. This variable doesn't exist, so then it creates the variable and gives it the default value "cfparam String Example," which ends our template. Next, we learn about some naming conventions for ColdFusion variables.

Naming Conventions for ColdFusion Variables

ColdFusion has its own set of rules concerning what makes a valid variable name. If you don't follow these rules, ColdFusion will throw an error. Here's a list of points to watch for:

- The first character in a variable name must be a letter.

- The remaining characters in your variable's name can be any combination of letters, numbers, or the underscore character.

- Variable names cannot have any spaces in them.

Let's look at a few examples of variable names:

Incorrect Variable Names	Correct Variable Names
Test$1	Test01
12MyNumber	MyNumber12
Sample Variable Name	Sample_Variable_Name

The first example is invalid because it uses a $ in the variable name. We correct it, as shown in the second column, by removing the dollar sign and replacing it with a number, 0. The second variable name is incorrect because it begins with a number. Valid variable names must start with a character. We can modify this value by moving the value to the end of the variable name, instead of having it at the beginning. The final example is invalid because it uses spaces in the variable name. We can replace the spaces with underscores to turn it into a valid variable name.

When naming variables always give the variable a descriptive name because this makes your code more readable and easier to maintain. For example, "ProductName" is much more descriptive than "Name," "UserID" is a better choice than "ID," and "LoopCounter" is more descriptive than "X."

1-Minute Drill

● Name two tags to set a variable.

● What should the first character of a variable name be?

Outputting Your Variables with cfoutput

Although we already know different ways to create ColdFusion variables, we don't know how to do anything with those variables yet. In traditional programming languages, printing a variable's value so it appears to the end user is common. ColdFusion doesn't have a print function, per say, but you should know how to output a variable's value. This section shows you how.

The ColdFusion tag that enables you to output a variable is the *cfoutput tag*. The cfoutput, like most other tags, needs both an open and a close tag. Some attributes exist to the cfoutput tag and you learn about them in Module 5. The format of the cfoutput tag is like this:

```
<cfoutput>
 Other Text or HTML statements here
</cfoutput>
```

In between the open and close cfoutput tags, you can put any text you want, including HTML, CFML tags, or ColdFusion variables. HTML is sent back to the browser as if you hadn't used the cfoutput tag around them. CFML tags are processed and any resultant text is streamed to the browser. The ColdFusion interpreter needs a way to separate ColdFusion variables that aren't within a CFML tag from other CFML tags, regular HTML, or plain text. We do this by using the pound sign on either end of the variable.

● cfset and cfparam are two tags to set a variable.
● The first character of a variable name should be a letter.

Hint

In Module 1, we learned about nesting one HTML table inside another. Just as we can nest HTML tables, many ColdFusion statements can be nested inside each other. For example, a cfset or cfparam can be put inside a cfoutput block.

Let's discover how to implement the cfoutput tag. This example demonstrates the wrong way and the right way to output a single value:

```
<cfset MyVariable = "Test Value">

<!-- output the variable -->
<cfoutput>
 Wrong Output: MyVariable <BR>
 Correct Output: #MyVariable# <BR>
</cfoutput>
```

This code segment first uses a cfset tag to create a variable and gives it a value. The second portion of the template is a cfoutput block to output that value. We demonstrate two ways to output the value: one of them incorrect and one of them correct. You can see the resulting page here.

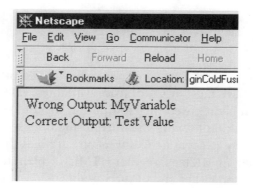

We output the variable's value in two separate ways. The first method is missing the pound signs surrounding the variable name. ColdFusion sees this as straight text, instead of as a variable that needs to be processed. You can see in the illustration that ColdFusion did, indeed, print the text instead of processing the variable. In the next line, when you correctly surround the variable name with pound signs, however, ColdFusion does process the variable and return its value.

Project 2-1: Using Variables for Our Navigation

For this project, we will revisit the simple site we created in Module 1 and modify the navigational elements, so they make use of some ColdFusion variables.

Step-by-Step

Let's start by looking at the original template—index.cfm—from the Project1-3 directory. We want to take some of the values from the navigation bar and re-create them using ColdFusion variables.

1. Examine the elements that make up your navigation bar and choose what should be moved into variables.

```
<!---
Description: Sample Home Page

Entering: N/A
Exiting: N/A

Dependencies: N/A
Expecting: N/A

Modification History
Date     Modifier           Modification
************************************************************
09/15/2001  Jeff Houser, DotComIt     Created
--->

<html>

<head>
 <title>A Sample Home Page</title>
</head>

<body>

<table border="1">
 <tr>
 <!--- Start Navigation Bar --->
 <td>
  <table>
  <tr>
```

```
  <td><a href="Index.htm">Home</a></td>
 </tr>

 <tr>
  <td><a href="LinkPage.htm">Links</a></td>
 </tr>
 </table>
<td>
<!--- End Navigation Bar --->

<!--- start content of the page --->
<td>Welcome to our Home Page<td>
<!--- End content of the page --->
 </tr>
</table>

</body>
</html>
```

Our navigation bar, as it currently stands, has two items in it: a link to the home page of the site and a link to the link page of the site. Each item in the navigation bar has the text displayed to the end user and the location of the page used in the href attribute of the anchor tag. We use variables to store the information for each of our links.

2. Create the variables. Because we have two links in our navigation bar and two elements for each link, we need four variables to create our navigation bar:

- **HomePageLink**   Contains the filename of the page we want to link to for the home page
- **HomePageText**   Contains the text to be displayed to the web browser for our home page link
- **LinkPageLink**   Contains the filename of the page we want to link to for the Link page
- **LinkPageText**   Contains the text to be displayed to the web browser for our link page link

We set these variables at the top of the template, using the cfset tag. All these variables are located in the variables scope, so specify that when creating the variables by prepending the scope name—variables—before the variable name. The following shows the code:

2

```
<!---
Description: Sample Home Page

Entering: N/A
Exiting: N/A

Dependencies: N/A
Expecting: N/A

Modification History
Date        Modifier                Modification
*************************************************************
09/15/2001  Jeff Houser, DotComIt  Created
--->

<!-- create our navigation variables -->
<cfset variables.HomePageLink = "Index.cfm">
<cfset variables.HomePageText = "Home">
<cfset variables.LinkPageLink = "LinkPage.cfm">
<cfset variables.LinkPageText = "Links">
<!-- end navigation variable creation -->

<html>

<head>
 <title>A Sample Home Page</title>
</head>

<body>

<TABLE border="1">
 <tr>
 <!--- Start Navigation Bar --->
 <td>
  <table>
  <tr>
   <td><a href="Index.htm">Home</a></td>
  </tr>

  <tr>
   <td><a href="LinkPage.htm">Links</a></td>
  </tr>
  </table>
 <td>
```

cfsets

```
<!--- End Navigation Bar --->

<!--- start content of the page --->
<td>Welcome to our Home Page<td>
<!--- End content of the page --->
</tr>
</table>

</body>
</html>
```

Note

Keeping as much of your code as possible at the top of the template is considered good form. This code is often called the *business logic* of your application. In ColdFusion development the bottom half of your template is usually reserved for HTML and output.

3. Examine the output section of our code. We can see the navigation bar column of our master table now starts out with a cfoutput tag, as the following shows.

```
<!---
Description: Sample Home Page

Entering: N/A
Exiting: N/A

Dependencies: N/A
Expecting: N/A

Modification History
Date     Modifier          Modification
**************************************************************
09/15/2001 Jeff Houser, DotComIt Created
09/26/2001 Jeff Houser, DotComIt Added Variables in
                          Navigation
--->

<!-- create our navigation variables -->
<cfset variables.HomePageLink = "Index.cfm">
<cfset variables.HomePageText = "Home">
<cfset variables.LinkPageLink = "LinkPage.cfm">
<cfset variables.LinkPageText = "Links">
```

```
<!-- end navigation variable creation -->

<html>

<head>
 <title>A Sample Home Page</title>
</head>

<body>

<table border="1">
 <tr>
 <!--- Start Navigation Bar --->
 <td>
   <cfoutput>
   <table>
    <tr>
    <td>
     <a href="#variables.HomePageLink#">
      #variables.HomePageText#
     </a>
    </td>
    </tr>

    <tr>
    <td>
     <a href="#variables.LinkPageLink#">
      #variables.LinkPageText#
     </a>
    </td>
    </tr>
   </table>
   </cfoutput>
 <td>
 <!--- End Navigation Bar --->

 <!--- start content of the page --->
 <td>Welcome to our Home Page<td>
 <!--- End content of the page --->
 </tr>
</table>

</body>
</html>
```

Dynamically generated links

Our navigation table is similar in structure to what it was before, so we can move on to look specifically at the links. This is the home page link from Module 1:

```
<a href="Index.htm">Home</a>
```

All the pertinent values, such as Index.htm and Home, are written directly into the code. This is our brand-new home page link:

```
<a href="#variables.HomePageLink#">
 #variables.HomePageText#
</a>
```

We have two variables in this line, although the resultant text is the same. `Index.htm` was replaced with the variable `HomePageLink`. `Home` was replaced with the variable `HomePageText`. When ColdFusion is processing the page, it sees the pound signs around the variable and knows it needs to return the value of the variable, not the name of the variable.

Following along with our code, we perform exactly the same operation for the next link in our navigation bar, except with different variables: LinkPageLink and LinkPageText. These variables are used to create a link to the link page, instead of to the home page. As you can see with your resultant home page in the following, these actions don't change the outlook of the page from the end user.

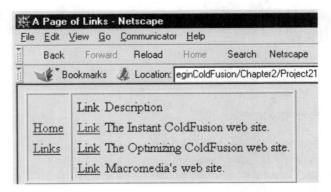

4. The final thing we want to note in our template is that we modified the documentation header. We added a new entry into the modification history. This type of paper-trail documentation helps us keep track of the history of

changes a document goes through. At this point in the game, it's trivial to write a line or two about what you're changing, but when you have to make modifications later, you'll be glad you did.

Project Summary

This project showed you a single use of variables within a ColdFusion application. While this isn't necessarily a real-world application, it is the start of one. In future modules, we can build and expand on the concepts learned here.

Module Summary

This Module introduced you to variables, and how to create and use variables in ColdFusion. We used the cfset and cfparam tags for creating variables, and the cfoutput tag for displaying a variable's value. In later modules, we use variables for many things, such as accepting user input, making decisions in our code, and executing a single block of code multiple times.

☑ *Mastery Check*

1. A variable can also be referred to as a _____ pair.

2. Choose which are valid variable scopes:

    A. URL

    B. Web

    C. Application

    D. Browser

    E. All of the above

    F. None of the above

3. A variable's _____ defines the extent of its availability.

4. What two tags can be used to create a variable?

_____

_____

☑ Mastery Check

5. What are the differences between cfset and cfparam?

_____

_____

6. The cfoutput tag is used to _____ a variable.

7. Which of these choices would be a valid variable name?

  A. $4rqst

  B. TheBVariable

  C. TheBVariable02

  D. 6twelvetwentyfour

  E. All of the above

  F. None of the above

8. What is the prefix for the local variable scope?

_____

_____

9. Which cfset tag is in the correct format?

  A. <cfset samplea = value

  B. cfset $sampleb = "myvalue">

  C. <cfset samplec = 1>

  D. <cfset sampled = "My Sample">

  E. <cfset 1samplee = "my sample">

10. Which attributes are valid cfparam attributes?

  A. Variable

  B. Name

  C. Default

  D. Value

Module 3

Database Design Theory

The Goals of This Module

- Introduce databases
- Explore the functions of databases and application development
- Discuss database design concepts
- Design a database

ColdFusion's functionality quickly becomes limited if you don't have a database residing behind the scenes on your web site. This module discusses databases fundamentals, some commonly used databases, and the theories behind designing a database. Many ColdFusion programmers say that understanding databases and good database design is more important than knowing CFML.

What Is a Database?

To start this discussion, we need to know what a database is at a conceptual level. We will learn about different kinds of databases, and the strengths and weaknesses of each one in this module.

Database Concepts

A *database,* in its simplest description, is a collection of related data. That data could be of any type—from a simple grocery list to a list of customers, products, and orders on an e-commerce site. First let's look at the elements that make up a database. This data is partitioned off into related groups, called *tables.* A single database table is similar to a spreadsheet, and it can be further broken down into columns and rows. A *row* is a single set of all columns and, in a single table, no two rows can be identical. All columns must contain a single value.

Earlier versions of databases were implemented so they would only support a single table of data. A row in the table was accessed in an iterative manner, starting from the first row, and moving to the last one. These types of databases were called *flat file databases.*

The following is a simple example that's relevant to web development. Many web sites today offer special features or support to users who register on their site, so let's create a table for the user's registration information. This sample table has only a few customers in it.

FirstName	LastName	Email	State	ZIP
Jeff	Houser	jeff@instantcoldfusion.com	CT	12345
Kyle	Manning	jeff@farcryfly.com	NY	15462
Fentra	Ackle	fentra@magonda.com	FL	19676
Marge	Milton	marge@magonda.com	FL	19676

The example table contains a subset of the complete data you might use in a real application, but it's fine for our purposes. We have five fields: FirstName, LastName, Email, State, and ZIP. Other fields, not in the list, that we might want to store are Address, City, Username, and Password.

Flat file databases create problems and the biggest problem is the replication of data. For instance, data is replicated in both the state and ZIP columns of the example table. If a piece of data was used in two different rows, then that text would be stored in two different places. This can create human error and lead to incorrect data because of data entry problems. Also, instead of storing a single piece of data once, you're now storing it once for each row that contains the data. In the example, we're storing the text FL two times, instead of once. This doubles our space requirements, which will probably grow even more as we have more users. To get to the final row of a table, you would have to iterate through every row in the table. This isn't time efficient, especially as more data is put into the system. Something had to be done to remedy these problems: enter the relational database management system.

A *relational database management system* is built from many of the table concepts described previously, with one important difference. Instead of storing all data in a single table, you can create multiple tables in which you store your data. This helps you avoid the problems of double data storage and data entry errors. You can store a piece of data in one place, and then use that data in many places. In the previous example, you want to split your single table into three tables. The State and ZIP columns are the two columns in your original table with replicated data. So, your original customer table is split into a customer table, a State table, and a ZIP table. This is the new customer table:

FirstName	LastName	Email
Jeff	Houser	jeff@instantcoldfusion.com
Kyle	Manning	jeff@farcryfly.com
Fentra	Ackle	fentra@magonda.com
Marge	Milton	marge@magonda.com

And this is the State table:

State
CT
NY
FL

This is the ZIP table:

ZIP
12345
15462
19676

As you can see, the State and ZIP tables have less data than the customer table. The separation of the tables does take more thought up-front, but the added benefits of separate tables far outweigh the additional up-front development costs.

With this added dimension of complexity, we need a way to keep track of which tables should be associated with other tables. In database design theory, we have two special types of data—called keys—to keep track of this database association and there are two types of keys: primary and foreign. A *primary key*, which can be a single column or a collection of columns, is used to identify a row uniquely. A *foreign key* is a primary key that resides in a table other than its own. We'll continue exploring the customer example.

Hint

Although, keys can be of any data type, they're often implemented as integer fields. Many times, these fields are set to increment integers automatically.

Because primary and foreign keys are unique identifiers for a row, they're often called identity (ID) fields. First, let's add a primary key to the ZIP table:

ZIPID	ZIP
1	12345
2	15462
3	19676

Our ZIPID is a field. Now you can safely use the ZIPID 1 to reference the ZIP 12345, the ZIPID 2 to reference the ZIP 15462, or the ZIPID 3 to reference the ZIP 19676. We can make a similar modification to the State table:

StateID	State
4	CT
5	NY
6	FL

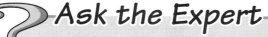

Ask the Expert

Question: Looking at the structure of the database tables, wouldn't keeping track of what data is located where be hard for the end user? How does the user access the data?

Answer: Yes, maintaining the data would be difficult if the users were accessing the database tables directly. In an ideal world, you wouldn't want the user to access the tables directly. Instead, you'd want to create an interface for users that gives them an intuitive way to access the data. In this module, though, we're concentrating on the best way to store data, not building an interface for maintaining the data. A user interface builder can be included in the database program or it can be built in a separate language, such as Visual Basic or ColdFusion. We'll start building one of these interfaces in Module 5.

As with the ZIP table, we can now access the state value with only the StateID. This is similar to the variable concept discussed, where we use one thing to reference another. When searching through a table, cycling through a list of IDs and finding a value is more efficient than searching through a text list for a particular value.

The updated Customer table looks like this:

CustomerID	FirstName	LastName	Email	StateID	ZIPID
1	Jeff	Houser	jeff@instantcoldfusion.com	4	1
2	Kyle	Manning	jeff@farcryfly.com	5	2
3	Fentra	Ackle	fentra@magonda.com	6	3
4	Marge	Milton	marge@magonda.com	6	4

We added a CustomerID field to the Customer table, which enables us to identify a single customer uniquely. In addition, we need to preserve our original associations that each customer has with their state and ZIP values. We'll add two foreign key columns into this table to preserve these associations: StateID, and ZIPID. Whenever we look at customer data, we can see the foreign keys and know we must look into other tables for the data.

1-Minute Drill

● What is a database in its simplest form?

● All rows in a table must be _____ ?

Database Choices

The two main types of databases are file-based databases and client/server databases. While both can be used with ColdFusion, client/server databases are usually a better choice. First, let's look at Microsoft Access, the most common file-based database.

Microsoft Access is one of the most commonly used databases for the back end of a web site. It's inexpensive, widely available as part of Microsoft Office, and easy for the nonprogrammer to use. Access has its place, but that place isn't on the Web. Access isn't scalable, so it isn't known for being a stable database when used for Web access. As the size and complexity of your site grows, the performance of Access drops because Access wasn't designed for high-volume, multiuser use. Article Q174496 of the Microsoft Knowledge Base states that you may experience unexpected results by using Access as a production database on the Web. Access doesn't have the built-in security features found in most of the enterprise-class databases.

Hint

Microsoft Access can be beneficial when creating proof of principal preproduction sites.

Sybase SQL Anywhere, Microsoft SQL Server, and Oracle are examples of client/server databases. *Client/server databases* are databases that have two components, as you can see in Figure 3-1. As the name suggests, one of those components is a client and the other is a database server. As someone who has surfed the Web, you've probably already had experience with what client/server architecture is, although you might not have heard it called this before. A *server* is something that can accept requests from an outside source, while a *client* is the piece of software that sends those requests. A *web server* is akin to a database server and a *web browser* is akin to a database client. The *server component* is an

---

● In its simplest form, a database is a collection of data.
● All rows in a table must be unique.

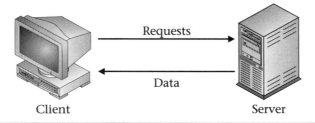

Figure 3-1   Client/server architecture

3

independent entity that controls all access to the database. The client simply
sends commands to the database server, but it's the job of the database server
to implement those commands based on the user's access privileges.

Client/server databases are more reliable, secure, and scalable than a file-
based database because they were designed from the ground up to support
simultaneous multiple users. The user doesn't directly access a specific file but,
instead, accesses the server. The server takes the clients' requests and processes
them. The server decides what access to give the client, based on the user's
login. With a *file-based database*, typically the only security options you have
are yes or no. Either the users have access, enabling them to get in and do
whatever they want, or they have no access at all. The client/server databases
enable you to set levels of access. A user might be able to get in and read existing
data, but can't modify it, for example.

From a development standpoint, you don't write your ColdFusion code
differently whether you're using a client/server database or a file-based database.
Isn't it nice to know you aren't going to be called in on the weekend to fix
something that broke because of a poor database choice?

With so many different databases to choose from, you might wonder how
to choose one that will best suit your ColdFusion development needs. When
developing in ColdFusion, you can access the database in the backend by using
SQL, the language of databases. ColdFusion easily integrates with any database
that's compliant to the open database connectivity (ODBC) standard. Because
most databases do this, you can easily write ColdFusion code that's portable to
any database backend. When you work in a team, having one person worry about
the database end of the equation and the other one worry about the ColdFusion
development can be beneficial. SQL and ODBC are discussed in Module 5.

1-Minute Drill

- What are the two types of databases?
- What is a primary key?

Relationships Between Your Data

After discussing some database basics, you should realize the key to understanding databases is understanding your data. Three types of data relationships exist (or, four types, if you count no relation whatsoever): one-to-one, one-to-many, and many-to-many. We'll look at each of these relationships and learn how we can turn those relationships into database tables. Let's start with the simplest form of relationship: a one-to-one relationship.

One-to-One Relationships

The simplest relationship between any two forms of data is *a one-to-one relationship*. This means for any one piece of data X, there's one piece of data Y. And, for every piece of data Y, there's only one piece of data X. Let's explore some examples.

To find some simple examples of a one-to-one relationship, let's begin by looking at the human body. Every person has a single nose. Every nose belongs to only one person. Every person has one right arm and, given any right arm, you can rest assured that arm belongs to only one person. You probably won't be trying to develop a database that will catalog the parts of the human body, though, so let's move on to some web development examples.

Tip

The relationship between two pieces of data depends entirely on the assumptions we make about that data. If those assumptions are wrong, your resulting application might have problems.

If your web site has a news section, some items are associated with each news release, such as a release date, a release title or headline, and the text of the release. All these items fall under a one-to-one relationship. For every

---

- The two types of databases are client/server databases and file-based databases.
- A primary key is a column or a group of columns that uniquely identify a row.

release, there's a single release date and, for each date, there's only one release. You wouldn't want two titles to be put on two separate releases. Now, let's turn our news releases into a database table.

When turning a one-to-one relationship into a database table, you have two options: the first option is to put all the data in a single table and the second option is to create two tables. We'll implement our news release table as a single table, and then examine an example where you might want to use two tables to implement a one-to-one relationship. This is our news release table:

NewsID	NewsDate	Title	BodyText
1	10/05/98	Halloween Bash	You're all invited to our annual Halloween party celebrating, blah, blah, blah, and so forth . . .
2	01/01/01	A Brand New Year	It's a new year and prospects are looking good for blah, blah, blah, and so forth . . .
3	03/16/99	Beware the Ides of March	People gathered yesterday to celebrate the Ides of March, the fateful day that, blah, blah, and so forth . . .
4	02/01/02	*ColdFusion: A Beginner's Guide* published	McGraw-Hill/Osborne publishes *ColdFusion: A Beginner's Guide,* blah, blah, and so forth . . .

Our table has four fields. As always, we have a primary key called NewsID. We have a date column called NewsDate to store the date of the news release. And, we have a Title column for the headline of the release and a BodyText column for the content of the release. We entered four separate releases into our example table to see how the data would be stored. The BodyText column contains values that are truncated for space. A real press release would have more information.

Hint

Date is a reserved word in many databases. A good practice is to avoid naming our columns after reserved words.

Let's look at an example of a place where you might want to split a one-to-one relationship data into separate tables. Let's say you're the web master of a site that offers advanced user customization. Your users can build their own home pages by customizing the colors and content on the page. Let's look at the colors of the page. This can be a one-to-one relationship. Each user can input a unique background page color, and each background color and each text color is only associated with one user. When we implement this, we might want to separate the user's preferences from the user table. This enables us to report on the preference data easily and efficiently, without having to deal with the user data.

The two tables we need to implement this are the Customer table, called Customers, and the Preferences table, called CustomerPreferences. We can use our Customer table from earlier in this module:

CustomerID	FirstName	LastName	Email
1	Jeff	Houser	jeff@instantcoldfusion.com
2	Kyle	Manning	jeff@farcryfly.com
3	Fentra	Ackle	fentra@magonda.com
4	Marge	Milton	marge@magonda.com

Our CustomerPreference table looks like this:

CustomerPreferenceID	BackgroundColor	TextColor
1	Aqua	Black
2	White	Black
3	Black	White
4	Orange	White

We have three columns in this table. The CustomerPreferenceID is your primary key. BackgroundColor and TextColor hold the user's color preferences, as previously discussed. In a real-world application, you would probably want to store additional preferences, but these two will suffice for example purposes.

The missing ingredient between these two tables is the relation. How do we associate the Customer table with the CustomerPreference table, or the CustomerPreference table with the Customer table? Separate tables are related to each other by the use of primary and foreign keys. In a one-to-one relationship, we have two options that can solve our problem. We can either take the primary key of the CustomerPreference table and put it in the Customer table or we can take the primary key of the Customer table and put it in the CustomerPreference table. Either option will sufficiently define our relationship. For our purposes, let's take the CustomerID and put in the CustomerPreference table, like this:

CustomerPreferenceID	CustomerID	BackgroundColor	TextColor
1	1	Aqua	Black
2	2	White	Black
3	3	Black	White
4	4	Orange	White

Let's move on to another type of relationship: a one-to-many relationship.

3

One-to-Many Relationships

In a *one-to-many relationship,* for every single piece of data X, there can be many pieces of data Y. For every piece of data Y, only one piece of data X can exist. Let's return to the example of the human body. Every human has two eyes. Each eye belongs to only one human. This is a one-to-many relationship between eyes and a person. Arms, legs, hands, and feet could also fall into the one-to-many relationship category. Let's look at more web-based examples.

If you were to create a categorized list of frequently asked questions, you would run into a one-to-many relationship. Each question would fall into a single category, while a single category could have multiple questions inside it. If you were developing an address book application, your employees might work for a single department, but each department would have multiple employees in it. Both of these are one-to-many relationships. Let's take an example and create database tables from it.

If you wanted to create a personal finance application to store information about all of a user's bank accounts, you would run into some one-to-many relationships. Each user could have multiple bank accounts, such as a checking account and a savings account. Each account can only be related to one user. This is a one-to-many relationship.

We need a user table to handle the users. Make this a simple table with three fields: a CustomerID, FirstName, and LastName.

CustomerID	FirstName	LastName
1	Jeff	Houser
2	Kyle	Manning
3	Fentra	Ackle
4	Marge	Milton

This data was taken from some previous examples in this module. Next, we want to create an account table, with the relevant account information. Our Account table should have an AccountID column, an AccountNumber column, a Bank column, and an AccountType column. Let's look at the table:

AccountID	AccountNumber	Bank	AccountType
1	12345	Bank 1	Savings
2	22-3334	Random Bank 2	Checking
3	BBN250034	1st Bank of Nowhere	COD
4	4567109	Bank 1	Checking

All this data is fabricated data. AccountID is the primary key of our table and AccountNumber is the unique identifier the bank assigns to an account. The reason for having these as two different fields is because different banks use different formulas for creating the AccountNumbers. Having your primary key be a consistent value is beneficial, and AccountNumber isn't a consistent value.

These tables are created, but they aren't yet related, so we need to understand how to relate the two tables to each other. Once again, to create our relationships, we take the primary key from one table and put it in the other. When creating a one-to-one relationship between two tables, it didn't matter which table got the primary key of the other. In one-to-many relationships, this does matter. The table on the "one" side of the relationship is the one that must get the primary key of the table on the "many" side of the relationship. Let's reexamine the Account table:

AccountID	CustomerID	Account Number	Bank	AccountType
1	1	12345	Bank 1	Savings
2	2	22–3334	Random Bank 2	Checking
3	2	BBN250034	1st Bank of Nowhere	COD
4	4	4567109	Bank 1	Checking

Putting the CustomerID in the Account table shows us that every account has a single customer associated with it. As we can see by examining the data, however, customer can have multiple accounts. CustomerID 2 has both a checking account and a COD account.

Many-to-Many Relationships

The final relationship type is a *many-to-many relationship,* which is the most complicated of the relationship types. For every value of X data, there can be many values of Y data. But also for every value of Y data, there can also be many values of X data. Unfortunately, the human body example used in the previous two sections doesn't hold up here. People don't share arms, legs, brains, noses, or eyes with other people, so let's jump right in to some more real-world web examples.

Perhaps you've searched a knowledge base on a web site, looking for information on a company's products. A single write-up in the knowledge base can often apply to many products. Likewise, many products can most likely have more than one article on them in the knowledge base. This is a many-to-many relationship.

Perhaps you were reading the previous bank account example and thought to yourself that you have a joint account with your spouse, child, or parents. This is contradictory to our original assumption that every account would have only one person associated with it because a joint account would have multiple people associated with it. The assumptions we make about our data define the functionality and, if we make wrong assumptions, the final application will be wrong. This isn't to say our original assumption was incorrect, however. It depends on the application you are trying to develop and knowing what will meet the needs.

Suppose we want to change our bank account example so the system will support an account with joint owners. This is no longer a one-to-many relationship; this now becomes a many-to-many relationship. A bank account can have multiple customers and a customer can have multiple bank accounts. Let's review our two tables. Here's the Customer table:

CustomerID	FirstName	LastName
1	Jeff	Houser
2	Kyle	Manning
3	Fentra	Ackle
4	Marge	Milton

Here is the Account table:

AccountID	AccountNumber	Bank	AccountType
1	12345	Bank 1	Savings
2	22-3334	Random Bank 2	Checking
3	BBN250034	1st Bank of Nowhere	COD
4	4567109	Bank 1	Checking

The real issue to discuss is how do we relate these two tables to each other. In a many-to-many relationship, you create a separate table with the primary key of each of the tables. This type of table is called an *intersection table*. Our intersection table would look like this:

CustomerID	AccountID
1	1
2	2
2	2
4	4

I like to name intersection tables by combining the names of the previous two tables, so this table would be named CustomerAccount. The intersection table contains only associations, not data. Also, I like to implement the primary key of an intersection table as a group of all the columns in the table. They don't need a special primary key field.

1-Minute Drill

- What are the three types of relationships between data?
- What is an intersection table?

Normalizing Your Database

After you collect your data, you need to build your database. The key to creating your table structure is to develop an understanding of the data. First, let's look at some steps we can take when developing your database and explain how to spot potential red flags in your data.

- The three types of relationships between data are One-to-One, One-to-Many, Many-to-Many.
- An intersection table is a table to store a many-to-many relationship.

Insertion and Deletion Anomalies

The process of analyzing your data and organizing it into tables is called *normalization.* Database normalization is the most important aspect of database design. The normalization of your database can prevent the replication of data storage, and avoid insertion and deletion anomalies.

Insertion and *deletion anomalies* happen when we can't add, or delete, one type of data without also adding, or deleting, another type of data. Continue using the bank example we've been following in this module. Pretend you were given a sample check register and you've been asked to model this in a database format. This is the check register:

Check Number	Date	Amount	Comment	Acount Number	BankName
341	10/05/2001	350.12	Flowers	BBN250034	1st Bank of Nowhere
348	10/05/2001	12.12	Gas	BBN250034	1st Bank of Nowhere
348	10/06/2001	52.97	Snacks	BBN250034	1st Bank of Nowhere
352	11/04/2001	56.00	N/A	BBN250034	1st Bank of Nowhere
354	11/10/2001	14.00	Stationery	BBN250034	1st Bank of Nowhere

If we were to take the structure directly like this and use it as our database, we would run into some logic problems.

Based on this structure, a checking account cannot exist in the database without a check written against it. This is known as an *insertion anomaly*. You cannot insert one piece of data—the checking account—without also inserting a check. We want to avoid situations like this. This also contains a deletion anomaly. We can't delete a check without also deleting the checking account information. We solve all these problems by separating all the information into separate tables.

One table would contain the CheckNumber, Date, Price, and Comment columns. The BankName would go into a table of its own. The AccountNumber would go into yet a third table. Let's start with the bank table:

Bank ID	BankName
1	1st Bank of Nowhere

The AccountNumber table would be like this:

AccountNumberID	BankID	AccountNumber
1	1	BBN250034

Finally, our check register:

Check Number	Date	Amount	Comment	Account NumberID
341	10/05/2001	350.12	Flowers	1
348	10/05/2001	12.12	Gas	1
348	10/06/2001	52.97	Snacks	1
352	11/04/2001	56.00	N/A	1
354	11/10/2001	14.00	Stationery	1

This three-tabled structure enables us to avoid any insertion and deletion anomalies.

The Normal Forms

Database normalization has six different levels and each level is called a normal form. Each *normal form* exists to handle a specific case of insertion or deletion anomalies. The levels build on each other, in a stepwise manner, so a database that's in the second normal form must also be in the first normal form.

The *first normal form* is any table that meets the definition of a relation. A table is a relation if all the columns are single-valued and all entries in a row are of the same type. I don't know of a database that allows you to create a table that doesn't meet the definition of a relation, so it's enough to say that anything you create will be, at the least, in first normal form. You need to make sure you don't store lists in a text field.

The *second normal form* avoids situations where some data in the table is only partially dependent on the primary key. If you follow a suggestion made earlier and always use an integer field—separate from the data you're modeling—as your primary key, all your table structures will be in second normal form. You'll experience problems with second normal form only when you're using a combination of fields as your primary key.

The *third normal form* eliminates transitive dependencies. A *transitive dependency* occurs when two pieces of data relate to each other via another piece of data. An example is a situation in which you want to store the fees for having a checking account at a particular bank. Every bank charges different fees for its checking accounts. The fields of your table would be AccountID, AccountNumber, BankName, and Fee. To put this structure into third normal form, you first separate the BankName field out into a separate table and add a BankID into your Account table, which puts the structure into second normal form. Then, you separate the Fee field out into a separate table and relate the fees with the bank. You could get the fee on the checking account through its bank type.

The next normal form is called Boyce-Codd normal form (BCNF), in which every relation is based off a primary key. If you have a table with multiple fields that can be used as a primary key, you need to make sure all database relations are based off the primary key. If you make sure you always use a special field as the unique identifier and base all your relations off your unique ID, then you won't have problems with BCNF. The *fourth normal form* is one with no multivalued dependencies. A *multivalued dependency* occurs where you have two unrelated bits of data that depend on the same key. A single person can have a checking account and a car, for example, but a car and a checking account are two completely unrelated items. If you were to implement both items in one table, you would experience a multivalued dependency because the user couldn't have a checking account without a car and couldn't have a car without a checking account.

The last two normal forms are the fifth normal form and Domain/Key normal form. The *fifth normal form* refers to obscure anomalies where, after you deconstruct your data, no way exists to reconstruct it. I have yet to come across a situation where this was the case. *Domain/Key normal form* is a fancy way to state that your database structure contains no modification anomalies. The name of this normal form comes from two important database attributes: a *key* is the unique identifier of a particular row and a *domain* is the description of valid values for each column in that row.

1-Minute Drill

- What do you do to avoid insertion and deletion anomalies?
- How many normal forms are there?

- To avoid insertion and deletion anomalies, you normalize the database.
- There are six normal forms.

Project 3-1: Designing a Product Database

Let's look at a real-world example of database development. Pretend you work for a music store and you've just been handed an Excel sheet of the available CDs the store wants to put on its web site.

Step-by-Step

1. Look at the data we've been given. You can see some of the sample data in Table 3-1 or you can download the full spreadsheet from instantcoldfusion.com. This sheet has five pieces of data. In a real-world situation, you would probably be given more data. Other data we might want to deal with is the price of the CD, the record label of the CD, the number of units in stock, or the order the songs appear on each disc. The data here is fine for the purpose of your example. Let's turn this spreadsheet into a database structure.

Artist	CD Name	Song	Genre1	Genre2
"Weird Al" Yankovic	Running with Scissors	The Saga Begins	Comedy	Folk
"Weird Al" Yankovic	Running with Scissors	Germs	Comedy	Rap
"Weird Al" Yankovic	Running with Scissors	Grapefruit Diet	Comedy	Swing
"Weird Al" Yankovic	Weird Al Yankovic	Ricky	Comedy	Rock
"Weird Al" Yankovic	Weird Al Yankovic	Gotta Boogie	Comedy	Disco
"Weird Al" Yankovic	Weird Al Yankovic	My Bologna	Comedy	Rock
"Weird Al" Yankovic	Off The Deep End	Smells Like Nirvana	Comedy	Grunge
"Weird Al" Yankovic	Off The Deep End	Polka Your Eyes Out	Comedy	Polka
"Weird Al" Yankovic	Off The Deep End	When I Was Your Age	Comedy	Rock
Nirvana	Nevermind	Smells Like Teen Spirit	Grunge	Alternative
Nirvana	Nevermind	Come As You Are	Grunge	Alternative
Nirvana	Nevermind	Lithium	Grunge	Alternative
Nirvana	Bleach	Paper Cuts	Grunge	Alternative
Nirvana	Bleach	Negative Creep	Grunge	Alternative

Table 3-1   Products

Artist	CD Name	Song	Genre1	Genre2
Nirvana	Bleach	Scoff	Grunge	Alternative
Teenage Fanclub	DGC Rarities Vol 1	Mad Dog 20/20	Alternative	Rock
Nirvana	DGC Rarities Vol 1	Pay to Play	Grunge	Alternative
Weezer	DGC Rarities Vol 1	Jamie	Rock	Surf
Cell	DGC Rarities Vol 1	Never Too High	Rock	Grunge

Table 3-1 Products (*continued*)

2. To create our database table structure, first we analyze the data in our columns to understand what we've been given:

- **Title** The title of the CD.
- **Artist** The artist on the CD.
- **Song** The title of a song by the particular artist from the album in question.
- **Genre1** The genre in which the song is located.
- **Genre2** A secondary genre with which the song is associated.

The most forthright element you might notice is your spreadsheet has two columns for Genre. We want to avoid this replication of data in our final table structure. Other than Genre, we have three pieces of data: the title of the CD, the artist on the CD, and the list of songs on the CD.

3. Now that we know the four pieces of data we have to deal with, we need to define the relationships that lie between our data. We can do this by stating clear facts about each piece of data:

- A CD has only one title
- A title relates back to a single CD
- A CD can have multiple songs
- A song can only be on a single CD
- A single artist can have multiple songs
- A song can be associated with only a single song

● A single song only shows up on a single CD

● A single song can have multiple genres

● A single genre can be associated with multiple songs

Caution

When defining the relationships between your data, make sure you have a sample large enough to document all assumptions.

I made some internal assumptions about the data, based on my knowledge of CDs, which may or may not be obvious from the previous specifications: An artist is associated with a song and the song is associated with a compact disc, and the artist isn't directly associated with a compact disc (this is an indirect association through the songs). Depending on the type of application you're developing, this assumption may or may not fill your needs. In this case, it will fill your needs, though.

4. The next step is to create your database tables from the assumptions we created in Step 2. First, you want a CD table. This table contains a primary key, DiscID, and the title of the disc, DiscTitle.

DiscID	DiscTitle
1	DGC Rarities Vol 1
2	Bleach
3	Nevermind
4	Off The Deep End
5	Weird Al Yankovic
6	Running with Scissors

Then, we want to associate the songs with the CD they're on. A single disc can have multiple songs, yet a song is only associated back with a single song. This is a one-to-many relationship. Create your song table and give it the primary key of the Disc table.

SongID	Song	DiscID
1	The Saga Begins	6
2	Negative Creep	2
3	Mad Dog 20/20	1
4	Smells Like Nirvana	4
5	Polka Your Eyes Out	4

This table segment contains only a subset of the data from Table 3-1, but it demonstrates our intent.

Next, we need to model the artist's relationship with a song. This is also a one-to-many relationship. An artist can have multiple songs, but a song can only have multiple artists. We accomplish this by taking the ArtistID from the one side of the relationship and putting it into the Song table from the many side of the relationship. Our Artist table looks like this:

ArtistID	Artist
1	Nirvana
2	"Weird Al" Yankovic
3	Weezer
4	Teenage Fanclub

We update the Song table by placing the ArtistID in it, like this:

SongID	Song	DiscID	ArtistID
1	The Saga Begins	6	2
2	Negative Creep	2	1
3	Mad Dog 20/20	1	4
4	Smells Like Nirvana	4	2
5	Polka Your Eyes Out	4	2

We still haven't touched on the Genre tables. This is a many-to-many relationship between a song and a genre. A song can have many genres and a genre can have many songs associated with it. First, let's create the Genre table:

GenreID	Genre
1	Comedy
2	Rock
3	Grunge
4	Alternative
5	Pop
6	Polka

To create the many-to-many relationship, we draw up a new intersection table between the two facets of data:

SongID	GenreID
1 (The Saga Begins)	1 (Comedy)
2 (Negative Creep)	3 (Grunge)

SongID	**GenreID**
2 (Negative Creep)	4 (Alternative)
3 (Mad Dog 20/20)	2 (Rock)
3 (Mad Dog 20/20)	4 (Alternative)
4 (Smells Like Nirvana)	1 (Comedy)
4 (Smells Like Nirvana)	3 (Grunge)
5 (Polka Your Eyes Out)	1 (Comedy)
5 (Polka Your Eyes Out)	6 (Polka)

When creating the intersection table, I included the name the ID references in parentheses. As always, these tables are only subsets of the actual tables. I implemented the database as a Microsoft Access file, which you'll use as the backend to your site in future modules. Figure 3-2 shows the database diagram.

Tip

A good idea is to enforce referential integrity at the database level, through the use of relationships, triggers, or other functions that your database of choice offers.

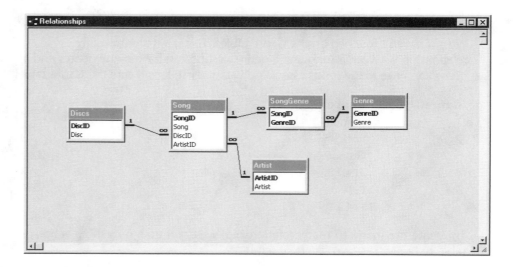

Figure 3-2 Database diagram

Project Summary

If you can get your data in a digital format, it's common to get the data as an Excel sheet or in a non-normalized Access database. Both are easy for nonprogrammers to use and maintain. This project stepped you through the process of analyzing data so you can build your database.

Module Summary

Your database is the foundation of nearly everything you'll do in ColdFusion applications. This module covered database relationships and techniques for normalizing your data. Being knowledgeable about database concepts and building good databases can help you well in all your ColdFusion development.

3

☑ *Mastery Check*

1. What are some characteristics of a database table?

_____

_____

2. What is a primary key? What is a foreign key?

_____

_____

3. When accessing databases through ColdFusion, you use ODBC. What does ODBC stand for?

A. Open Database Connectivity

B. Only Data Before Calling

C. One Database Call

D. Open Door Base Cylinder

4. On examination of our Account table in the section of one-to-many relationships, you might notice the table isn't completely normalized. What must be done to normalize the table further?

_____

_____

5. When you normalize a database, you are _____ data anomalies.

6. An insertion anomaly occurs when:

A. You cannot create one piece of data without creating a second type of unrelated data.

B. You cannot delete one piece of data without also deleting a second piece of unrelated data.

C. You cannot create one piece of data without creating a second type of related data.

D. You cannot delete one piece of data without also creating a piece of related data.

3

☑ *Mastery Check*

7. What's wrong with this table? How would you fix it?

ID	Student	Grade	Teacher
1	Jeff	First	Mr. Smith
2	Mary	First	Mr. Smith
3	Angela	Third	Ms. Teeker
4	Jude	Fourth	Ms. Tilly

8. What are some characteristics of a one-to-one relationship?

_____

_____

9. Pick the two main types of databases:

A. File based

B. Data Warehouse

C. Web based

D. Client/server

Module 4

Parameter Passing and Forms

The Goals of This Module

- Demonstrate how to send variables from one template to another
- Introduce HTML forms
- Create a valid HTML form

After learning about variables in Module 2, we'll now learn how to share variables between separate pages, which is called parameter passing. Then, we'll learn about HTML forms and accepting user input.

Parameter Passing via the URL

This section gives you an overview of how to share variables between two ColdFusion template pages. We start with an overview of the Web as a stateless environment. Then, we learn about the query string of the URL and how we can use it to pass variables from one application to another. Finally, we see examples of passing parameters.

The Stateless Web

The Web is a stateless environment. This means every request for a page is unique, with no correlation between requests. This causes problems when creating web applications. In traditional programming languages, you can easily keep track of user information and variables. For example, if you were to open an HTML or ColdFusion document in the HTML editor of your choice, the program would need to keep track of many things. The program would need to know the name and file location of the current document, as well as the location of the cursor in the document. Most likely, the program will keep track of any changes you made to the document. It needs to know if you selected any text. The program also needs to know of any other open documents. All these things contribute to the state of your application, and the list of contributors can go on and on. The program knows what's going on. There's no way to keep track of such things when you're creating web applications.

In a web application, you might want to keep track of a number of things during the user's use of your application. For instance, in a secure application, has the user logged in? What type of access does the user have to what information? What section of the site is the user looking at? We can deal with this issue in many ways. One is to pass state information via the URL. Another is to use browser cookies to store state information. A third option is to use technologies, such as Java or Flash. This module investigates the URL option.

Tip

ColdFusion is designed to use cookies to handle advanced state management. We learn about this in detail in Module 7.

Passing Parameters

Variables and parameters are different names for the same thing. *Parameter passing* means creating variables on one page and making them available to a second page. To make variables available, we put them in the URL. The portion of the URL that contains parameters is called the *query string*.

A simple URL to a ColdFusion page might look like this:

```
HTTP://www.myserver.com/Dir/Page.cfm
```

The code starts with the command HTTP, which stands for Hypertext Transfer Protocol. This portion of the URL tells the browser what type of action it's performing. Next is the colon and two backslashes, which separates the command from the item on which the command is being performed. Third comes the server or domain name, www.myserver.com. Following the server name is the directory name, Dir, and the filename, Page.cfm. This URL is perfectly valid, but an optional portion of this URL isn't located here. This portion is called the query string and it's located after the filename.

The *query string* defines the variables that will be available during the HTTP request. The query string is located right after the filename and is separated from the filename by a question mark. Variables are defined in the query string much the same way they're defined using ColdFusion's cfset tag. The variable name is followed by an equal sign, which is then followed by the value of the variable. Here's an example:

```
HTTP://www.myserver.com/Dir/Page.cfm?Var1=value1
```

This example creates a variable called Var1 and gives it the value of value1 when executing the page Page.cfm. If you want to pass multiple parameters in the URL, you can separate each parameter by an ampersand (&). A URL with two variables would look like this:

```
www.myserver.com/Dir/Page.cfm?Var1=value1&Var2=value2
```

With this URL, the page.cfm template will have two variables available: Var1 and Var2.

1-Minute Drill

● What is another name for a variable?

● How are variables defined in the query string portion of a URL?

In our discussion of variable scopes, one of the scopes was termed the URL scope. Parameters passed in the URL exist in the URL variable scope. In the preceding example, we could access these variables using the following variable names: url.Var1 or url.Var2. ColdFusion does this automatically, with no extra development work on your part. Here's a project that uses URL variables.

MessagePage.cfm

Project 4-1: Putting URL Variables to Use

URL variables come in handy when we create our web applications. This project teaches how you to put URL variables to use. We'll take the site we've been building in the past chapters and add a page that displays any message passed through the variable.

Step-by-Step

1. Let's create the new page to your web site. You can find the finished MessagePage.cfm file on InstantColdFusion.com/index.cfm/LinkPage.cfm. We can start by creating our standard page structure with a documentation header and the page structure we're using for our site.

```
<!---
Description: A page to display the URL
        variable message.

Entering: N/A
Exiting: N/A

Dependencies: N/A
```

● Parameter is another name for a variable.
● Variables are defined in the query string portion of a URL as variablename=variablevalue.

```
Expecting: Message : a URL variable

Modification History
Date           Modifier              Modification
****************************************************************
09/15/2001    Jeff Houser, DotComIt  Created
--->

<!-- create our navigation variables -->
<cfset variables.HomePageLink = "Index.cfm">
<cfset variables.HomePageText = "Home">
<cfset variables.LinkPageLink = "LinkPage.cfm">
<cfset variables.LinkPageText = "Links">
<!-- end navigation variable creation -->

<html>

<head>
 <title>A Message Page</title>
</head>

<body>

<table border="1">
 <tr>
  <!--- Start Navigation Bar --->
  <td>
    <cfoutput>
     <table>
      <tr>
       <td>
        <a href="#variables.HomePageLink#">
         #variables.HomePageText#
        </a>
        </td>
      </tr>

      <tr>
      <td>
       <a href="#variables.LinkPageLink#">
          #variables.LinkPageText#
        </a>
        </td>
      </tr>
```

4

```
   </table>
  </cfoutput>
  </td>
 <!--- End Navigation Bar --->

 <!--- start content of the page --->
 <td>
 </td>
 <!--- End content of the page --->
 </tr>
</table>

</body>
</html>
```

Start by filling in our documentation header, stating that this page will display a URL variable. Then we move on to the portion of the template where we create our URL variables. Then we come to the navigation column of our page layout, followed by the content column. Creating that portion is the first step in our project.

2. The next step is to add our new page to the navigation bar. Do this by creating two new navigation variables for our links. Following our naming conventions, we create MessagePageLink and MessagePageText. MessagePageText is simple enough; it states that our link text will display the words "Message Page." We want to pay a little more attention to the MessagePageLink.

```
<!---
Description: A page to display the URL
       variable message.

Entering: N/A
Exiting: N/A

Dependencies: N/A
Expecting: Message : a URL variable

Modification History
Date      Modifier        Modification
***********************************************************
09/15/2001   Jeff Houser, DotComIt  Created
--->
```

```
<!-- create our navigation variables -->
<cfset variables.HomePageLink = "Index.cfm">
<cfset variables.HomePageText = "Home">
<cfset variables.LinkPageLink = "LinkPage.cfm">
<cfset variables.LinkPageText = "Links">
<cfset variables.MessagePageLink =
   "MessagePage.cfm?Message=YouCameFromMessagePage">
<cfset variables.MessagePageText = "Message Page">
<!-- end navigation variable creation -->

<html>

<head>
 <title>A Message Page</title>
</head>

<body>

<table border="1">
 <tr>
 <!--- Start Navigation Bar --->
 <td>
   <cfoutput>
   <table>
    <tr>
     <td>
      <a href="#variables.HomePageLink#">
      #variables.HomePageText#
       </a>
     </td>
    </tr>

    <tr>
    <td>
      <a href="#variables.LinkPageLink#">
      #variables.LinkPageText#
       </a>
      </td>
    </tr>

    <tr>
    <td>
      <a href="#variables.MessagePageLink#">
      #variables.MessagePageText#
```

New navigation variables

4

New navigation link

```
        </a>
       </td>
      </tr>
    </table>
   </cfoutput>
  </td>
  <!--- End Navigation Bar --->

  <!--- start content of the page --->
  <td>
  </td>
  <!--- End content of the page --->
 </tr>
</table>

</body>
</html>
```

The MessagePageLink contains the page that's going to load up when the user clicks the link it's used to create. In addition to the filename of the page we're linking to, we placed a query string in the URL. We create the variable Message and give it the value of YouCameFromMessagePage (see the following illustration). If you downloaded the files from the web site, you'll see Index.cfm and LinkPage.cfm have similar, but different, values for this variable.

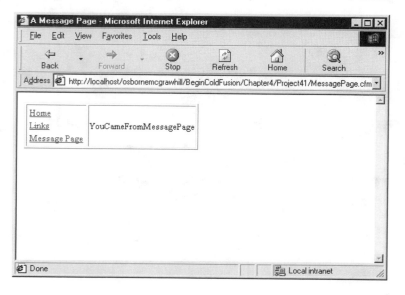

3. Our next step is to output the message variable in the body portion of the page. We simply surround your message variable with a cfoutput block.

```
<!---
Description: A page to display the URL
      variable message.

Entering: N/A
Exiting: N/A

Dependencies: N/A
Expecting: Message : a URL variable

Modification History
Date        Modifier            Modification
*************************************************************
09/15/2001   Jeff Houser, DotComIt  Created
--->

<!-- create our navigation variables -->
<cfset variables.HomePageLink = "Index.cfm">
<cfset variables.HomePageText = "Home">
<cfset variables.LinkPageLink = "LinkPage.cfm">
<cfset variables.LinkPageText = "Links">
<cfset variables.MessagePageLink =
   "MessagePage.cfm?Message=YouCameFromMessagePage">
<cfset variables.MessagePageText = "Message Page">
<!-- end navigation variable creation -->

<html>

<head>
 <title>A Message Page</title>
</head>

<body>

<table border="1">
  <tr>
  <!--- Start Navigation Bar --->
  <td>
    <cfoutput>
    <table>
      <tr>
      <td>
      <a href="#variables.HomePageLink#">
```

```
                    #variables.HomePageText#
                  </a>
                </td>
              </tr>

              <tr>
                <td>
                  <a href="#variables.LinkPageLink#">
                    #variables.LinkPageText#
                  </a>
                </td>
              </tr>

              <tr>
                <td>
                  <a href="#variables.MessagePageLink#">
                    #variables.MessagePageText#
                  </a>
                </td>
              </tr>
            </table>
          </cfoutput>
        </td>
        <!--- End Navigation Bar --->

        <!--- start content of the page --->
        <td>
          <cfoutput>
            #url.Message#
          </cfoutput>
        </td>
        <!--- End content of the page --->
      </tr>
    </table>

  </body>
</html>
```

Output block

We can load the site onto your web server and click to the message page from the other pages to see the different results.

Project Summary

This project demonstrated a simple use of passing parameters via the URL. This concept is important to understand both in ColdFusion and all web development. In Module 5, you see some places where this can be a real benefit.

An Introduction to Forms

Passing variables via the URL is an important skill when developing web applications, but you must define the parameters being passed. It is also important to know how to collect information from the user. This section introduces you to HTML forms, which are used for collecting user input. We also learn about some specialized ColdFusion form elements.

The HTML Form Tag and cfform

4

We need to understand the HTML form tag. Then we'll learn about *cfform,* a specialized ColdFusion version of the form tag. Let's begin with an overview of what a form is.

Two pages are needed to process a single form: an input page and an action, or processing, page. The input page contains the form and various form elements that collect the user's input. The action page contains the processing to be performed on the data entered. We learn about the different types of form elements later in this module. First, let's look at the form tag.

As with most HTML tags, the *form tag* has an open and close tag. Become acquainted with these attributes to the open form tag:

- **Action**   This attribute contains the value of the page onto which we're submitting a form.

- **Method**   Two types of actions that can be performed with the form tag. The two valid values for this attribute are post and get. The *post value* is for passing data on to an action page and we use this value exclusively throughout this book. The *get value* is for collecting information from another page. Covering the get use of the form tag is beyond the scope of this book.

- **Enctype**   This specifies what Multipurpose Internet Mail Extensions (MIME) type of data that the form tag is passing to the action page. The most common value for this attribute, if it is specified at all, is multipart/form-data.

- **Name**   The *name* attribute is used to define a name of the form. This is used primarily to access form, or form elements, via JavaScript or some other client-side scripting language.

Other attributes are associated with the form tag, but these are the most common and the ones we'll use throughout this book.

Before delving into ColdFusion's cfform, let's look at how to set up our form tag:

```
<form action="ActionPage.cfm"
    method="post">
 <!--- insert other form elements here --->
</form>
```

Our form tag states we are posting our form information on the ActionPage.cfm. In between our open and close form tags, a comment that states other form elements would belong between the open and close form tags. We learn about the elements of a form in the next section. First, let's look at ColdFusion's replacement for the form tag: cfform.

The *cfform tag* is a ColdFusion way to create an HTML form that will provide greater built-in functionality than a standard HTML form tag. This isn't to say the cfform tag provides anything new over HTML—it simply takes some work to get there. If you're using cfform, then you also have access to ColdFusion specific form elements, described later in this module. Look at some of the attributes to the cfform tag:

- **Action** This attribute specifies the page the form information is passed on to for processing. This acts the same as the action attribute on the HTML form tag.

- **Enctype** This attribute defines the MIME type used to encode data sent via the post method. This is the same attribute as the HTML enctype attribute.

- **Name** This attribute provides a way to name the form you're creating and is identical to the name attribute of the normal form tag.

- **Passthrough** The *passthrough* attribute lets you define attributes for the form tag that aren't explicitly referenced in the cfform tag.

- **Enablecab** The *enablecab* attribute accepts a yes or no value. The default is no, but if it's set to yes, the user is asked if they want to download some Microsoft Java classes. These Java classes are necessary to run some of the custom ColdFusion form elements.

- **Onsubmit** The *onsubmit* attribute is an optional attribute. It takes the name of a JavaScript function you want to execute before the form is submitted.

Now, we can see an example of the cfform tag and examine what happens when the ColdFusion parses the cfform tag.

Tip

We aren't discussing all the attributes of the html form or the CFML cfform tags. We only discuss some basics you'll use in this book.

Let's look at an example cfform tag:

```
<cfform action="ActionPage.cfm">
 <!-- insert other form elements here -->
</cfform>
```

This tag creates a simple form. Remember, ColdFusion is a server-side language. The cfform tag executes and turns itself into an HTML form tag. The resulting code you get is this:

```
<script LANGUAGE=JAVASCRIPT TYPE="text/javascript" >
<!--

function _CF_checkCFForm_1(_CF_this)
  {
  return true;
  }

//-->
</script>

<form name="CFForm_1"
   action="ActionPage.cfm"
   method=POST
   onsubmit="return _CF_checkCFForm_1(this)">
 <!-- insert other form elements here -->
</form>
```

This code begins with some JavaScript. This is automatically generated JavaScript, used for form validation if you're using some of the other ColdFusion form elements. In this case, the JavaScript does nothing. Following the script, we have our html form tag. The browser never sees our cfform ColdFusion tag. Our form tag has an action, which we defined via the cfform. It automatically created a name and method for the form. The method is, of course, post. The form

4

tag also created the onsubmit that calls the JavaScript function when the form tries to submit. We needn't worry about the JavaScript right now, other than to realize that cfform gives us a way to create validation scripts automatically.

If you want to compare the cfform and the html form tag, you'll notice relatively no difference exists. ColdFusion's cfform gives you some built-in JavaScript functions and Java applets used to verify the form or provide specialized form elements. Because of this, most experienced developers stray away from using the built-in controls, preferring to code the functionality themselves. Next, we look at the actual form elements used in the form tag.

Form Elements

This section discusses the different elements you can use to accept input from the user. We also learn about the ColdFusion variations of these elements that can be used within a cfform tag. We examine four elements: text boxes, radio buttons, check boxes, and select boxes.

Text boxes, radio buttons, and check boxes are all created using the html input tag. The input tag has three important attributes:

- **Name** The *name* attribute defines a name to the form element. On the action page of your form, you will access the value the user entered through this name.

- **Value** The *value* attribute sets a default value for the attribute. If the user doesn't input or select a value for the form control, then it will contain the text in the value attribute when processing its value on the action page.

- **Type** The *type* attribute defines the type of form element we're creating. Some values for this attribute we'll discuss are text, radio, check box, and hidden.

Next, we see each of the form elements you can create with the input tag and how to create them.

The text form element fills a simple-enough purpose. It enables the user to enter text data into your form. Here's an example:

```
Text Box 1: <input type="text" name="TextBox1">
```

This creates a text form element with no default value. Notice we placed some text—Text Box 1:—before the input tag. This type of text is called an *identifier,* and it's entirely optional and completely unrelated to the input tag.

Identifiers are almost always used, though, because they tell the user what type of information you're looking for. A form with ten text boxes is simply too confusing to complete without some form of guidance. You can see some text boxes in Figure 4-1.

The input tag can also be used to create radio buttons. *Radio buttons* are best when you want the user to select a single item from your choices. Each choice for your radio button list must have a separate input statement. Set the name attribute of your radio button to the same value for each entry and specify the value attribute. By convention, the values are usually different for each entry, although this needn't be the case. It doesn't usually make sense to have multiple choices all refer to the same value.

4

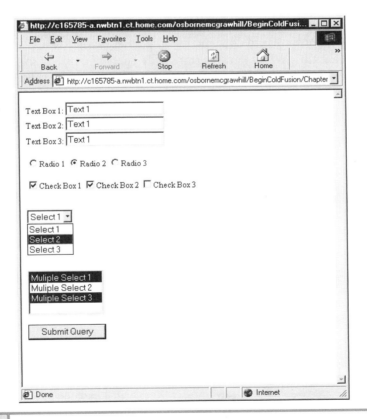

Figure 4-1   Text form element page

You can see some radio buttons in Figure 4-1. Let's look at the code behind them:

```
<input type="Radio" name="RButton" value="R1">Radio 1

<input type="Radio" name="RButton" value="R2">Radio 2

<input type="Radio" name="RButton" value="R3">Radio 3
```

This creates a single set of radio buttons, with three different options. The type of the input tag is set to radio. The name for all three input tags is set to the same thing: Rbutton and the value for each one is different. In the case of our radio buttons, put the identifier text after the input tag, instead of before it. As with the identifier text for our text box, this is a convention and nothing prevents us from leaving it out completely.

Check boxes are similar in concept and implementation to radio buttons. The main difference is this: While radio buttons only enable your user to select a single value, *check boxes* allow for the selection of multiple values. The value for the type attribute is check box. Similar to radio buttons, you have a separate input tag for each possible option. When we set the name attribute to the input tags, they are all set identically. The values, most commonly, are different for each option.

Let's look at some check box code:

```
<input type="Checkbox" name="CBBut" value="CB1">Cbox1

<input type="Checkbox" name="CBBut" value="CB2">Cbox2

<input type="Checkbox" name="CBBut" value="CB3">Cbox3
```

As you can see in Figure 4-1, the radio buttons are round and the check boxes are square. A black dot appears in the selected radio button, while a check appears in the check box square.

The fourth type of value to examine with the input tag is the hidden attribute. When you create a value that you want to pass on to the action form, but that you don't want the user to see or be able to change, you can set the type to *hidden*. This prevents the form element from being displayed to the user. The code is as follows:

```
<input type="hidden" name="HiddenVar"
       value="hiddenval">
```

The type is set to hidden, and the name and value are any values of our choosing.

A Coldfusion tag—cfinput—can be used as a replacement for the HTML input. As with the cfform tag, the cfinput is an attempt to provide more functionality than the HTML input tag. These are the attributes for the cfinput tag:

- **Type** The *type* accepts the values of text, radio, or check box, and creates the corresponding HTML element as previously described. If you leave this option out, the default is text.

- **Name** The *name* attribute is a parallel to the name attribute for the HTML form tag. It defines the name of the input tag and we use this name to access the value on the action page.

- **Value** The *value* attribute is optional and defines a default value for our form element. This is identical to the value attribute in the HTML input tag.

- **Required** The *required* attribute is an option attribute that accepts a yes or no value. If set to yes, an error is thrown when we try to submit the form without filling in a value.

- **Range** The *range* attribute is a way to validate numeric data. You give it the minimum value and the maximum value, separated by a comma.

- **Validate** The *validate* attribute is an optional attribute that sets up your resulting HTML input tag to verify certain types of data as the form is submitted. Valid values are: date, eurodate, time, float, integer, telephone, zipcode, creditcard, and social_security_number.

- **Message** The *message* attribute accepts the message to display if validation of the form data fails.

- **Passthrough** The *passthrough* attribute enables us to add attributes to the resulting html input tag, which aren't readily set up in the CFML cfinput tag.

The validation functionality built in to the cfinput tag is performed by precoded JavaScript functions. While some good built-in functionality exists, most advanced developers prefer to code that functionality manually, instead of allowing ColdFusion to insert tag. The fewer CF tags the developers have to use, the more efficient the final application will be.

4

Hint

If you want to make a form field required, the easiest way to do this is to create a hidden form field called *formfieldname*_required.

It isn't unheard of simply to copy the ColdFusion-generated JavaScript functions. The functions are usually located in the script subdirectory of your ColdFusion master directory.

Caution

All html form elements must reside between an open and close form tag. Likewise, the ColdFusion form elements must reside between an open and close cfform tag.

The final form element is the select box. The *select box* gives a user the opportunity to select something from a drop-down list. This is the final form element from Figure 4-1. Select boxes are a form element that doesn't stem from the input tag and are created through the use of two different tags: the select tag and the option tag. The *select tag* is the one that sets up the drop-down list. It needs an open and close tag. The select tag only takes one attribute that we need to worry about, which is the name attribute. As with the input tag, the name attribute gives a name to your select box and you can use that name to reference the value of the select box on the action page.

Put the option tag or, more commonly, a list of option tags, between the open and close select tags. The *option tag* defines the choices for your select list. It accepts a single attribute: the value attribute. Let's look at your code:

```
<select name="TestSelect">
 <option value="Select1">Select 1
 <option value="Select2">Select 2
 <option value="Select3">Select 3
</select>
```

The identifier text for elements in the drop-down list is located after the option tag. In the input tags, it didn't matter where the identifier was placed, but it does matter with a select list. Set up like this, the select tag acts like a radio button, in that you can only select a single element. If you add an attribute called *multiple* to the select tag, the resulting form element will allow multiple selections, such as a group of check boxes.

As with your input tag, there's also a ColdFusion version of the select tag called cfselect. Let's look at the attributes of the cfselect tag:

- **Name** The *name* attribute is the name of the select tag and is analogous to the name attribute of the HTML select tag.

- **Required** The *required* attribute is optional and accepts a yes or no value. If selected yes, then some JavaScript is created by ColdFusion to force a value to be entered.

- **Message** The *message* attribute is an optional attribute that contains the error shown if the required attribute is set to yes and nothing is selected.

- **Multiple** The *multiple* attribute has an identical effect as to the multiple attribute of the HTML select tag. It sets up a box to allow for multiple selections, instead of a drop-down list.

- **Query** The *query* attribute enables you to populate the drop-down list with information from a ColdFusion query. You learn about queries in Module 5.

- **Value** The *value* attribute is used in conjunction with the query attribute. It defines the column of the query used to fill in the values of the option attributes.

- **Display** The *display* attribute is used in conjunction with the query attribute. It defines the column of the query used as the identifier for the option attributes.

- **Passthrough** The *passthrough* attribute enables you to add attributes to the resulting html input tag that aren't readily set up in the CFML cfinput tag.

The option tags inside a cfselect are no different than the html option tags. As with the cfinput and cfform tags, the cfselect tag is translated into standard html before being streamed to the browser.

1-Minute Drill

- ColdFusion provides some specialized version of html form elements. They must be used within a _____ tag.
- All the special cfform elements must reside between an _____ and _____ cfform tag.

- Cfform
- Open and close

If you've done any web surfing, you know you also need a Submit button on your form. The Submit button is also created with the HTML input tag. We create a Submit button by setting the type attribute to submit. When the Submit button is pressed, all the form data is passed on to the action page. ColdFusion has a scope, the form scope that contains all the form variables. This makes the form variables easy to access from your ColdFusion code. Reset buttons, commonly used to put a form back to its default state, are created much the same way. You set the type attribute to reset.

formi.cfm
formp.cfm

Project 4-2: Creating a Functional Form

This project steps you through the process of creating a functional form. We'll create the user input page and a simple action page that outputs the values of the variables. In future modules, we'll perform some more complicated processing in the action page, but the important concepts demonstrated here will remain constant.

Step-by-Step

1. The first step in this tutorial is to create our action page. You can download the finished files from InstantColdFusion.com. The form input page is named Formi.cfm. Start with the following code:

```
<!---
Description: Page to accept user input

Entering: N/A
Exiting: N/A

Dependencies: N/A
Expecting: Formp.cfm

Modification History
Date      Modifier         Modification
*************************************************************
10/17/2001  Jeff Houser, DotComIt Created
--->

<form action="Formp.cfm" method="post">  ←  [Open form tag]

</form>  ←  [Close form tag]
```

Begin the template with the documentation header and fill in the relevant information. The body portion of the template has the open and close form tags. Send the form to the action page—Formp.cfm—using the post method. The next step is to create some form elements.

2. For this project, create three simple text input blocks. Do that with three different input tags, setting the type of text for each one. This gives your user the option to enter three different values. If you were to create a registration form on your web site, for example, you would use something similar on your input form.

```
<!---
Description: Page to accept user input

Entering: N/A
Exiting: Formp.cfm

Dependencies: N/A
Expecting: N/A

Modification History
Date      Modifier         Modification
*************************************************************
10/17/2001  Jeff Houser, DotComIt Created
--->

<form action="Formp.cfm" method="post">

  Text Box 1: <input type="text" name="TextBox1"><br>
  Text Box 2: <input type="text" name="TextBox2"><br>
  Text Box 3: <input type="text" name="TextBox3"><br>
  <BR>

  <input type="Submit">
</form>
```

Form input boxes

Create our three text boxes quite simply. The types are text, and we can give them names TextBox1, TextBox2, and TextBox3. Before our end form tag, put the Submit button on the form. You can see these in the following illustration.

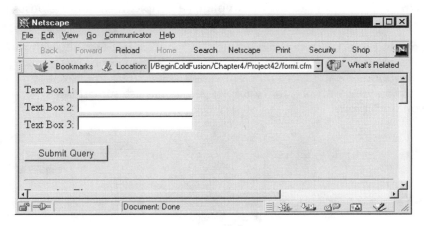

Let's look at how to create your processing page.

3. The next step to create our form is to create the processing page. You can find it with the files for this chapter as Formp.cfm. Create it by starting with our documentation header:

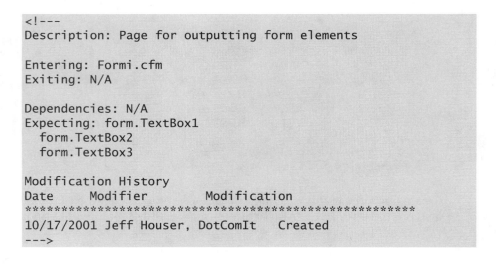

```
<!---
Description: Page for outputting form elements

Entering: Formi.cfm
Exiting: N/A

Dependencies: N/A
Expecting: form.TextBox1
   form.TextBox2
   form.TextBox3


Modification History
Date     Modifier        Modification
***********************************************************
10/17/2001 Jeff Houser, DotComIt   Created
--->
```

Add a description stating that we're using this page to output form variables from the previous template. Enter this page from Formi.cfm and we can expect three different variables to be defined when we get here. Let's move on to the body of this template.

4. The body section of the form contains a cfoutput block. We have three lines between our cfoutput, one for each form variable. You can see the form variables are scoped, with the form. text in front of them. To output them, we also surround them with pound signs. The pound sign helps ColdFusion distinguish the variables from the normal text.

4

```
<!---
Description: Page strictly for demonstrating form
             elements

Entering: Form.cfm
Exiting: N/A

Dependencies: N/A
Expecting: form.TextBox1
   form.TextBox2
   form.TextBox3

Modification History
Date       Modifier        Modification
****************************************************
10/17/2001 Jeff Houser, DotComIt   Created
--->

<cfoutput>
 Your first Entry was: #form.TextBox1# <br>
 Your second entry was: #form.TextBox2#<br>       ── cfoutput block
 Your third entry was: #form.TextBox3#<br>

</cfoutput>
```

You can see the results of our submitted form in the following screenshot:

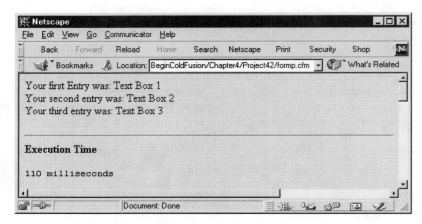

Project Summary

This project shows us how to take input from a user using an html form and process it in ColdFusion after the user submits the forms value. In future chapters, we use our knowledge of forms to create and maintain database data.

Module Summary

We have been examining a number of important ColdFusion concepts in the first four modules and our projects have become more and more complex. The next module teaches us how to get information from the database we created in Module 3. It combines all the knowledge we learned so far and creates your first real-world application.

☑️ *Mastery Check*

1. What are the differences between variables and parameters?

_____

_____

2. Variables are passed in a URL via the _____.

3. If you have multiple variables in a URL, what character would you use to separate them?

   A. ?

   B. #

   C. &

   D. $

4. Take the site you created in Project 2-1 and modify the pages, so they'll work with the new page you created in Project 4-1. The finished files are located on the web site.

5. Name two attributes to the form tag.

_____

_____

6. HTML forms usually have an _____ page and a _____ page.

7. Select the two types of form elements you can create with the html input tag:

   A. Radio buttons

   B. Select list

   C. Hidden

   D. Large text field

4

✓ Mastery Check

8. What are the fallbacks of specialized ColdFusion form tags and cfform?

_____

_____

9. The select tag and the _____ tag are usually used together.

10. Why are form fields named?

_____

_____

Module 5

SQL: The Language of the Database

The Goals of This Module

- Learn how to incorporate database data into your web site
- Introduce SQL select, insert, update, and delete
- Create a drill-down product interface
- Create forms for updating product data

This module teaches you all about the structured query language (SQL), which is the way you can communicate with your open database connectivity (ODBC) databases. This chapter brings together much of the information discussed in previous chapters, such as database design from Module 3, and URL parameters and HTML forms from Module 4. We learn how to get data from our database, and how to create new data, update existing data, and delete data. Let's begin by looking at how to use the SQL language to get data out of your database.

Getting Your Data

The most common use of your database data is displaying it, so the following section discusses the SQL SELECT statement. The cfquery tag is then introduced and I'll show you how to use it to execute SQL queries. First, though, here's how to write a simple SELECT statement.

The SQL SELECT Statement

You'll use a SQL SELECT statement to tell your data source you want to get data from your database. We'll see the elements of the SELECT statement, and then look at some examples where you might use it.

A SQL SELECT statement has three different parts: the select portion, the conditional portion, and the ordering portion. The select portion of the statement is the only required part and it always comes first.

Note

Any group of SQL commands is called a *query*. When we refer to a SELECT statement, we could as easily say a SELECT query.

The select portion of a SELECT statement looks like this:

```
SELECT ColumnList
FROM TableList
```

The query begins with the keyword SELECT. This tells us the type of query we're performing. Following that, we have a list of database columns we're selecting. This list can be something as simple as a wildcard—*—

to select all columns or it could be a list of the specific columns you want to select. The use of wildcards might, and usually does, have a detrimental impact on performance. You can separate multiple columns in your list by using a comma.

Following the column list, we put in the FROM keyword and a list of tables. The table list tells us from what tables we're selecting data. If we're selecting from multiple tables, we separate each table name with commas. A single table is listed without commas.

Hint

When creating the column list of your SELECT statement, it's good to specify what table the column is coming from, especially in queries where you're selecting from multiple tables. You do this, just like you were scooping ColdFusion variables: `TableName.Column`.

5

If we have a table named, users, that looks like this:

UserID	UserName	FirstName	LastName	Email
1	Partner	Jeff	Houser	jeff@instantcoldfusion.com
2	Random	Kyle	Manning	jeff@farcryfly.com
3	Garbage	Fentra	Ackle	fentra@magonda.com
4	Rats	Marge	Milton	marge@magonda.com

So far, we only have enough knowledge to write a SELECT statement to return all the rows in the table. We can do this in two ways. The first is by using wildcards, like this:

```
SELECT *
FROM Users
```

The second way is to specify each column individually:

```
SELECT Users.UserID, Users.UserName, Users.FirstName,
    Users.LastName, Users.Email
FROM Users
```

While the first method is easier, the second is more efficient, although the performance difference is marginal for most queries. Often, you won't need all the data in a table and writing out the list of columns that are needed tells the database not to return the columns you don't need. This means less information is being passed back to you, which makes everything more efficient.

The second part of a SELECT statement is the conditional part. When we don't want to return all the rows of a table, then we want to include a conditional portion of your SELECT statement. A SELECT statement with a conditional portion is set up like this:

```
SELECT ColumnList
FROM TableList
WHERE Conditions
```

The first part of the SELECT statement is as discussed earlier. The second part is new and begins with the keyword WHERE. Our conditions follow. A single condition uses the format of:

```
ColumnName operator Value
```

The ColumnName of our condition refers to any column that resides in the tables of our query. The operator is a comparison operator (see Table 5–1). The most common operator is the equal sign, to test for equality. After the operator of our choosing, we have the value. This value can be a column, a literal value, or even a ColdFusion variable.

Here's an example of how we would use a conditional clause in a SELECT statement:

```
SELECT *
FROM Users
WHERE Users.UserID = 1
```

Condition Tested	Operator
Equal	=
Greater Than	>
Less Than	<
Not Equal	<>
Greater Than or Equal	>=
Less Than or Equal	<=

Table 5-1   SQL Operators

This query is similar to an earlier example, so we'll go right to the conditional portion. We want to return all rows where the UserID is equal to 1. Because the UserID is the primary key of the Users table, you get this row back:

UserID	UserName	FirstName	LastName	Email
1	Partner	Jeff	Houser	jeff@instantcoldfusion.com

We can change our query to return all the rows that aren't equal to 1:

```
SELECT *
FROM Users
WHERE Users.UserID <> 1
```

If we do this, we get these rows back:

UserID	UserName	FirstName	LastName	Email
2	Random	Kyle	Manning	jeff@farcryfly.com
3	Garbage	Fentra	Ackle	fentra@magonda.com
4	Rats	Marge	Milton	marge@magonda.com

Note

The results returned by a query are referred to as a *Result Set*.

The final portion of a SELECT statement is the ordering portion. If we want to order the results, use this portion. A query with an ordering portion looks like this:

```
SELECT ColumnList
FROM TableList
WHERE Conditions
ORDER BY ColumnList
```

At the end of our query, we have a new addition, which starts with the two keywords, ORDER and BY. After that, we have a column list. The *column list* is a list of columns we want to sort by. The columns we list here must be located in tables referenced in the query. In many cases, you'll only be sorting on a single column, but examples with multiple columns do appear. A good example is if you want to sort by last name, and then by first name. In multiple sorting column cases, the first column is sorted for the full result set and the second column is sorted within the boundaries of the first column. Here's an example.

Ask the Expert

Question: You described how to use a single condition in a SELECT statement. Can I apply multiple conditions to my SELECT statement?

Answer: Yes, multiple conditions are allowed in the conditional clause of a SELECT statement. You can use as many conditions as you want, as long as the whole condition will simplify down to only one value. You can connect multiple conditions with Boolean logic. George Boole developed Boolean logic in the mid-1800s. Between each condition, you can use the Boolean operators AND, OR, and NOT. You use truth tables to find the results of the combination of the conditions. A *truth table* lists all the possible values for each condition and the results. The following is a sample truth table:

Condition 1	Condition 2	Condition 1 AND Condition 2	Condition 1 OR Condition 2	NOT Condition 1	NOT Condition 2
True	True	True	True	False	False
True	False	False	True	False	True
False	True	False	True	True	False
False	False	False	False	True	True

For example, say Condition 1 states the sky is blue, while Condition 2 says the sky is red. To find the answer, we can look it up in the truth table. Condition 1 is true and Condition 2 is false. If we were to compare these answers with the AND operator, the result would be false because both conditions aren't true. If we were to compare these with the OR operator, the result would be true. With the OR operator, only one condition needs to be true for the whole statement to be considered true. The NOT operator strictly reverses the current condition.

If we were to perform the query

```
SELECT *
FROM Users
ORDER BY Users.LastName
```

we would achieve these results:

UserID	UserName	FirstName	LastName	Email
3	Garbage	Fentra	Ackle	fentra@magonda.com
1	Partner	Jeff	Houser	jeff@instantcoldfusion.com
2	Random	Kyle	Manning	jeff@farcryfly.com
4	Rats	Marge	Milton	marge@magonda.com

The result set is sorted by the LastName column. The order isn't the default order. As you can see, the UserIDs don't iterate in order, as with the past examples.

Let's add some data to our original User table:

UserID	UserName	FirstName	LastName	Email
1	Partner	Jeff	Houser	jeff@instantcoldfusion.com
2	Random	Kyle	Manning	jeff@farcryfly.com
3	Garbage	Fentra	Ackle	fentra@magonda.com
4	Rats	Marge	Milton	marge@magonda.com
5	Hammer	Hammer	Manning	jeff2@farcryfly.com
6	DHouser	David	Houser	dave@magonda.com

I added some additional data, so you can see duplicate last names, which appear when you order by multiple fields:

```
SELECT *
FROM Users
ORDER BY Users.LastName
```

The result set from this data looks like this:

UserID	UserName	FirstName	LastName	Email
3	Garbage	Fentra	Ackle	fentra@magonda.com
6	DHouser	David	Houser	dave@magonda.com
1	Partner	Jeff	Houser	jeff@instantcoldfusion.com
5	Hammer	Hammer	Manning	jeff2@farcryfly.com

UserID	UserName	FirstName	LastName	Email
2	Random	Kyle	Manning	jeff@farcryfly.com
4	Rats	Marge	Milton	marge@magonda.com

This demonstrates how the data is sorted on multiple fields. Sorting with the LastName field is performed and within the LastName field, the results are sorted by the First Name.

1-Minute Drill

- What is the reserved word for the select portion of a SELECT statement?
- When you have a list of column names in your select list, they're separated by a ____?

Selecting Data from Multiple Tables

The process of selecting data from multiple tables is called a *join*. This section describes how joins work and examines the different types of joins. Two types of joins exist: inner joins and outer joins. The most common joins are inner joins.

Let's revisit the example from Module 3. First, we have a State table:

StateID	State
4	CT
5	NY
6	FL
7	MA

Second, we have a Customer table:

CustomerID	FirstName	LastName	Email	StateID	ZIPID
1	Jeff	Houser	jeff@instantcoldfusion.com	4	1
2	Kyle	Manning	jeff@farcryfly.com	5	2
3	Fentra	Ackle	fentra@magonda.com	6	3
4	Marge	Milton	marge@magonda.com	6	4

These are two normalized tables and we already know how to perform simple queries to get data from a single table. Given these tables, though, how do we get

---

- The reserved word for the select portion of a SELECT statement is SELECT.
- A comma separates a list of column names in your select list.

a customer's information and state? The Customer table only contains an ID, not the actual data. Let's look at the generalized SELECT statement:

```
SELECT ColumnList
FROM TableList
WHERE Conditions
```

We need the SELECT keyword, and then a list of columns we want to select. Now we can use just the asterisk wildcard. Then we have the FROM keyword and a list of tables. We want to specify the State table and the Customer table, so the query comes together like this:

```
SELECT *
FROM Customer, State
```

If we were to perform this query, all rows in the first table—Customer—are matched with the rows in the second table. This operation is called a *union*. We'll get a result set like this:

Customer ID	FirstName	LastName	Email	StateID	ZIPID	StateID	State
1	Jeff	Houser	jeff@instantcoldfusion.com	4	1	4	CT
1	Jeff	Houser	jeff@instantcoldfusion.com	4	1	5	NY
1	Jeff	Houser	jeff@instantcoldfusion.com	4	1	6	FL
1	Jeff	Houser	jeff@instantcoldfusion.com	4	1	7	MA
2	Kyle	Manning	jeff@farcryfly.com	5	2	4	CT
2	Kyle	Manning	jeff@farcryfly.com	5	2	5	NY
2	Kyle	Manning	jeff@farcryfly.com	5	2	6	FL
2	Kyle	Manning	jeff@farcryfly.com	5	2	7	MA
3	Fentra	Ackle	fentra@magonda.com	6	3	4	CT
3	Fentra	Ackle	fentra@magonda.com	6	3	5	NY
3	Fentra	Ackle	fentra@magonda.com	6	3	6	FL
3	Fentra	Ackle	fentra@magonda.com	6	3	7	MA
4	Marge	Milton	marge@magonda.com	6	3	4	CT
4	Marge	Milton	marge@magonda.com	6	3	5	NY
4	Marge	Milton	marge@magonda.com	6	3	6	FL
4	Marge	Milton	marge@magonda.com	6	3	7	MA

These results are a jumbled mess and they don't give us the information we want. It's rare to perform a join and not to include the conditional portion of a SELECT statement.

To find more useful values, we want to include the values where the StateID in the Customer table is equal to the StateID in the State table. This is the updated SELECT statement:

```
SELECT *
FROM Customer, State
WHERE Customer.StateID = State.StateID
```

The first action performed by this query is the union that creates the previous table. Then the table will be limited to meet the condition, where the StateID from the Customer table is equal to the StateID from the State table. The resulting table looks like this:

CustomerID	FirstName	LastName	Email	StateID	ZIPID	StateID	State
1	Jeff	Houser	jeff@instantcoldfusion.com	4	1	4	CT
2	Kyle	Manning	jeff@farcryfly.com	5	2	5	NY
3	Fentra	Ackle	fentra@magonda.com	6	3	6	FL
4	Marge	Milton	marge@magonda.com	6	3	6	FL

These results are much more common—and useful—when developing web sites. In many cases, we'll want to limit your query further not to return multiple ID fields, in this case, the StateID is returned twice in the final query.

This type of join is known as an inner join. When performing an inner join, the union of the tables is created, and then the results are limited by the conditional part of the SELECT statement. Let's look at an outer join.

An outer join is set up a little differently than an inner join. An *inner join* performs the union of two tables and returns all the rows with equal elements. An *outer join* also performs the union of the two tables, yet it returns all values for one of the tables given precedence. Here's how to set up an outer join:

```
SELECT ColumnList
FROM Table1 RIGHT OUTER JOIN Table2
ON Condition
```

We begin with the SELECT keyword, followed by a list of columns we want to select. Then we have the FROM keyword. This is where things change from the inner join discussed previously. First, we place the name of the first table, and then we have a keyword—either RIGHT or LEFT—to define which table will take precedence. If the keyword is set to RIGHT, then the second table, table2, takes precedence. If the keyword is set to LEFT, then table1 takes precedence. All rows are returned from the table that is given precedence, whether or not matches exist in the second table. After the name of the second table, we have the keyword ON. Then we have the condition.

Note

The outer join syntax can be easily modified to create an inner join. Remove the LEFT or RIGHT keywords because they don't apply to inner joins. Also remove the word OUTER, leaving only the keyword JOIN between the two tables.

Here's an example:

```
SELECT *
FROM Customer RIGHT INNER JOIN State
ON Customer.StateID = State.StateID
```

This join will select all the entries in the State table and all the equivalent entries in the Customer table:

Customer ID	FirstName	LastName	Email	StateID	ZIPID	StateID	State
1	Jeff	Houser	jeff@instantcoldfusion.com	4	1	4	CT
2	Kyle	Manning	jeff@farcryfly.com	5	2	5	NY
3	Fentra	Ackle	fentra@magonda.com	6	3	6	FL
4	Marge	Milton	marge@magonda.com	6	3	6	FL
---	---	---	---	---	---	7	MA

1-Minute Drill

● What are the two different types of joins?
● Outer joins give precedence to one table over the other. What keywords give this precedence?

● Inner joins and outer joins are the two different types of joins.
● RIGHT or LEFT are the keywords that give outer joins precedence to one table over the other.

ColdFusion's cfquery

Now that we know about the SELECT statement and how to select from multiple tables, we can learn how to implement this functionality within ColdFusion. ColdFusion provides a tag specifically designed to pass query information to your database, via ODBC: cfquery.

Tip

ColdFusion doesn't perform any validation of the SQL commands you execute using the cfquery: it merely acts as a pass-through between your text and the database. If the database returns an error, ColdFusion simply regurgitates it.

As with many ColdFusion and HTML tags, cfquery needs both an open and a close tag. The important attributes you need to know about are:

- **Name**   The *name* attribute defines the name of the variable to which the query will be returned. This name is used to perform any further processing on the output.

- **Datasource**   The *datasource* attribute is the name of the ODBC data source against which we want to run the query.

- **Username**   The *username* attribute is an optional attribute that enables us to specify the user name login to the database we're accessing. This is usually used in conjunction with the password attribute.

- **Password**   The *password* attribute is an optional attribute that enables you to specify the password login to the database we're accessing. This is usually used in conjunction with the username attribute.

- **Maxrows**   The *maxrows* attribute specifies the maximum number of rows to be placed in the result set.

- **Blockfactor**   The *blockfactor* attribute is optional and defines how many rows the database will return to ColdFusion once. It accepts a value between 1 and 100.

- **Cachedwithin**   The *cachedwithin* attribute allows for query caching. When you cache a query, the query is run once, and then stored in memory. The second time ColdFusion executes the query, it grabs the query in memory without having to run the query again. Its value is created using a ColdFusion function: createtimespan. The time span defines how long the query will reside in memory before executing it again.

Here's how we put the SQL statements and the cfquery tag together. Building on the examples discussed earlier in this chapter, we can take one of the queries and make them ColdFusion-ready:

```
<cfquery datasource="TestDatasource" name="TestName">
 SELECT *
 FROM Customer, State
 WHERE Customer.StateID = State.StateID
</cfquery>
```

When ColdFusion comes across this statement, it sends the query text to the database and returns the result set as the variable TestName.

One final word on how to output the data: As in past modules, we output data using the cfoutput tag. The cfoutput tag includes an attribute specifically designed for outputting query data and that attribute is the query attribute. The attribute accepts the name of the query from which we're outputting data. When you use the query attribute as part of the cfoutput tag, ColdFusion executes the code within the cfoutput block once for every row in the result set of the query, which makes processing queries easy. To output on the previous example query, you would write a cfoutput block like this:

```
<cfoutput query="TestDatasource">
 #TestName.LastName#, #TestName.FirstName#
</cfoutput>
```

This code will output all the LastName and FirstName sets for each row returned by the query.

DiscList.cfm
GenreList.cfm
SongList.cfm

Project 5-1: Creating a Drill-Down Interface for Your Products

This project teaches you how to create a drill-down interface for the product database created in Module 3. A *drill-down interface* is a common type of code segment you'll use routinely in your coding. Let's start with a list of genres, then display all the songs in the selected genres, and finally display the information on the disc, which the song resides on.

Step-by-Step

1. We need to create three main pages for this project: a genre page, a song-listing page, and a disc-listing page. You can download these finished pages from

InstantColdFusion.com. The following shows the start of the page to list all the song genres:

```
<!---
Description: A page to list all the genres

Entering: N/A
Exiting: SongList.cfm

Dependencies: N/A
Expecting: N/A

Modification History
Date     Modifier        Modification
*************************************************************
10/23/2001 Jeff Houser, DotComIt  Created
--->

<!-- HTML header -->
<html>
<head>
 <title>Genre Page</title>
</head>
<!-- end HTML header -->

<!-- Start Main Content-->
<body>

<table>
 <tr>
 <td>Genre</td>
 </tr>

</table>
<!-- end the content table -->

</body>
</html>
```

Begin by creating your documentation header and fill in the proper information. Make note of the next page, SongList.cfm, in your logic flow. Next, we define the basic layout to your page, creating a table to display our content. Then, add a single header row to your table. Finally, you want to add our ColdFusion code to the template.

2. Taking our GenreList.cfm template, we want to add the ColdFusion code to it. Examine the following code:

```
<!---
Description: A page to list all the genres

Entering: N/A
Exiting: SongList.cfm

Dependencies: N/A
Expecting: N/A

Modification History
Date    Modifier          Modification
*********************************************************
10/23/2001 Jeff Houser, DotComIt  Created
--->

<!--- a query to get the list of all Genres --->
<cfquery datasource="Chapter5" name="GetGenre">
 SELECT *
 FROM Genre
 ORDER BY Genre
</cfquery>

<!-- html header -->
<html>
<head>
 <title>Genre Page</title>
</head>
<!-- end HTML header -->

<!-- Start Main Content-->
<body>

<table>
 <tr>
 <td>Genre</td>
 </tr>
 <!-- cfoutput over the query -->
 <cfoutput query="GetGenre">
 <tr>
  <td>
```

Simple query to get genre information

```
<a href="SongList.cfm?GenreID=#GetGenre.GenreID#">
 #GetGenre.Genre#
</a><br>
</td>
</tr>
</cfoutput>
<!-- end cfoutput -->
</table>
<!-- end the content table -->

</body>
</html>
```

Output the query

Examine your query first. This is a simple SELECT statement. We select all the information from the Genre table and order it by the Genre. If you draw your attention lower into the template, we can see the output block, where we use a cfoutput tag with the query attribute. Inside the block, create a single row in our table. Then, pass URL parameters on to the SongList.cfm template and pass the GenreID. We use the Genre column for the link text. The resulting page is shown here:

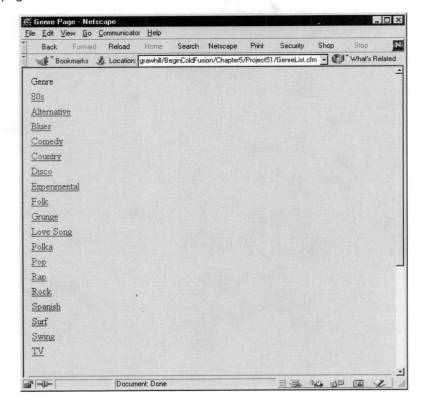

3. In the SongList.cfm template, start by setting up our standard documentation
header. Enter this page from the GenreList.cfm page and leave it to go to
the DiscList.cfm template. We expect the GenreID to be passed into this
template. Add a simple description and the date the template was created.
The template is shown as follows:

```
<!---
Description: A page to list all the songs in a genre

Entering: GenreList.cfm
Exiting: DiscList.cfm

Dependencies: N/A
Expecting: GenreID

Modification History
Date    Modifier             Modification
********************************************************
10/23/2001 Jeff Houser, DotComIt    Created
--->

<!-- a query to get all the songs for
    the specific genre -->
<cfquery datasource="Chapter5" name="GetSongs">
 SELECT Song.*, Artist.Artist
 FROM Song, Artist, SongGenre
 WHERE SongGenre.GenreID = #url.GenreID# AND
  SongGenre.SongID = Song.SongID AND
  Song.ArtistID = Artist.ArtistID
</cfquery>

<!-- html header -->
<html>
<head>
 <title>Song List</title>
</head>
<!-- end HTML header -->


<!-- Start Main Content-->
<body>

<table>
 <!-- cfoutput over the query -->
 <cfoutput query="GetSongs">
 <tr>
 <td>
```

A complex query

```
   <a href="DiscList.cfm?DiscID=#GetSongs.DiscID#">
   #GetSongs.Song#
   </A>
   </td>
   <td>
   #GetSongs.Artist#
   </td>
   </tr>
   </cfoutput>
   <!-- end cfoutput -->
   </table>
   <!-- end the content table -->

   </body>
   </html>
```

The next part of the template is the query and it is a complex query. We want to display all the songs and their artists in this query. But, the only information we have is the GenreID, so we do a join of three tables: SongGenre, Song, and Artist. To perform this query, you have three conditions. The first condition selects the GenreID from the SongGenre table. The second condition associates the SongID between the SongGenre table and the Song table. The final condition draws the association between the ArtistID in the Song table and the ArtistID in the Artist table.

Moving deeper into the body of our template, create a table for formatting purposes. Inside the table we use, once again, the CFOUTPUT tag displays all the resulting information from our query. And, once again, we're passing parameters via the URL. The DiscList.cfm page will need the DiscID to perform its function. Let's move on to the next template.

4. The final page in our drill-down structure is the DiscList.cfm. We create our template, starting with the documentation header and body layout. The finished template is as follows:

```
<!---
Description: A page to list all songs on a disc
         based on the DiscID

Entering: SongList.cfm
Exiting: N/A

Dependencies: N/A
Expecting: DiscID
```

```
Modification History
Date      Modifier           Modification
*************************************************************
10/23/2001  Jeff Houser, DotComIt   Created
--->

<!-- a query to get all the songs for
   the specific genre -->
<cfquery datasource="Chapter5" name="GetDisc">
 SELECT Discs.*, Song.*, Artist.Artist
 FROM Song, Artist, Discs
 WHERE Song.DiscID = #url.DiscID# AND
  Discs.DiscID = Song.DiscID AND
  Song.ArtistID = Artist.ArtistID
</cfquery>

<!-- html header -->
<html>
<head>
 <title>Disc List</title>
</head>
<!-- end HTML header -->

<!-- Start Main Content-->
<body>

<table>
 <!-- cfoutput over the query -->
 <cfoutput query="GetDisc" group="Disc">
 <tr>
  <td colspan="2">Album: #GetDisc.Disc#</td>
 </tr>
 <tr>
  <td>Song</td>
  <td>Artist</td>
 </tr>

 <cfoutput>
 <tr>
  <td>#GetDisc.Song#</td>
  <td>#GetDisc.Artist# </td>
 </tr>
 </cfoutput>
 </cfoutput>
 <!-- end cfoutput -->
```

Grouping the query output

5

```
</table>
<!-- end the content table -->

</body>
</html>
```

Moving into the template, we begin with a query. We've been given the DiscID and we want to output the disc name, as well as the song and artist information on the disc. To get all this information in a single query, draw information from three different tables: Song, Artist, and Disc. Compare the DiscID from the Song table to the DiscID passed in the URL. Then, we compare link the Song table and the Disc table using the DiscID field. We link the Artist table and the Song table using the ArtistID field. This puts all the information we need into our query.

Before looking at the cfoutput loop, let's look at the data the query will return.

Disc	Song	Artist
Bleach	Blew	Nirvana
Bleach	Paper Cuts	Nirvana
Bleach	Negative Creep	Nirvana
Bleach	Scoff	Nirvana
Bleach	Swap Meet	Nirvana
Bleach	Mr Moustache	Nirvana
Bleach	Sifting	Nirvana
Bleach	Big Cheese	Nirvana
Bleach	Downer	Nirvana

The Disc field contains the same value for every entry in the list. Do we want to display it once for every song? Or, do we want to display it multiple times for each song? The answer depends on what you're doing. We can process the query normally if we want to display the album name once for each song. There's an easy way, though, to display the album title only once, even though it shows up in your resulting query multiple times. Do this with the group attribute of the cfquery tag.

The group attribute's value is one of the columns in your query. It will display the grouped column once and display all the other columns with the same value as the grouped column. Then the cfoutput will move on to the next value for the grouped column. If you can't guess from our table, we want to group on the Disc column.

Caution

If you aren't using the group attribute in a cfoutput tag, you won't be able to nest cfoutput tags.

Our cfoutput tag is grouped on the Disc column. It displays the disc name, and then enters into a nested cfoutput block. The secondary cfoutput block displays the song and the Artist fields of the query. You can see the results in the following illustration.

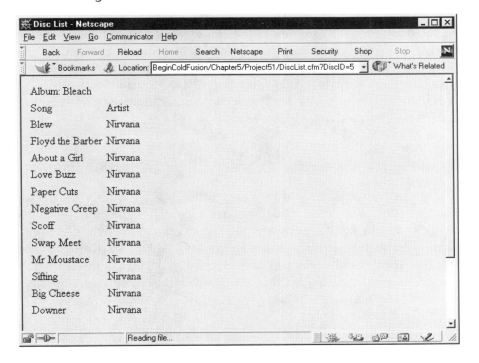

Project Summary

This project stepped us through the process of creating a series of drill-down structures to display the data associated with our CDs. This is a common implementation that will show up many times in your web development days.

Data Maintenance with SQL

We've already learned how to get data from a database using the SQL SELECT command. As you might expect, we can perform other operations against data. We can create new data and update existing data. We can even write a query to delete data from a database. This section teaches you how to do these things.

Creating a New Database Record

Understanding how to create new entries into your database tables is important. In a web site, whenever we use a form and collect information from the user, we'll want to do something with that information and we'll usually want to put it into a database. We can do that using the SQL Insert command.

A SQL insert command has two main parts: the column list and the value list. Both parts are required. Let's look at the format of a SQL insert:

```
INSERT INTO TableName ( ColumnList )
VALUES ( ValueList )
```

The statement starts out with two keywords: INSERT and INTO. Then we add the name of the table. Next, we have a list of columns into which we insert the data. The columns are separated by a comma. The whole column list is surrounded by parentheses. Then we have the VALUES keyword, followed by a value list. The value list contains each element of data we're inserting into the database. Commas separate the values and, as with the column list, the value list is surrounded by parentheses.

Here's an insert example:

```
INSERT INTO Customer
 (FirstName,
 LastName,
 Email,
 StateID,
 ZIPID)
VALUES ('Jargon',
    'Mint',
    'test@magonda.com'
    6
    3 )
```

This query creates a new record in the Customer table from earlier examples. We assume the CustomerID is automatically generated, so we needn't explicitly list that in our column list or give it a value in our value list. The remaining fields are all there: FirstName, LastName, Email, StateID, and ZIPID. Now we list the values. The text values for FirstName, LastName, and Email are surrounded by single quotes. The numerical values for StateID and ZIPID are left alone.

A SQL INSERT statement will create a new entry into a Database table. ColdFusion provides a tag—cfinsert—to accomplish the same thing. Cfinsert is built to work easily with HTML forms and is placed on the action page. Here are some of the attributes for the tag:

- **Datasource** The *datasource* attribute contains the name of the data source we're inserting data into. This is a required attribute.

- **Tablename** The *tablename* attribute contains the name of the table we're inserting data into. This is a required attribute.

- **Username** The *username* attribute is an optional attribute that contains the user name for access to the database. The username attribute is used in conjunction with the password attribute and is optional.

- **Password** The *password* attribute contains the password needed for access to the database. It's used in conjunction with the username attribute and is optional.

- **Formfields** The *formfields* attribute is optional and contains a list of form fields you want to insert into the specified database table. If you leave this attribute out, all form fields will be inserted into the table. This could cause problems if your form fields aren't in the table you're trying to insert into.

Be aware of the cfinsert tag because, as with the cfform tag, it isn't used commonly. When we use the cfinsert tag, we give up considerable control over our insert statement.

Update Our Database Records

In addition to giving you a way to create new data in your database, SQL also provides a way to update existing records. The SQL command for this is UPDATE. Anytime you want to make any changes to dynamic data on your database, we use the UPDATE statement.

A sample update statement takes this form:

```
UPDATE TableName
SET Column1 = Value1,
Column2 = Value2,
Column3 = Value3,
...
Columnn = Valuen
WHERE Conditions
```

The UPDATE keyword begins the statement, and then we have the name of the table where we're updating our data. After that is the SET keyword, followed by a list of column name and value pairs. The column name comes first, and then the equal sign and the new value for the column. As many of these name value pairs can exist as there are columns in the table. Each assignment operator is separated by a comma. The WHERE keyword follows next, and then we have the conditional part of our query. If the conditional part of our query is left out, all rows in a table will be updated.

Let's review the Customer table we've been using in the past few chapters, and then look at some examples of this query.

CustomerID	FirstName	LastName	Email	StateID	ZIPID
1	Jeff	Houser	jeff@instantcoldfusion.com	4	1
2	Kyle	Manning	jeff@farcryfly.com	5	2
3	Fentra	Ackle	fentra@magonda.com	6	3
4	Marge	Milton	marge@magonda.com	6	3

Some of the most common update queries we write will be to update a single record. Let's execute this query:

```
UPDATE Customer
SET FirstName = 'Jeffry',
  Email = 'jhouser@instantcoldfusion.com'
WHERE CustomerID = 1
```

This will update all the records where the CustomerID is equal to 1. Our updated table will look like this:

CustomerID	FirstName	LastName	Email	StateID	ZIPID
1	Jeffry	Houser	jhouser@instantcoldfusion.com	4	1
2	Kyle	Manning	jeff@farcryfly.com	5	2
3	Fentra	Ackle	fentra@magonda.com	6	3
4	Marge	Milton	marge@magonda.com	6	3

As we can see from this table, only one row was modified. When developing a web interface, these are the most common types of update queries we'll be writing. Imagine a client calls you and says all its Connecticut customers have moved to Massachusetts. The client wants you to change that in its database. The StateID for Connecticut is 6 and it's 7 for Massachusetts. You can write the query like this:

```
UPDATE Customer
SET StateID = 7
WHERE StateID = 6
```

After we execute the query, our update table will look like this:

CustomerID	FirstName	LastName	Email	StateID	ZIPID
1	Jeffry	Houser	jhouser@instantcoldfusion.com	4	1
2	Kyle	Manning	jeff@farcryfly.com	5	2
3	Fentra	Ackle	fentra@magonda.com	7	3
4	Marge	Milton	marge@magonda.com	7	3

Notice the last two rows—3 and 4—have changed, but the first two rows haven't been touched. Queries like this have greater effect and usefulness in real world situations where you are dealing with thousands of rows, instead of our small example set.

As with the insert command, ColdFusion also provides its own version of the update statement and the tag is called cfupdate. Many of the attributes are similar to the cfinsert tag. Here are some of them:

- **Datasource**   The *datasource* attribute is a required attribute that contains the name of the data source for which we're updating your data.

- **Tablename**   The *tablename* attribute, a required attribute, contains the name of the table for which we're updating data.

- **Username**   The *username* attribute is an optional attribute that contains the user name for access to the database. The username attribute is used in conjunction with the password attribute.

- **Password**   The *password* attribute is an optional attribute that contains the password needed for access to the database. It's used in conjunction with the username attribute.

- **Formfields**   The *formfields* attribute contains a list of form fields you want to insert into the specified database table. One of the form fields must be the primary key of the item you're updating. If you leave this out, all form fields will be inserted into the table, which could cause problems if your form fields aren't in the table you're trying to update.

As with the cfinsert, the cfupdate tag isn't used for advanced development, but it does have its place for a down-and-dirty quick update. The biggest limitation of the cfupdate tag is you can't use it to update multiple records.

Deleting Data

The final SQL statement to review is the delete statement. No matter how much time you spend creating your data, eventually, a time will come when you want to delete it. The delete statement gives you a way to do that.

Here's how the delete statement comes together:

```
DELETE FROM TableName
WHERE Conditions
```

The delete statement begins with the DELETE and FROM keywords. Then we have the name of the table from which we want to delete data. Following that, we have the conditional portion of the statement. If the conditions are left out, then every piece of data in the table will be deleted. This usually isn't what you want.

1-Minute Drill

● What SQL command can you use to create a new entry in a database table?

● What does the acronym SQL stands for?

● The username attribute of cfupdate and cfinsert is usually used in conjunction with what other attribute?

I'm about to share one of those hidden IT secrets. Never, ever delete anything. Once the system is in the hands of the end user, sooner or later someone will call you to ask how they can retrieve data they just deleted. There's a better way

---

● INSERT is the SQL command you can use to create a new entry in a database table.
● SQL is the acronym for structured query language.
● The username attribute of cfupdate and cfinsert is usually used in conjunction with the password attribute.

to do this. Create a column, called Deleted, in your important database tables. Make this column a bit, yes/no, or Boolean column. These types of columns only have two possible values: 1 or 0. When you create data in the table, automatically set the Deleted column to 0. When you delete the column, instead of running a DELETE statement, run an UPDATE statement and change the Deleted column to 1. Add a condition to all your display queries to filter out the data where Deleted is equal to 1. That way, when your end users call you to ask you to magically restore data, you don't have to tell them the data is gone for good. For space considerations, it might be good to cycle through all the database information on a routine basis and delete data older than one month, six months, one year, or whatever other date you choose. An on-off field like this is called a *flag*.

SongList.cfm
Songp.cfm
Songu.cfm

Project 5-2: Maintaining Our Product List from a Browser

This project shows you how to create a form to update your data. We focus on creating a form we can use to update the Song information in the database. If a song was accidentally associated with the wrong artist or disc, this update form enables you to change that information.

Step-by-Step

1. We want to create two pages to update the information on a song: our form input page and your action page. You can download our resulting files from the web site. Let's look at the code for the input page: Songu.cfm.

```
<!---
Description: Page to update Song Data

Entering: N/A
Exiting: Songp.cfm

Dependencies: N/A
Expecting: SongID

Modification History
Date    Modifier          Modification
**********************************************************
10/23/2001 Jeff Houser, DotComIt    Created
--->
```

5

```
<!-- get the song info -->
<cfquery datasource="chapter5" name="GetSongInfo">
 SELECT Song.*
 FROM Song
 WHERE Song.SongID = #url.SongID#
</cfquery>

<!-- get all artists -->
<cfquery datasource="chapter5" name="GetArtists">
 SELECT Artist.*
 FROM Artist
 ORDER BY Artist
</cfquery>

<!-- get all Discs -->
<cfquery datasource="chapter5" name="GetDiscs">
 SELECT Discs.*
 FROM Discs
 ORDER BY Disc
</cfquery>
```

Queries to get song data

To create this page, begin with our documentation header. We'll want to define the SongID before coming into this page. Three different pieces of data are directly associated with the Song table: song data, disc data, and artist data. To make a page to update all this information, we must address all three items. First, perform a query to get the song info for the current song we're updating, and then perform a query to get the artists. Finally, we have a query to get all the disc information. Use this query information when we create your forms.

2. Next, we want to create our form. After the queries, we add the outline for our form with the open and close form tags. Specify that we're posting data with the method attribute; the action attribute states we're sending the form data on to Songp.cfm template. The code follows:

```
<!---
Description: Page to update Song Data

Entering: N/A
Exiting: Songp.cfm

Dependencies: N/A
Expecting: SongID

Modification History
```

5

```
Date    Modifier           Modification
*********************************************************
10/23/2001 Jeff Houser, DotComIt     Created
--->

<!-- get the song info -->
<cfquery datasource="chapter5" name="GetSongInfo">
 SELECT Song.*
 FROM Song
 WHERE Song.SongID = #url.SongID#
</cfquery>

<!-- get all artists -->
<cfquery datasource="chapter5" name="GetArtists">
 SELECT Artist.*
 FROM Artist
 ORDER BY Artist
</cfquery>

<!-- get all discs -->
<cfquery datasource="chapter5" name="GetDiscs">
 SELECT Discs.*
 FROM Discs
 ORDER BY Disc
</cfquery>

<!-- the form -->
<form action="Songp.cfm" method="post">
 <table>
 <cfoutput>
 <!-- pass the hidden songID -->
 <input type="Hidden" name="SongID"
    value="#GetSongInfo.SongID#">         Hidden form field

 <!-- The Song Name -->
 <tr>
  <td>Song Name: </td>
  <td>
  <input type="Text" name="Song"
     value="#GetSongInfo.Song#">
  </td>
 </tr>
 </cfoutput>
```

```
<tr>
 <td colspan="2"><INPUT type="Submit"></td>
</tr>

</table>

</FORM>
```

Inside the form tag are two input tags. The first is a hidden tag containing the SongID and the second is a text field containing the song name. We prefill each of these values with data from our GetSongInfo query.

3. We still have two pieces of data to deal with. We need the way to choose the album and the artist a song is associated with. The finished code for our template follows.

```
<!---
Description: Page to update Song Data

Entering: N/A
Exiting: Songp.cfm

Dependencies: N/A
Expecting: SongID

Modification History
Date    Modifier            Modification
************************************************************
10/23/2001 Jeff Houser, DotComIt    Created
--->

<!-- get the song info -->
<cfquery datasource="chapter5" name="GetSongInfo">
 SELECT Song.*
 FROM Song
 WHERE Song.SongID = #url.SongID#
</cfquery>

<!-- get all artists -->
<cfquery datasource="chapter5" name="GetArtists">
 SELECT Artist.*
 FROM Artist
 ORDER BY Artist
</cfquery>

<!-- get all discs -->
<cfquery datasource="chapter5" name="GetDiscs">
```

```
 SELECT Discs.*
 FROM Discs
 ORDER BY Disc
</cfquery>

<!-- the form -->
<form action="Songp.cfm" method="post">
 <table>
 <cfoutput>
 <!-- pass the hidden songID -->
 <input type="Hidden" name="SongID"
     value="#GetSongInfo.SongID#">

 <!-- The Song Name -->
 <tr>
  <td>Song Name: </td>
  <td>
  <input type="Text" name="Song"
      value="#GetSongInfo.Song#">
  </td>
 </tr>
 </cfoutput>

 <!-- Select the Artist -->
 <tr>
  <td>Artist:</td>
  <td>
  <select name="ArtistID">
   <cfoutput query="GetArtists">
   <option value="#GetArtists.ArtistID#">
    #GetArtists.Artist#
   </cfoutput>
  </select>
  </td>
 </tr>

 <!-- Select the Disc -->
 <tr>
  <td>Disc:</td>
  <td>
  <select name="DiscID">
   <cfoutput query="GetDiscs">
   <option value="#GetDiscs.DiscID#">
    #GetDiscs.Disc#
   </cfoutput>
  </select><br>
  </td>
```

Artist drop-down

Disc drop-down

5

```
</tr>

<tr>
 <td colspan="2"><INPUT type="Submit"></td>
</tr>

</table>

</form>
```

We create both of our select boxes in much the same way. One is for the disc information and the other is for the artist information. To create the artist information, start with the HTML select statement and name it ArtistID. Then enter into a cfoutput block, using the GetArtists query. In the cfoutput block, create our option tags for the select box. The value of the option is the ArtistID. The identifier text next to the option tag is the Artist Name column. We implement our disc select field in much the same way. The results follow:

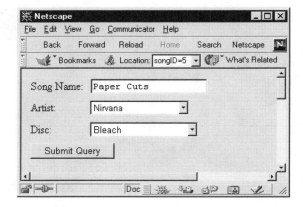

4. The final set in this project is to create the processing page for our template. This processing page is a simple page and the page is shown here:

```
<!---
Description: Page to update Song Data

Entering: Songp.cfm
Exiting: N/A
```

```
Dependencies: N/A
Expecting: form.SongID
   form.Song
  form.ArtistID
  form.DiscID

Modification History
Date     Modifier    Modification
*****************************************************************
10/23/2001  Jeff Houser, DotComIt     Created
--->

<cfquery datasource="chapter5" name="GetDiscs">
 UPDATE Song
 SET Song = '#form.Song#',
 DiscID = #form.DiscID#,
 ArtistID = #form.ArtistID#
 WHERE Song.SongID = #form.SongID#
</cfquery>

<cfoutput>
 <a href="Songu.cfm?SongID=#form.SongID#">
 Back to the Song
 </a>
</cfoutput>
```

As always, we start with our documentation header. Describe the flow of the template, from Songu.cfm to the current template, Songp.cfm. Define all the form variables necessary to make this code work. The content of this page is simple: We perform our update query using the cfquery tag. Modify the Song, DiscID, and ArtistID based on the user's selections on the input page and specify in our conditional clause that we're updating the template where the SongID is equal to the SongID passed in from the previous template. Finally, place a link back to the original song page, which finishes this project.

Project Summary

This project demonstrated the important concept of using ColdFusion to create an interface for maintaining data through our web browser. We only looked at one portion of what would be a full interface for our data: updating the information in a table. You can easily expand on these concepts to write an interface for creating or updating new artists, discs, or genres.

Module Summary

This module covered the basics of the structured query language (SQL). We learned how to use SQL to get information from databases and how to use it to put information into a database. The next module explains ColdFusion expressions and shows us how to perform string and numerical processing.

☑ *Mastery Check*

1. What is a query?

_____

_____

2. What is the only required portion of a SELECT query?

A. Select portion

B. Conditional portion

C. Where portion

D. Ordering portion

3. When performing a join, the _____ of two tables is taken. What is the difference between an inner join and an outer join?

_____

_____

4. What are the required attributes of a cfquery tag? Select two:

A. Name

B. Cachedwithin

C. Query

D. Datasource

✓ Mastery Check

5. What are the four main types of SQL queries you can execute?

_____

_____

6. ColdFusion provides its own versions of two important SQL statements. What are the tags?

_____

_____

7. The _____ command can involve multiple tables.

8. Why wouldn't you want to give your end users the capability to delete data?

_____

_____

9. The group attribute of the cfoutput is used to _____.

10. The concepts demonstrated in Project 5-2 are important, however, the project is a bit limited. Based on the pages you created, you must explicitly define the SongID in the URL. This isn't as user friendly as it could be. Create a page, SongList.cfm, that displays a list of songs. Make the song name clickable, so it goes to the edit song page.

5

Module 6

Getting Things
Done in ColdFusion

The Goals of This Module

- Introduce ColdFusion functions
- Learn how to create and manipulate strings
- Learn how to deal with numbers in ColdFusion

This module examines ColdFusion *expressions,* which are used to manipulate data. We learn about different forms of string processing, how ColdFusion deals with numbers, and how to perform math functions from within ColdFusion.

Expressions Overview

This section tells us what expressions are. We learn about the different ColdFusion data types and how ColdFusion handles these data types internally. We also look at ColdFusion functions: what they are and how to use them when developing your ColdFusion applications.

What Is an Expression?

A *ColdFusion expression* is a way to process data. Expressions evaluate to a single piece of data and two types of expressions exist: simple and complex. A *complex expression* is the result of one or more simple expressions linked together by an operator. We learn how to link them together later in this module. For now, let's look at the elements of a simple expression.

Many elements can be used to build a simple expression. All the elements are shown in Table 6-1, but we'll look at the basic types. This list is similar to the data types a ColdFusion variable can have. A *simple expression* can be made up of simple data types like integers, real numbers, strings, lists, Boolean values, or date and time values. A simple expression can also contain complex data types, such as structures, arrays, queries, or COM objects. We learn about complex data types in ColdFusion in Module 13.

An additional element of a ColdFusion expression could be a variable. The variable could be pointed to any of the simple data types. In past modules, we used cfoutput to evaluate one of the simplest ColdFusion expressions. We displayed the value of the variable. Although we didn't know it at the time, when we put the variable's name between two pound (#) signs, we were creating a simple ColdFusion expression.

You can create complex expressions by separating multiple simple expressions with specific operators. Four different types of operators exist: Arithmetic, String, Decision, and Boolean. You learn about string and arithmetic manipulation operators later in this module and both decision and Boolean operators are examined in Module 8.

When to Use Pound Signs

As we learned in previous modules, pound signs have a special meaning in ColdFusion. When the ColdFusion server is processing a page and comes

Type	Description
Integer	Integers are numbers with no decimal point.
Real Number	Real numbers are numbers that contain a decimal point.
Strings	Strings are text values enclosed in either single quotes or double quotes.
Boolean Values	Boolean values can either be TRUE or FALSE. As integers, TRUE is 1 and FALSE is 0. As strings, TRUE is YES and FALSE is NO.
Date-Time Values	Date-time values contain values for a specified date or time. If no time is specified, then it's automatically set to 12.
Lists	Lists are a specialized version of strings and are covered in Module 13.
Structures	Structures are a series of name value pairs and are covered in Module 14.
Arrays	Arrays are a way to store groups of related data and are covered in Module 14.
Queries	Queries contain the result set of a SQL query and are created using the CFQUERY tag. ColdFusion queries are discussed in Module 5.
COM Objects	Common Object Model (COM) objects are components that encapsulate specific functionality you can call from your ColdFusion applications. Covering COM objects is beyond the scope of this book.
Variables	When the variable is used in an expression, the variable's value is returned. The variable must contain a simple type.
Functions	All ColdFusion functions return basic objects, so they can be used safely inside a ColdFusion expression.

Table 6-1   Elements of a ColdFusion Expression

6

across a pound sign, the server knows it must perform special processing on that text. Here's a simple example with cfoutput:

```
<cfset MyVariable = "Test">
<cfoutput> My Variable #<yVariable# </cfoutput>
```

First, we set our variable, and then we output it. ColdFusion processes the cfset tag. Then it comes across the cfoutput tag. Within the cfoutput block, it rolls over the My Variable text and leaves it alone. Then it comes across the MyVariable variable names, surrounded by pound signs. The pound signs tell the ColdFusion server it needs to perform some additional processing. Because the expression between the pound signs is a variable name, ColdFusion gets the variables value Test and returns it to the browser. The person browsing this page will see My Variable Test as the results of our execution.

Simple expressions can be used safely within a cfoutput block; however, complex expressions cannot be used. The workaround for this is to execute your complex expression within a cfset block and set its result to a single variable name. After that, you can successfully output the variables within the cfoutput block.

ColdFusion lets you use a simple expression located inside a single string. To do this, you must place the pound signs around the expression:

```
<cfset MyVar1 = "My Variable 1">
<cfset MyString = "MyVar1 is #MyVar1#">
```

Both cfset statements are perfectly valid and the resulting value for the mystring variable is "MyVar1 is My Variable 1". As with the cfoutput tag, complex expressions can't be used inside a string.

Avoid the overuse of pound signs. One of the previous examples could be rewritten like this:

```
<cfset #MyVar1# = "My Variable 1">
```

Although this is a valid ColdFusion statement, the pound signs around the variable name aren't needed. They make the code harder to read and force the ColdFusion server to perform additional processing. In some instances when you use ColdFusion functions, you might come across the need for nested pound signs but, usually, this detracts from the readability of the code and isn't recommended. Code can easily be written to avoid such circumstances.

ColdFusion Functions

In addition to the tags that are the meat and potatoes of ColdFusion development, numerous functions constitute the gravy of your development dinner. ColdFusion provides numerous functions that provide more intricate data manipulation capabilities than you can get through the use of tags.

ColdFusion functions provide considerable functionality that would be cumbersome to achieve using the tag syntax. Numerous functions exist for performing math operations, dealing with complex data types, handling dates, manipulating strings, and formatting display data.

The specific use of each function is defined by the function name. This is the general syntax for a function:

```
FunctionName(ArgumentList)
```

Begin with the function name, which is the name of the function we want to call. Then we have an open parentheses statement. Following that, we have a list of all the arguments the function accepts. As with most lists, a comma separates each argument. Some functions don't take any arguments, while others have a certain set of required arguments. Some functions even have optional requirements.

When dealing with ColdFusion tags, the order in which you list your tag attributes doesn't make a difference to the performance of a tag. Specifying the arguments for a function is different because you don't list the argument name, only the argument value. The order of the arguments in the argument list determines how the arguments get assigned to the argument values when ColdFusion processes the function. This is something the ColdFusion server handles internally.

Let's use NumberFormat as an example. The *NumberFormat* function is used to format a number before displaying it to the end user. NumberFormat accepts one required value: the number you want to format. It also accepts one optional value, the mask. The *mask* defines how you want to display the data. Here's a code example:

```
<cfset MyVar1 = 1.5>
<cfoutput>
 My variable unformatted: #MyVar1#<BR>
 My variable formatted: #NumberFormat(MyVar1,"___")#
<BR>
</cfoutput>
```

The mask in the number format line says we want to display, at most, three numbers, with no decimal point. First, we set the value of a variable to 1.5. Then we output the value as it is. Our output gives us 1.5. And, then we output the value using the NumberFormat function, which outputs the value with no decimal place. The number is automatically rounded to 2.

This demonstrates how functions are used within a ColdFusion expression. We learn more about this topic in this module. Next, we learn how ColdFusion processes strings.

6

1-Minute Drill

- What are pound signs used for?
- What is the simplest type of expression?

Strings in ColdFusion

A *string* is any grouping of text and strings can have numerous uses in ColdFusion. Whenever a user enters data into a form or pulls data from a database, ColdFusion treats those values as string values. Knowing how to deal with strings will be important to your ColdFusion development. First, we show how to concatenate strings, and then we look at some ColdFusion functions that can be used to process strings.

String Concatenation

Only one operator can be used on strings and this is for string concatenation. ColdFusion uses the ampersand (&) to concatenate strings. When you hear the term *string concatenation*, we're talking about creating a single string out of two, or more, separate strings.

Here's an example of how to use the string concatenation operator:

```
<cfset MyVar1 = "string1" & "string2">
```

Remember when we discussed using the cfset tag to create variables? The variable's value, to the right of the equal sign, is a ColdFusion expression. In the string concatenation example, we have one complex expression, which is two simple expressions brought together through the use of the & operator. The results that get stored in the MyVar1 variable would be string1string2.

Hint

Lists are only specialized versions of strings. Lists are covered in Module 13.

- Pound signs are used to distinguish regular text from a ColdFusion expression.
- The simplest type of expression is to output a variable's value.

String Functions

Many functions are provided for the manipulation of strings in ColdFusion and you're going to examine some of them. First, we learn about different ways to extract substrings, and then we learn how to do find and replace operations to modify strings.

When performing any sort of string processing, knowing the length of the string is often beneficial. ColdFusion provides the Len function to help you achieve that purpose. The *Len* function accepts one string parameter and returns the length of that string. Here's an example:

```
<cfset MyString = "This is My String">
<cfset MyStringLength = Len(MyString)>
```

We create a string variable, MyString, whose value is a string literal, surrounded by quotes. Then we create a second variable called MyStringLength. This variable's value is the result of an expression. We use the Len function on the MyString variable. ColdFusion recognizes the function and processes it, returning the value 17.

Note

The Len function can also be used on binary objects; however, that use is beyond the scope of this book.

In the previous section, we learned how to use the concatenation operator to create a new string from one or more strings. This is an additive process, meaning we start with something and add to it. We're about to learn how to create new strings through a subtractive process or by removing characters from the original string

The Left, Right, and Mid functions are all used to extract a portion of a string from a bigger string. The *Left* function is to extract characters from the beginning of a string. The *Right* function is used to extract characters starting from the last character of a string. The *Mid* function is used to take a group of characters out of the middle of a string. First, look at the Left and Right functions.

The Left function accepts two values into it. The first value is the string we're extracting our substring from. The second value is the length of the string we're extracting. Say, for example, we want to extract the first five characters from a string. This is how we do it:

```
<cfset Sentence = "This is a test sentence">
<cfset FirstFive = Left(Sentence, 5)>
```

We store our initial string in a variable. Then, we use another cfset tag to create our substring. We use the left function. The first attribute is the Sentence variable we create in our first line of code and the second variable is the number 5. The FirstFive variable will now have the value of "This." The space is intentionally left in there because this is the fifth character.

Note

The string we're extracting substrings from remains unchanged by the functions. We're creating new variables, not changing existing ones.

Here's an example of the right function. Following our left example, extract the last five characters of the same string:

```
<cfset Sentence = "This is a test sentence">
<cfset LastFive = Right(Sentence, 5)>
```

Starting from the rightmost portion, or the end, of the string, ColdFusion counts five characters toward the start of the string. The LastFive variable will contain the value "tence."

The Mid function is a bit more complicated than either the Right or Left function. Instead of two parameters, the *Mid* function needs three. In addition to the string we're processing and the number of characters we're extracting, we need to specify the character from which we're going to start extracting. Say we want to extract the second five characters from our string:

```
<cfset Sentence = "This is a test sentence">
<cfset SecondFive = Mid(Sentence, 6, 5)>
```

The first value of our Mid function is the string we're going to extract from. The second value is the starting character. To get the second five characters, we start at character 6. The final value is the number of characters we're trying to extract. The value of our SecondFive variable will be "is a."

To have to perform a find or replace within strings is common. ColdFusion provides some functions to perform these actions and two of them are Find and Replace. The *Find* function returns the first index of the found string. If a character we're searching for shows up in multiple places, only the first index will be returned.

Tip

Strings are indexed by the order in which the characters appear, from left to right. The index of the first character is 1, the index of the fourth character is 4, and so on.

The Find function takes three different arguments. The first argument is the string you're searching for. The second argument is the string you're searching against. Both of these arguments are required. The third argument is an optional argument, which tells you where to begin your search. The default starting point is the first character of the string. If we want to find the location of the first space in a string, we would use this:

```
<cfset Sentence = "This is a test sentence">
<cfset FirstSpace = Find(" ",Sentence)>
```

The value of the FirstSpace variable contains the number 5, which is the index of the first space character in the Sentence variable.

In addition to a Find function, ColdFusion also contains a Replace function. The *Replace* function accepts four parameters, with three of them being required. The first parameter is the string we're searching through and the second parameter is the string we're replacing. The third parameter is the string we're replacing it with and the fourth parameter is a scope parameter. You can specify ONE to replace only the first occurrence of your string or ALL to replace all occurrences of your string. The default is to replace only the first item in the string.

1-Minute Drill

● What is the only operator you can use on strings?

● What are the Left, Right, and Mid functions used for?

● The only operator you can use on strings is the concatenation operator (&).
● The Left, Right, and Mid functions are used to extract substrings from a string.

Say we want to cycle through our sentence variable and replace the spaces with underscores:

```
<cfset Sentence = "This is a test sentence">
<cfset FirstReplaced = Replace(Sentence," ","_")>
<cfset AllReplaced = Replace(Sentence," ","_","all")>
```

The first line in our code segment defines our sentence. Then we move on to use the replace function to replace the first space with an underscore. Our resulting variable is "This_is a test sentence". The second replace statement creates the variable AllReplaced and its value is "This_is_a_test_sentence".

This section explored some of the basic ColdFusion string-processing functions and string-processing rules. We learned how to extract substrings and modify the values of strings using the Right, Mid, Len, and Left functions. We also learned how to search through strings to find or change values within those strings using the Find and Replace functions.

Genrei.cfm
Genrep.cfm

Project 6-1: Processing User Input

Let's revisit our interface for product maintenance, which we started creating in Module 5. Perhaps we're giving our end users the capability to create a new genre, but we want to limit the amount of characters that can be in a genre name. This project steps us through the process of creating a template to do this.

Step-by-Step

1. Because we're creating a way to create a new genre, we need to create two different pages: an input page and a processing page. Begin by looking at the input page. This page, Genrei.cfm, is downloadable from the web site InstantColdFusion.com:

```
<!---
Description: Page to create a new genre

Entering: Genrep.cfm
Exiting: N/A

Dependencies: N/A
Expecting: N/A

Modification History
```

```
Date    Modifier          Modification
********************************************************
11/06/2001 Jeff Houser, DotComIt  Created
--->

<!-- the form -->
<form action="Genrep.cfm" method="post">
 <!-- the input text box for genre -->
 <INPUT type="text" name="Genre">

 <!-- the submit button -->
 <INPUT type="Submit" name="Submit">
</form>
```

Our page starts with the documentation header. This page contains a simple form. Post the form information onto the Genrep.cfm page. We have two input boxes: one is a text box for the genre info and the other is the Submit button for the form, which completes this template. We can now move on to examine the processing page.

2. The second page in this project is the processing page for the form. We can make the page without any additional processing, and then learn how to add in our code to limit the length of the user's genre input. This is the code for our Genrep.cfm page:

```
<!---
Description: The processing page for creating a
       new genre

Entering: Genrei.cfm
Exiting: N/A

Dependencies: N/A
Expecting: form.Genre

Modification History
Date    Modifier          Modification
********************************************************
11/06/2001 Jeff Houser, DotComIt  Created
--->

<!-- insert query -->
<cfquery datasource="Chapter6" name="InsertGenre">
 INSERT INTO Genre (Genre)
```

6

```
VALUES ('#Genre#' )
</cfquery>

<cfoutput>
 Your new genre <b>#Genre#</b> was
 created. <BR>
</cfoutput>
```

The documentation header starts this page. The header states we're expecting the Genre variable to be created in the form scope at the time we execute this page template. We begin the processing portion of our template with the insert query and insert the Genre field into the Genre table. We display a thanks message, which ends our template.

3. The whole purpose of this project was to create a way to create a new genre, while limiting the length of the user's input. We can do this using the Left function discussed earlier in this chapter. This is the code:

```
<!---
Description: The processing page for creating a
        new genre

Entering: N/A
Exiting: N/A

Dependencies: N/A
Expecting: form.Genre

Modification History
Date     Modifier         Modification
*************************************************************
11/06/2001 Jeff Houser, DotComIt  Created
--->

<!-- insert query -->
<cfquery datasource="Chapter6" name="InsertGenre">
 INSERT INTO Genre (Genre)
 VALUES ('#Left(Genre,25)#' )
</cfquery>                            [ Left functions ]

<cfoutput>
 Your new genre <b>#Left(Genre,25)#</b> was
 created. <BR>
</cfoutput>
```

We refer to the user's input in two places: the insert query and the thank you message. Use the Left function to truncate the user's input automatically, if necessary. By doing this, we limit the user's input to 25 characters.

Note

Perhaps an easier way to accomplish this task might be to use the maxlength attribute of the input tag. This accepts a number value and prevents the user from entering strings with more characters.

Project Summary

What we did in this project was to modify the user's input automatically without telling the user we were going to modify it. Modifying your user's input without their knowledge might not be a good idea. Perhaps a better solution would be to give the user the opportunity to change their data or at least warn them before you change it. We don't have enough knowledge to implement something like this yet, but the necessary concepts are covered in Module 8.

6

Numbers in ColdFusion

In addition to strings, ColdFusion can also manage numerical data. *Integers* are numbers without a decimal and *real numbers* are numbers with a decimal. ColdFusion can handle either one of them without problems. First, we learn about arithmetic operators that can be used to combine simple expressions together, and then we learn about some of the built-in functions ColdFusion provides for dealing with mathematical concepts.

Arithmetic Operators

ColdFusion provides the standard mathematical functions you would expect. You can specify the sign of a number, either negative or positive. You can also perform math functions such as addition, subtraction, multiplication, and division. ColdFusion supports the div and mod operators, and it allows for exponents to be used within a number. Let's move into some specifics. The arithmetic operators are in Table 6-2.

The unary operator for a positive number is the plus (+) sign. It you don't specify this, it's implied. For a negative number, the minus (-) sign is used. This

Operator	Description	Order of Operations
+	Tells us the sign of a number is positive	First
-	Tells us the sign of a number is negative	First
^	Exponents	Second
*	Perform multiplication	Third
/	Perform division	Third
\	Perform division and return the integer result without a remainder	Fourth
MOD	Perform division and return the integer remainder	Fifth
+	Perform addition	Sixth
-	Perform subtraction	Sixth

Table 6-2 Arithmetic Operators in ColdFusion

example creates one variable that contains a negative number and one that contains a positive number. For example:

```
<cfset PositiveNumber = +5>
<cfset NegativeNumber = -5>
```

Use a cfset to create our variables. We assign the literal values to variable names, using a +5 to create the positive number and a –5 to create the negative number. This should be easy to understand because it's written out the same way when we do math by hand.

ColdFusion lets us perform addition, subtraction, multiplication, and division. The operator for addition is a + sign. The operator for subtraction is a – sign. Multiplication uses an asterick (*) and division uses a forward slash (/). Here are some examples:

```
<cfset AdditionExample = 1 + 1>
<cfset SubtractionExample = 1 - 1>
<cfset MultiplicationExample = 1 * 1>
<cfset DivisionExample = 1 / 1>
```

The AdditionExample variable will be set to 2 because 1 plus 1 equals 2. For the subtraction example, we get 0 because 1 minus 1 equals 0. Both multiplication and division examples return 1 because that's how the math pans out.

Tip

When performing division, make sure the right side of the slash isn't equal to zero. This will cause an error.

The next two operators we need to learn about are the div and mod operators. The *div* operator is represented by a backward slash. When you perform a div operation, the number on the left is divided by the number on the right. The result returned is an integer without any remainder. Using the *mod* operator will divide the first number by the second and the integer remainder is returned. The mod symbol is MOD. Here's an example of each:

```
<cfset MODExample = 11 mod 4>
<cfset DivExample = 11 \ 4>
```

In the first example, a 3 will be returned because that's the integer remainder when you divide 11 by 4. In the second example, we get a 2 because that's how many times 4 goes evenly into 11.

Finally, let's look at the caret (^) symbol, which is used for exponents.

```
<cfset ExponentExample = 5^2>
```

The previous short snippet will take 5 and multiple it by itself two times. Five times five is 25. That result will be stored in the ExponentExample variable.

Before moving on to look at some of the mathematical functions, I want to specify the order of operations of these things. Table 6-2 has an Order of Operations column. When it comes across a complex expression, first ColdFusion looks for the unary operators to tell the sign—either positive or negative— for each number. Then it processes all exponents. Next, it performs all the multiplication and division operations. It performs these in the order from left to right. Following multiplication and division, ColdFusion first performs the div operator, and then the mod operator. Next, ColdFusion performs addition and subtraction. As with math we'd do by hand, parentheses can be used to change the order of operations. Here are some examples:

```
<cfset MyVar1 = 5+3*6/9>
<cfset MyVar2 = (5+3)*6/9>
```

The first example will multiply 3 by 6, resulting in 18. It will divide the answer by 9, resulting in 2. Then it will add the 2 to 5, thus, giving the MyVar1 a value of 7. The next example first adds 5 and 3, creating a value of 8. Then it will multiply 8 by 6, resulting in 48. 48 is divided by 9, giving 5.33. The same numbers give different results because of the different priorities the parentheses give the operator. Paying attention to your order of operations is important.

Mathematical Functions

In-depth coverage of ColdFusion's mathematical functions are beyond the scope of this book, but you should be aware of them. ColdFusion has over 30 built-in functions that can be used to perform mathematical processes.

If we need to subtract from or add to a number quickly, we can use the DecrementValue or IncrementValue functions, respectively. These functions are discussed in Module 9 when looping constructs are covered. ColdFusion also provides some functions for the comparison of two numbers. We can use the Max and Min functions to compare two numbers, and return the bigger, or smaller, value, respectively.

1-Minute Drill

● What does ColdFusion look at first when dealing with arithmetic operators?

● What is the difference between the forward (/) slash and the backward (\) slash in ColdFusion?

If you need to find the absolute value of a number, you can use the Abs *f* function. For those who need to perform advanced math, you can use Sin, Cos, and Tan functions to find the sine, cosine, and tangent. You can find the opposite of sine, cosine, and tangent by using the arc functions: Asin, Acos, and Atn, respectively. ColdFusion also provides various bit functions for operating on numbers at the bit level. You can explore many more ColdFusion functions at your leisure.

● ColdFusion first looks at the unary operators of plus and minus when dealing with arithmetic operators. Parentheses would also be a valid answer.

● The forward slash performs normal division. The backward slash performs a div statement.

AveragePrice.cfm

Project 6-2: Calculating the Average Cost of All Our Products

Pretend we're creating a report on the products in our database. We want to add up the price of each product and compute the average. This can be easily done using some simple ColdFusion math functions.

Step-by-Step

1. The first step in this project is to modify our database structure. We don't currently store the price in any of our database tables. We can easily add it to the disc table. Your resultant table will look like this:

DiscID	Disc	Price
1	Running with Scissors	$5.00
2	Weird Al Yankovic	$10.00
3	Off The Deep End	$15.00
4	Nevermind	$17.99
5	Bleach	$12.15
6	DGC Rarities Vol 1	$19.00

2. Now we can move on to look at some ColdFusion code. The first thing we want to do is create our template file, AveragePrice.cfm. You can download this file from the InstantColdFusion.com web site. Look at the code:

```
<!---
Description: A page to compute the average price of
      all the discs in the database

Entering: N/A
Exiting: N/A

Dependencies: N/A
Expecting: N/A

Modification History
Date     Modifier         Modification
*************************************************************
11/06/2001  Jeff Houser, DotComIt  Created
--->

<!-- get all the discs in the database -->
```

6

```
<cfquery datasource="Chapter6" name="GetProducts">
 SELECT *
 FROM Discs
 ORDER BY Discs.DiscID
</cfquery>
```

Query to get all discs

The first step we perform in our code is to create the documentation header. The purpose of this page is to compute the average of all the products in the database. Our first functional step is to get all the products in the database, which we do with a query.

3. After we get all the products in our database, we need to get a total of the price field in each record returned to us. Remembering back to Module 5, we were able to process each record of a result set individually by using the query attribute of the cfoutput tag. This is how we total all the prices:

```
<!---
Description: A page to compute the average price of
      all the discs in the database

Entering: N/A
Exiting: N/A

Dependencies: N/A
Expecting: N/A

Modification History
Date      Modifier        Modification
**********************************************************
11/06/2001  Jeff Houser, DotComIt  Created
--->

<!-- get all the discs in the database -->
<cfquery datasource="Chapter6" name="GetProducts">
 SELECT *
 FROM Discs
 ORDER BY Discs.DiscID
</cfquery>

<!-- initialize the total to zero -->
<cfset variables.Total = 0>

<!-- calculate the total for each disc in
   the database -->
```

```
<cfoutput query="GetProducts">
 <cfset variables.Total =
    variables.Total + #GetProducts.Price#>
</cfoutput>
```

Performing calculations on query data

Inside our cfoutput block, we create a local variable called Total. The same variable is initialized to zero before we enter the block. We set the value of Total equal to the current value of Total, plus the price of the current disc we're processing. This technique of setting the same variable we're referencing is common in programming languages.

4. The final step in our code block is to compute the average. An average is computed by taking the sum of all the prices and dividing it by the number of entries we counted to get the sum. When ColdFusion creates a query set, it contains a special variable we can use to get the number of records that were returned. The variable is named *queryname*.RecordCount. We use this variable to compute the average.

6

```
<!---
Description: A page to compute the average price of
      all the discs in the database

Entering: N/A
Exiting: N/A

Dependencies: N/A
Expecting: N/A

Modification History
Date      Modifier          Modification
***************************************************************
11/06/2001  Jeff Houser, DotComIt  Created
--->

<!-- get all the discs in the database -->
<cfquery datasource="Chapter6" name="GetProducts">
 SELECT *
 FROM Discs
 ORDER BY Discs.DiscID
</cfquery>

<!-- initialize the total to zero -->
<cfset variables.Total = 0>

<!-- calculate the total for each disc in
    the database -->
```

```
<cfoutput query="GetProducts">
 <cfset variables.Total =
    variables.Total + #GetProducts.Price#>
</cfoutput>

<!-- compute the average -->
<cfset variables.Average =
    variables.Total/#GetProducts.RecordCount#>

<!-- output the average -->
<cfoutput>

 <b>Average Price Per Disc</b>: #variables.Average#<BR>

</cfoutput>
```

Code to compute the average

After we compute the average by dividing the sum total with the query's recordcount, we output the value to the end user.

Project Summary

This successfully demonstrates how you might need to use ColdFusion arithmetic in a real-world example. This is a ColdFusion-centric way to solve the problem. You might be able to find other database solutions through the use of an aggregate function that will improve the efficiency of your solution. Covering specific SQL aggregate functions is beyond the scope of the book, but you can research the topic in the documentation of your database of choice.

Other Data Types

Before concluding this chapter, I want to make you are aware of how ColdFusion handles some of the data types we haven't discussed. First, we'll learn about date-time values, and then you'll review Boolean values.

Date and Time Values

Some special ColdFusion functions recognize string value as being in a date and time format. We learn what ColdFusion will recognize as a date-time value but, now, let's examine the different forms of a date, and then start to add the time to those values.

ColdFusion date and time objects are stored as strings. ColdFusion recognizes a variety of different date formats.

```
"October 5, 1975"
"Oct 5, 1975"
"Oct. 5, 1975"
"10/5/75"
"1975-5-10"
```

The month is written out, followed by a space and the day, and then followed by a comma, and followed by the year. Next, we have two different variations on the first theme: the month abbreviation, and then the day, a comma, and the year. Then comes a variation that includes a period after the month text. It is followed by the United States standard date format: month, day, and year. Next, is the European date format, which is year, month, and date. Both the United States and the European formats could be separated by a forward slash or a dash.

Caution

We can't have a date-time value without both date and time values. If you create a date value without the time, the time portion is automatically set to 12:00 A.M.

6

Next come the ColdFusion time values. We can't create the time formats in any combination with the date formats. The time can be accurate, up to the second. Keeping a constant date, these are the time formats:

```
"October 5, 1975 02:34:12"
"October 5, 1975 2:34a"
"October 5, 1975 2:34am"
"October 5, 1975 02:34am"
"October 5, 1975 2am"
```

The first format displays the hour, minute, and second, separated by colons. The second, third, and fourth formats include the time and minute. They also have an A.M./P.M. indicator. The first specifies using either an *a* or a *p*, while the second two have added the A.M. back into the fold.

Given a specific date, ColdFusion provides numerous functions for manipulating that date. We can extract information, such as the year, day, month, hour, minute, and second. We can also add or subtract dates. ColdFusion also provides functions for creating dates and time objects in different formats, most notably ODBC format. This makes it pass data to and from the database.

Boolean Values

ColdFusion also has a Boolean data type. A Boolean variable is one that contains either one of two values. These values are either yes or no, on or off, 1 or 0, or true or false. Boolean values are known for being efficient in permanent data storage and memory storage. And, because Boolean values only contain two values, they only take one bit to store: that bit is either on or off.

The uses for these values are numerous when programming. We can use them for loop control, as discussed in Module 9. We can also use them in conditional statements, which we explore in Module 8. And, in Module 3, we learn that database columns can also have a Boolean type. Microsoft Access calls Boolean fields *Yes/No fields*. Microsoft SQL Server calls them *bit fields*.

Boolean values in ColdFusion are usually the result of a logical operation. They can be created using the cfset or cfparam tag. The values are either true or false, but can also be used as numbers or text. In a numerical format, true is 1 and false is 0. The text value for true is yes, while, for false, the value is no. We use Boolean values in later programming topics; for now it's only important for you to know they exist.

Module Summary

This module taught us about ColdFusion expressions and how we can manipulate data using expressions. We learned in depth about the different data types in ColdFusion, such as strings and numbers. We also briefly learned about how ColdFusion handles date and Boolean data. The next section takes us more in depth into ColdFusion as ColdFusion's application scope is introduced.

Mastery Check

1. What is an expression?

    _____

    _____

2. What are elements of an expression?

    A. Variables

    B. Functions

    C. Strings

    D. Equal signs

3. What is the difference between a simple and a complex expression?

    _____

    _____

4. What are the different types of operators that can be used to build complex expressions from simple ones?

    A. Arithmetic

    B. String

    C. Decision

    D. Boolean

    E. All of the above

    F. None of the above

5. In addition to tags, ColdFusion provides an extensive library of _____ to help in your development needs.

6. What will the value of MyVar1 be after these statements are executed?

    ```
    <cfset MyVar1 = 10*((5*2)-4)/(5*(2-4))>
    ```

    _____

6

☑ Mastery Check

7. To get the number of records returned in a query, what property of the query object can you use?

_____

_____

8. Why are Boolean values different from other variables?

_____

_____

9. If a date is created without a time, ColdFusion creates a default time and associates it to that date. What is the time?

   A. 12:00 A.M.

   B. 12:00 P.M.

   C. 11:59 A.M.

   D. 2:15 P.M.

10. Which statement(s) has the correct use of pound signs?

   A. `<cfset myvar1 = #myvar2# + #1#>`

   B. `<cfset myvar1 = #myvar2 + 1#>`

   C. `<cfset #myvar1# = myvar2 + #1#>`

   D. `<cfset myvar1 = myvar2 + 1>`

Part 2

Programming Concepts in ColdFusion

Module 7

ColdFusion's Application Framework

The Goals of This Module

- Learn how to set up the application framework for ColdFusion
- Learn about ColdFusion's Application and Session scopes
- Introduce the cfapplication tag
- Introduce Application.cfm and OnRequestEnd.cfm
- Create a sample Application.cfm

This module teaches us how to set up the application scope for ColdFusion. The *application framework* provides a way to keep track of users as they move from page to page on your web site.

Setting Up a ColdFusion Application

ColdFusion has an application framework designed to help you keep track of a session's state in your application. We learn what state management and sessions are, and then we see how to implement them in ColdFusion.

An Introduction to State Management

To understand the concept of sessions and state management on the Web, we must understand state management. The *state* is the condition of the application. Think about your favorite HTML editor for a moment. The state of the application would include information like the number of opened documents, the currently active documents, where the cursor resides in each document, or if you have any selected text.

State management is simply a way to remember what the state is. Let's stick with the HTML editor example. Say you opened a document. Scroll down to the bottom of that document and place the cursor there. Now, open a second document, type some text, and highlight it. Switch back to the first document. You'll notice the cursor is still at the bottom of the first document. Switch back to the second document and you'll see your new text is still highlighted. This is an example of an application's state management within an application. Your HTML editor is programmed to remember all the open documents and the selected text.

Now, leave your HTML editor alone while you spend the next hour answering your e-mail using your favorite e-mail program. When you come back to your HTML editor, it still knows you have two open documents: the cursor is at the bottom of the first document and the second document has certain text selected at the top. Even though you left the program to do other things, the program is still maintaining the state. There's no inherent way to provide this functionality on the Web.

The Web has no inherent state management. The web server makes no distinction between page requests: It doesn't know where you came from or where you might go next. It sends you the page you asked for and that's the end of it.

We can approach the problem of state management on the Web in multiple ways. One option is to code your web site in self-contained programs, such as Java or Flash. This way, the web server only serves up one file that contains the whole site. URL or form variables can also be used to maintain state, but we must pass the relevant state information to each page of the site.

Another way to deal with state management on the Web is to use cookies. *Cookies* are pieces of data stored in the browser on the client's machine, which are only accessible by the server that created them. ColdFusion is designed to use cookies for its state management capabilities, although URL variables can be used as an alternate method. ColdFusion was set up for this state management using the cfapplication tag.

The cfapplication Tag

ColdFusion provides a tag—cfapplication—for defining its application framework. This section looks at the cfapplication tag, and explores how it can be used and what it can do. The tag is set up to define how ColdFusion will handle variables that reside in the application, session, and client scopes. These scopes are known as persistent scopes and are examined in the section "The Persistent Scopes." The tag is also used to define a name for the application.

Here are some attributes to the cfapplication tag:

7

- **Name**   The *name* attribute gives a name to your application. This is the only required attribute for the cfapplication tag.

- **Setclientcookies**   The *setclientcookies* attribute tells ColdFusion whether you want to use browser cookies to manage client state. This is a yes or no value, with yes as the default.

- **Setdomaincookies**   The acceptable values for the *setdomaincookies* attribute are yes or no. When dealing with clustered servers, this makes the ColdFusion created cookies available to all servers in the cluster.

Note

Clustered servers are a group of servers that operate together to serve the same site, resulting in less server load and a more efficiently running site.

- **Clientmanagement**   The *clientmanagement* attribute accepts a yes or no value that tells ColdFusion whether this application allows the use of client variables. The default is no. We learn about client variables in the upcoming section "Client Variables."

- **Clientstorage** The *clientstorage* attribute defines how we want to store the client variables. A default method is defined in the ColdFusion administrator. You can select Cookie, Registry, or the name of a data source.

- **Sessionmanagement** The *sessionmanagement* attribute is a yes or no value, which tells ColdFusion to enable session variables for this application. The default is no. Session variables are discussed in the upcoming section "Application and Session Variables."

- **Sessiontimeout** The *sessiontimeout* attribute defines the amount of time session variables exist in memory before timing out. This value can be overridden by settings in the ColdFusion administrator and is created using a ColdFusion function, CreateTimeSpan.

- **Applicationtimeout** The *applicationtimeout* attribute is used to define the length of time application variables exist before timing out. This also accepts a value created by CreateTimeSpan. This is a setting that can be overridden in the ColdFusion administrator. We learn about application variables in the upcoming section "Application and Session Variables."

You might have noticed that a few of the attributes refer to the CreateTimeSpan function. Let's see what that function does before reviewing an example of the cfapplication tag.

The *CreateTimeSpan* function is used to create a date/time object that can be used for adding and subtracting from other date/time objects. The date/time this function creates doesn't specify a specific date; it specifies an interval. The CreateTimeSpan function has four attributes: days, hours, minutes, and seconds. All of these attributes accept integer values. Because ColdFusion date/time objects are precise up to the second, this function needs to provide a way to create time spans up to the second. If we want to create a time span for two days, four hours, and fifteen seconds, we would use this code: `Createtimespan(2,4,0,15)`. If we want to create a time span for 14 minutes, we would use the code `Createtimespan(0,0,14,0)`. One of this function's primary uses is to define the timeout length for application and session variables in the cfapplication tag.

Here's an example of cfapplication:

```
<cfapplication name="example" setclientcookies="Yes"
    clientmanagement="Yes"
    applicationtimeout=
        #CreateTimeSpan(1,0,0,0)#
sessionmanagement="Yes" sessiontimeout=
        #CreateTimeSpan(0,4,0,0)#>
```

We begin by naming the tag with the name attribute. The name is used to keep track of all application-specific information. If you were to put a cfapplication tag on every page and give it a different name, ColdFusion would view each pages as separate applications and no correlation would exist among any application, session, or client variables.

Note

Many hosting providers set their machines to reboot automatically at least once a day, usually at a low-traffic time, early in the morning. This allows the server to reclaim lost memory. When the machine is shut down, all session and application variables are lost.

The next attribute is the *client management* attribute, which allows client variables to be used with our application. Then we define the timeout for application variables within our application. I set the value to one day, and then we have the two attributes to define our session variable behavior. Yes, we want session variables to be available during our application's execution. I set the timeout expiration to four hours.

7

Caution

Maximum timeouts for application and session variables can be set in the ColdFusion administrator. The default is 20 minutes. You'll have to ask your server administrator to expand the values if you need them greater.

We've referred to the application, client, and session scopes a few times in this module, so we'll learn about them next.

Ask the Expert

Question: Can you tell me more about how ColdFusion uses cookies to handle session management? You also mentioned that session management could be handled through the use of URL variables. Tell me more about this.

Answer: When the cfapplication tag runs with the setclientcookie set to yes or is left out because yes is the default, ColdFusion automatically creates two cookies: CFID and CFTOKEN. The values for both of these cookies are automatically generated. *CFID* is a number that iterates for each user on the site and *CFTOKEN* is a randomly generated number. These two values are used together to keep track of the user's state throughout the application. The use of an iterating number and a random number are for security purposes to prevent one user from easily hijacking another's session.

If you decide you don't want to, or are unable to, use cookies in your application, ColdFusion can still provide you with session management capabilities. You must pass the CFID and CFTOKEN variables in every URL on the site. Both of these variables are automatically created in the session scope to give you easy access to them. A third variable is also automatically created in the session scope: urltoken. The *urltoken* variable contains the query string you need to pass in the URL: CFID=*xx*& CFTOKEN=*xxxxx*.

ColdFusion also creates a third cookie called CFMAGIC if the setdomaincookies attribute is set to yes. CFMAGIC exists strictly to tell ColdFusion that domain cookies have been set.

1-Minute Drill

- Web servers have no inherent way for session management. True or false?
- What tag does ColdFusion use to set up its application framework?
- The CreateTimeSpan function accepts four integer values: hour, minute, second, and ____.

The Persistent Scopes

The application, client, and session scopes are known as the *persistent scopes* throughout ColdFusion, which means they exist for more than one page request. We begin by looking at each of these scopes and see what they're used for, and then we learn about the cflock tag, an important tag that's used in relation to persistent scopes.

- True, web servers have no inherent way for session management.
- ColdFusion uses the cfapplication tag to set up its application framework.
- The CreateTimeSpan function accepts four integer values: hour, minute, second, and days.

Application and Session Variables

Application and session variables are the two persistent scopes that reside in the server's memory, and both have an important place in ColdFusion development. An *application variable* is a variable associated with a particular application. Remember, we use the cfapplication tag to define our application. It doesn't matter how many users are using that application. The variable only exists once in memory and all users have access to the same value. The name attribute of the cfapplication tag distinguishes one application from the other. Application variables are good for values such as file path of the web server root or absolute directories paths. These are values that won't change, no matter how many users are surfing on your site.

Session variables are a bit different than application variables. While an application variable only exists once for each application, *session variables* are unique to each user of an application. Session variables are great for user specific information, such as a user preference or login information.

Both session and application variables are stored in a shared memory space on the server. Preventing simultaneous access to this memory space is important because doing so could corrupt the memory or provide inconsistent or unexpected results. The ColdFusion server is *multithreaded,* which means it can handle multiple page requests at the same time. To prevent all those requests from accessing the shared memory space at the same time, ColdFusion provides a way to set your server into a single-threaded mode. You can do this programmatically by using the cflock tag.

The *cflock* tag was created in ColdFusion to allow for certain sections of your code to run as a single thread. This can prevent other page requests from requesting the same resources the current request is accessing. These are the important attributes to the cflock tag:

- **Timeout**   The *timeout* attribute tells us how long we want to wait for the lock before throwing an exception or continuing your code. This is a required value, which accepts an integer value as seconds. If the lock is achieved within this time frame, the code within the cflock tag is executed and execution continues normally. If it isn't achieved, execution continues based on the value of the throwontimeout attribute.

- **Throwontimeout**   The *throwontimeout* attribute specifies how the cflock tag will react if the lock isn't achieved. This tag accepts a yes or no value. If the value is yes, the tag can throw an exception or it can continue processing the template after the cflock block. The default is to throw an exception.

- **Scope**   The *scope* attribute accepts three values: application, session, or server. You select the value based on the type of variable we're accessing within the cflock block. This attribute can't be used with the name attribute.

- **Name**   The *name* attribute is an optional attribute and is similar in function to the scope attribute. You can use this attribute to make any portion of your code single-threaded. The introduction of the scope attribute in ColdFusion 4.5 made the name attribute used primarily for writing to files or single-threading cfx custom tags. ColdFusion's file management capabilities and cfx custom tags are beyond the scope of this book.

- **Type**   The type attribute specifies the type of lock we want to use: either exclusive or read-only. Use exclusive locks when we want to write to a variable's value. Use read-only locks if we're only going to read the variable's value.

The cflock tag is important when accessing variables in the session or application scopes. The variables in these scopes are stored in a shared memory space, and multiple simultaneous access of the shared memory space can cause data corruption. Here's an example:

```
<cflock scope="application" type="exclusive"
    timeout="30">
 <cfset application.WebServerRoot = "W:\www\">
 <cfset application.ImageDir = "/image/">
</cflock>
```

The cflock tag has a start tag and an end tag. The scope attribute specifies we're accessing variables in the application scope. The type attribute specifies we'll be writing variables to the application scope. I set the timeout to 30 seconds. The cflock tag is a simple tag to use.

When you access our newly created application variables, remember to lock them at that point. Say we want to output their values:

```
<cfoutput>
 <cflock scope="application" type="readonly"
     timeout="30" throwontimeout="no">
 Web Server Root: #application.WebServerRoot# <BR>
 Image Directory: #application.ImageDir#<BR>
 </cflock>
</cfoutput>
```

Our reading code segment is similar to the writing code segment. To minimize the amount of code being locked, I included the cfoutput tags outside the lock. The cfoutput tag doesn't access the application scope, so no need exists for the tags to be within the lock. I set the code not to throw an exception on timeout. Because we're only outputting the variables, this probably won't be a mission-critical, stop the template, code. The type attribute is changed to read-only instead of exclusive. The scope attribute remains the same.

Hint

When accessing variables in the session or application scopes, you must scope your variables by prefixing them with the name of the scope.

Client Variables

The client scope is persistent scope, which hasn't been discussed yet. Unlike application and session variables, client variables aren't stored in memory. Three different storage methods exist: registry, cookies, and database. We'll learn about each of these storage methods and some of the uses for client variables.

Tip

Because client variables aren't stored in memory, they don't need locking.

Directly out of the box, ColdFusion is set up to use the registry to store client variables. Storing client variables in the registry is easy to set up and provide good performance. This generally isn't considered a good idea, however, especially on shared servers. The registry is important to the health of the machine and isn't designed as a data store for constant reading and writing. Client variables can quickly clutter the registry, causing server errors, or possibly reaching the maximum size. Most server administrators change this default setting as soon as possible.

Caution

While session and application variables can contain complex variables, as discussed in Module 13, client variables can only be simple data types.

Another way to store client variables is to use browser cookies. This gives you the advantage of not having to deal with their storage requirements. Implementing this type of storage is easy, they have good performance, and this also makes it easy to expire them. This does limit the amount of data you can store, though, because of browser limitations.

For example, Netscape Navigator only allows one particular server to set 20 cookies, and 3 might be taken up with ColdFusion's CFID, CFTOKEN, and CFMAGIC variables, leaving only17 remaining slots for your application. This won't work if you need lots of client variables. Also, the user can set the browser to deny cookies. If this happens, your application most likely will experience unexpected results. Cookies should be used sparingly as your method of client variable storage if you aren't planning on storing lots of data.

The preferred method for client variable storage is to use a database. Although they require more setup initially, they are much more stable and flexible than the alternate implementations. You don't have the size limitations with a database that you might with the registry or cookies and they are easily accessible from different servers. One potential drawback of this method is this: Every time you access a client variable, the data source must be queried. This could provide performance degradation of your application. The performance hit, however, is considered minimal and is far outweighed by the additional benefits of using a data source as the preferred storage method.

Tip

As the developer, you can usually leave the client variables in the hands of your capable server administrators.

Ask the Expert

Question: How do I set up a data source for use with client variables? What tables are needed?

Answer: If you create an empty database and an ODBC connection to it, your ColdFusion administrator provides an easy way to create the tables for the client database under the variables link. When you select a data source for use with client variables, an option exists to create the client database tables within your data source. When you select this option, ColdFusion automatically creates your client tables. The two tables that get created are called CData and CGlobal. *CGlobal* contains data about the user's surfing habits and has three fields:

- **CFID** The CFID field contains the CFID cookie value—the CFTOKEN cookie values—separated by a colon.

- **Data** The Data field contains some special client variables such as hitcount, lastvisit, and timecreated.

- **Lvisit** The Lvisit field contains the date and time of the user's last visit.

The CData table is the table that stores your client variables. Its fields are:

- **CFID** As with the CGlobal table, the values here are the CFID cookie value—the CFTOKEN cookie values—separated by a colon.

- **App** The app field contains the name of the app the client variables are associated with.

- **Data** The data field contains your client variables.

These two tables make up the client storage mechanism for databases.

Client variables are great for values you want to persist for an extended period of time. Perhaps you have a shopping cart application. When your user leaves the site and comes back two days later, it would be good if the items they put in their cart are still there. Session variables timeout and are great for situations like this. They are also good in nonsession-aware clustered environments. The client variables stored in a data source aren't lost if a user moves from one machine to the other.

 **1-Minute Drill**

- What are the three methods for storing client variables?
- What ColdFusion tag is used to prevent corruption of shared memory space?

- Cookie, registry, and a data source are the three methods for storing client variables.
- cflock is the ColdFusion tag used to prevent corruption of shared memory space.

Application.cfm and OnRequestEnd.cfm

To complete this discussion of ColdFusion's application framework, we need to know about two file names that are reserved for ColdFusion development: Application.cfm and OnRequestEnd.cfm. Before ColdFusion executes a template, it looks for Application.cfm and executes all the code within it. After ColdFusion executes a template, it looks for the OnRequestEnd.cfm file and executes the code within that file. Let's explore the uses for these files further.

The *Application.cfm* is an important file in all ColdFusion development. When ColdFusion executes a page, it first looks in the root directory for the Application.cfm file. If ColdFusion doesn't find the page there, it looks in the current directory's parent directory. If ColdFusion doesn't find the page there, it looks in that directory's parent directory. This process repeats until ColdFusion either finds the Application.cfm or comes to the root directory of the web server. The template continues to process the page request normally if it doesn't find the Application.cfm.

Because the Application.cfm executes for every page in a directory, this is the ideal place to put code you want to execute on every page. If nothing else, your cfapplication tag is the most common element in this template. Setting up default values for application, session, and client variables is also common here. If your application needs to be security conscious, this template is a good place to do security checks. If the user does not have access, we'll often redirect the user to a login page.

Because session variables must be locked every time we access them, it isn't uncommon to copy the session scope to the local or request scopes in the Application.cfm. This way, you can have one cflock command on your page. If we're modifying variables that also need to be changed in the session scope, you can always copy your local copy of the session variables back into the session scope at the end of your template.

Note

Officially, the Application.cfm and OnRequestEnd.cfm files are case-sensitive. Application.cfm needs a capital *A*. OnRequestEnd.cfm needs a capital *O, R,* and *E.* In the real world, the case sensitivity depends on your operating system.

The ColdFusion server receives a request for a page. It processes the Application.cfm, and then it processes the page. Is it done? Not quite yet. The ColdFusion server looks for the OnRequestEnd.cfm file in the same directory where it found the Application.cfm. It executes the code in that file, if found, before streaming the resultant HTML and text back to the browser. The OnRequestEnd.cfm isn't used that often. In fact, I've never come across a use for it, but it's good to be aware of its existence, just in case.

Application.cfm

Project 7-1: Your First Application.cfm

This project steps you through the process of creating a sample Application.cfm and brings together all the content we've learned about so far in this module. Let's begin with a blank Application.cfm and populate it with the relevant information you need.

Step-by-Step

1. Open your favorite HTML editor and create a blank document. The first thing we should do to create a sample Application.cfm is add our documentation header to the top of our document, like this:

```
<!---
Description: A Sample Application.cfm

Entering: N/A
Exiting: N/A

Dependencies: N/A
Expecting: N/A

Modification History
Date      Modifier         Modification
*************************************************************
11/09/2001  Jeff Houser, DotComIt  Created
--->
```

Our template description is a sample Application.cfm. Our Application.cfm will rarely expect any dependant files or expected variables, and we won't have any entering or exiting parameters. Finish the documentation with an entry into our modification history and the date we created it.

7

2. The next thing we want to do in our Application.cfm is to set up our application using the cfapplication tag. The modified code follows.

```
<!---
Description: A Sample Application.cfm

Entering: N/A
Exiting: N/A

Dependencies: N/A
Expecting: N/A

Modification History
Date       Modifier          Modification
******************************************************
11/09/2001  Jeff Houser, DotComIt  Created
--->

<cfapplication name="SampApp"
    applicationtimeout=#CreateTimeSpan(1,0,0,0)#
    setclientcookies="Yes" clientmanagement="Yes" ◄────── cfapplication tag
    sessionmanagement="Yes"
    sessiontimeout=#CreateTimeSpan(1,0,0,0)#>
```

Our application is named SampApp. This application has a timeout for application variables of one day. We want to use cookies for our state management and we want to initialize client management. The way we're going to store client variables wasn't specified because this setting is usually left to the server's default. This tag also turned on session management, with a session variable timeout of one day.

3. The next step in our Application.cfm is to create our application variables. We create two application variables, as the following shows.

```
<!---
Description: A Sample Application.cfm

Entering: N/A
Exiting: N/A

Dependencies: N/A
Expecting: N/A

Modification History
```

```
Date        Modifier              Modification
***********************************************************
11/09/2001  Jeff Houser, DotComIt   Created
--->

<cfapplication name="SampApp"
    applicationtimeout=#CreateTimeSpan(1,0,0,0)#
    setclientcookies="Yes" clientmanagement="Yes"
    sessiontimeout=#CreateTimeSpan(1,0,0,0)#
    sessionmanagement="Yes">

<!-- define the application variables -->
<cflock scope="application" type="exclusive"
    timeout="30">
 <cfset application.WebServerRoot =
            "C:\Projects\htdocs">
 <cfset application.ImageDir = "/image/">
</cflock>
```

Creating application variables

Our first application variable contains the *web server root,* which is a file location. The second application variable contains the location of an image directory, relevant to our web server's root. Notice the exclusive lock surrounding the cfset tags, where the application variables were set up.

4. After the application variables, we can set up some session variables. I created a session variable called IsLoggedIn, which you can see in the following code.

```
<!---
Description: A Sample Application.cfm

Entering: N/A
Exiting: N/A

Dependencies: N/A
Expecting: N/A

Modification History
Date        Modifier              Modification
***********************************************************
11/09/2001  Jeff Houser, DotComIt   Created
--->

<cfapplication name="SampApp"
    applicationtimeout=#CreateTimeSpan(1,0,0,0)#
    setclientcookies="Yes" clientmanagement="Yes"
```

```
        sessiontimeout=#CreateTimeSpan(1,0,0,0)#
        sessionmanagement="Yes">

<!-- define the application variables -->
<cflock scope="application" type="exclusive"
    timeout="30">
 <cfset application.WebServerRoot =
                "C:\Projects\htdocs">
 <cfset application.ImageDir = "/image/">
</cflock>

<!-- define the session variables -->
<cflock scope="session" type="exclusive" timeout="30">
 <cfset session.IsLoggedIn = "False">  ←──── Creating session variables
</cflock>
```

The *IsLoggedIn* variable is a common variable used on sites with security. This variable is an easy way to check whether the user is logged in.

5. Finally, we have one more element to add to our Application.cfm. As previously discussed, we copy the session scope into the request scope. This is done to avoid locking for performance reasons within our templates that access variables in the session scope.

```
<!---
Description: A Sample Application.cfm

Entering: N/A
Exiting: N/A

Dependencies: N/A
Expecting: N/A

Modification History
Date       Modifier           Modification
***********************************************************
11/09/2001  Jeff Houser, DotComIt  Created
--->

<cfapplication name="SampApp"
     applicationtimeout=#CreateTimeSpan(1,0,0,0)#
     setclientcookies="Yes" clientmanagement="Yes"
     sessiontimeout=#CreateTimeSpan(1,0,0,0)#
     sessionmanagement="Yes">
```

```
<!-- define the application variables -->
<cflock scope="application" type="exclusive"
    timeout="30">
 <cfset application.WebServerRoot =
            "C:\Projects\htdocs">
 <cfset application.ImageDir = "/image/">
</cflock>

<!-- define the session variables -->
<cflock scope="session" type="exclusive" timeout="30">
 <cfset session.IsLoggedIn = "False">
</cflock>                                    Copy session scope

<!-- copy the session scope into the request scope -->
<cflock scope="session" type="exclusive" timeout="30">
 <cfset request.TempSession = Duplicate(Session)>
</cflock>
```

The final lines of code in our template move the session scope into the request scope. To do this, use the duplicate function. If we were to do a straight assignment with cfset, then a pointer to the session scope would be created, instead of the copy. This is because of the nature of session scope and complex data structures. This topic is discussed in depth in Module 13.

Project Summary

An Application.cfm is a powerful tool when you develop ColdFusion applications and it resides in the center of ColdFusion's application framework. When we create ColdFusion code, Application.cfm will almost always be in the background, performing some function. Knowing what an Application.cfm is and what it can be used for is important.

Module Summary

This module covered ColdFusion's application framework. We learned about some important variable scopes and how they relate to the users on the site. We also learned about the importance of locking variables that reside in shared scopes. The Application.cfm template was introduced and we created a sample that you can modify to meet the needs of your own application. Future modules begin to explore specific programming concepts, starting with conditional statements in Module 8.

☑ Mastery Check

1. The session, application, and client scopes are called _____ scopes.

2. What are the differences between the application variables and session variables?

   _____

   _____

3. What is the only required attribute to the cfapplication tag?

   A. Sessiontimeout

   B. Setdomaincookies

   C. Name

   D. Setclientcookies

4. What file is the opposite of the Application.cfm?

   _____

   _____

5. ColdFusion automatically creates two cookie values to help handle session management. What are these values?

   A. SessionID

   B. CFID

   C. URLToken

   D. CFTOKEN

6. The cflock tag provides locking for ColdFusion variables located in shared scopes. The two types of locking the cflock tag provides are _____ and _____.

7. Where does ColdFusion look for the Application.cfm file? Where does it look for the OnRequestEnd.cfm file?

   _____

   _____

✓ Mastery Check

8. How do you use the createtimespan function?

_____

_____

9. What are the three potential methods for storing client variables?

_____

_____

10. When you implement _____ management on your web site, you provide a way to manage users' preferences as they surf from one page to another.

7

Module 8

Making Decisions with ColdFusion

The Goals of This Module

- Introduce conditional logic
- Learn how to create if statements in ColdFusion
- Learn the cfif and cfswitch statements

Up to this point, all the code written gets executed, no questions asked. But, what if we want to execute a certain piece of code only if certain conditions are true? For instance, we probably won't want to execute the code on the processing page of a form if the relevant form variables aren't defined. The answer to this is conditional logic. This module explains what conditional logic is and shows you how to implement it in ColdFusion.

An Overview of Conditional Logic

Conditional logic is something we experience every day. We'll talk a little about Boolean logic and operators but, first, let's look at some real-world examples of conditional logic.

What Is Conditional Logic?

Imagine you're in your car, driving down South Street. South Street ends at an intersection with Main Street. You have two options: you can make a right turn onto Main Street or a left turn onto Main Street. If you take a right, you'll be traveling east on Main Street. If you take a left, you'll be traveling west on Main Street. This is an example of conditional logic. You make a choice based on a certain condition and perform an action based on that choice.

Conditional logic is an important concept in computer programming. For example, say you're editing a document in your favorite HTML editor. You try to save it. Is your document a new document, which means you'll have to enter a file name for the document? Or, is it an existing document where the program can save the document without additional input from you? The program will use conditional logic to decide whether this is a new or an old document.

The most common form of conditional logic is the if statement. Later in this module, you'll see how to create if statements in ColdFusion but, first, you can examine some pseudocode to see how if statements can be implemented:

```
If Condition then
  Perform actions
Endif
```

If some condition is equal to true, then we go ahead and perform some function. I used an endif identifier to specify where the ending code lies. Let's look back to our driving example:

```
If Take Left Turn onto Main Street then
 You drive west on Main Street
EndIf

If take right turn onto Main Street then
 You drive east on Main Street
EndIf
```

If you take a left turn onto Main Street, then you'll be driving west on Main Street. If you take a right turn onto Main Street, then you will be driving east on Main Street. These are the two separate conditions from the original example.

In the world of coding, though, you would probably want to make steps to ensure both of these conditions don't have the opportunity to happen at once. After all, you probably won't be able to drive both west and east on Main Street at the same time. The way to do this is called an else-if statement. *Else-if statements* enable you to group conditions together. This is the basic structure:

```
If Condition1 then
 Perform action1
Elseif Condition2 then
 Perform action2
Endif
```

If condition1 is true, then we go ahead and perform action1. If condition1 is false, then we check to see if condition2 is true. If condition2 is true, then we go ahead and execute action2. If condition2 is false, we end our statement block and continue executing code.

Hint

In our pseudocode if statements, the actions performed if the condition is true can be either a single action or a group of multiple actions.

Let's rework the driving example to take advantage of our else-if statement:

```
If Take Left Turn onto Main Street then
 You drive west on Main Street
ElseIf take right turn onto Main Street then
 You drive east on Main Street
EndIf
```

8

This code says if you take a left turn onto Main Street, then you drive west on Main Street, or else, if you take a right turn onto Main Street, then you drive east on Main Street. This is exactly what will happen and it ensures we aren't driving both west and east on Main Street at the same time. Else-if statements can be repeated endlessly until you're out of potential conditions.

One potential problem with the previous code is we don't have a default action. What happens if condition1 is false and condition2 is false? The code will continue to execute at the end of the if statement without executing any commands. Thankfully, else statements exist to achieve this type of code. Instead of an else-if, we simply use an else statement. There is no additional condition, only additional actions if none of the other conditions are true.

```
If Condition1 then
  Perform action1
Elseif Condition2 then
  Perform action2
Else
  Perform Action3
Endif
```

If condition1 is true, then we perform action1. If condition1 is false, we check condition2. If condition2 is true, we perform action2. Now comes the new concept. If condition1 and condition2 are false, we perform action3. After that, the execution of our template continues after the end-if statement.

Let's see how the else statement works into your driving example:

```
If Take Left Turn onto Main Street then
  You drive west on Main Street
ElseIf take right turn onto Main Street then
  You drive east on Main Street
Else
  You stop driving.
EndIf
```

If you take a left turn onto Main Street then you will be driving west on Main Street, or else if you take a right turn onto Main Street, then you will be driving east on Main Street, or else you will stop driving. The else statement action could be anything. Perhaps the user turns around and continues to drive, back the way he came. Perhaps the car stalls and he stops driving. The final else action could be anything you want. This is only a way to provide some default logic into your code so something will happen.

Boolean Logic and Operators

In the previous section, we learned about if statements and how they can react to certain conditions. This section teaches you about how to use Boolean logic to create more advanced conditions. As discussed in past modules, a Boolean value is one that can have only one of two values: 0 or 1, true of false, yes or no, on or off. When you're performing Boolean logic, the intent is to get the result down to one of these two values. We're going to review the following Boolean operators: AND, OR, NOT, XOR, EQV, and IMP.

To understand how Boolean logic operates, first we need to examine a truth table. A *truth table* is a table that lists all possible value combinations for the variables in question and the final result of the whole expression. The conditions discussed in the last section of this module only had one condition. This is the simplest of all truth tables:

Condition	Condition
True	True
False	False

If the condition is true, then the result is true. If the condition is false, then the result is false.

The first Boolean operator—the NOT operator—can work on a single condition. The remainder of the operators are ways of comparing two separate conditions. The NOT operator merely reverses the value of a condition. The symbol for NOT is ~, however, writing out the word NOT is also a valid approach and the one ColdFusion uses. Here's the truth table for a not condition:

Condition	Not (Condition)
True	False
False	True

The two most commonly used operators are the AND and OR operators, so let's look at them first.

The AND operator compares two conditions like this:

- If both conditions are true, the result is true.

- If both conditions are false, the result is false.

- If one condition is true and the other is false, the result is false.

8

Both conditions must be true for the AND operator to return a true value. Our truth table with two conditions must be expanded from our original single condition truth table. We have more options. Let's call these conditions *X* and *Y*:

X	Y	X AND Y
True	True	True
True	False	False
False	True	False
False	False	False

For example, say *X* represents "The sky is blue" and *Y* represents "The ocean is blue." Because both *X* and *Y* are true, the final result is true. If we change *Y* to represent "The sky is black" then *X* is true, while *Y* is false. The final result will be false.

The OR operator compares two values like this:

● If both conditions are true, then the result is true.

● If both conditions are false, then the result is false.

● If one condition is true and the other value is false, then the result is true.

The OR operator is similar to the AND operator when both values are equal, but it's the exact opposite when the values are different. Only one condition must be true for an or statement to return true.

X	Y	X OR Y
True	True	True
True	False	True
False	True	True
False	False	False

If *X* is "The sky is blue" and *Y* is "The ocean is blue," our result value for the OR operator will be true because both *X* and *Y* are true. If we change *Y* to "The sky is black," then *X* is true, while *Y* is false. The final result will be true because at least one condition is true.

The next operator is the XOR operator. The XOR operator is known as the exclusive or, which means either or, but not both. The exclusive or is governed by these facts:

● If both conditions are true or both values are false, then the result is false.

● If one condition is true and the other value is false, then the result is true.

Let's look at the truth table:

X	*Y*	*X* XOR *Y*
True	True	False
True	False	True
False	True	True
False	False	False

Based on the rules of the exclusive or, if *X* says "The sky is blue" and *Y* states "The ocean is blue," your result would be false. Both of the values are true. If we change *Y* to "The sky is black," then *X* is true, while *Y* is false, and the final result would be false. If we then change *X* to "The ground is orange," that is also false, so false exclusive or false will return false.

The opposite of the exclusive or is known as equivalent. The ColdFusion symbol for equivalent is EQV. Equivalent computes values like this:

● If both values are true, then the result is true.

● If both values are false, then the result is true

● If one value is true and the other value is false, then the result is false.

The truth table for the equivalent operator can be seen here:

X	*Y*	*X* EQV *Y*
True	True	True
True	False	False
False	True	False
False	False	True

Following along with the example we've been using for equivalence, if *X* is "The sky is blue" and *Y* is "The ocean is blue," the result would be true because both conditions are true. If we change *Y* to be "The sky is black," then *X* is true, while *Y* is false, so the final result would be false. If we then change *X* to "The ground is orange," then both *X* and *Y* are false, making the result value false.

8

The final operator to examine is the implication operator. ColdFusion uses IMP to refer to implication. To say *X* IMP *Y* is the equivalent of "If *X*, then *Y*." *Implication* is the only operator where the order of the conditions will make a difference. *X* IMP *Y* might not be the same as *Y* IMP *X*. Implication follows these rules:

- If condition1 is true and condition2 is false, then the result is false.
- If condition1 is true and condition2 is true, then the result is true.
- If condition1 is false, then the result is true.

The implication truth table is this:

X	*Y*	**X IMP Y**
True	True	True
True	False	False
False	True	True
False	False	True

If *X* states "The sky is blue" and *Y* says "The ocean is blue," then your result would be true because *X* IMP *Y*. If we change *Y* to "The sky is black," then *X* is true, while *Y* is false, then the final result would be false. If we then change *X* to "The ground is orange," then both *X* and *Y* are false, making the result value true. False implies false.

Truth tables can easily be expanded to include more than two conditions. Let's look at a more complex condition that includes three variables:

```
((X and Y) or Z)
```

I used parentheses to make the order of operators more apparent. Because different operators are in this expression, we have a larger truth table than we had before. To simplify the process of creating the truth table, we'll figure out the first condition—*X* and *Y*—in its own column. Then we have the values there for comparison as we find our final result. This is the truth table:

X	*Y*	*Z*	(*X* and *Y*)	((*X* and *Y*) or *Z*)
True	True	True	True	True
True	True	False	True	True

X	Y	Z	(X and Y)	((X and Y) or Z)
True	False	True	False	True
True	False	False	False	False
False	True	True	False	True
False	True	False	False	False
False	False	True	False	True
False	False	False	False	False

Expanding on the example from earlier in this module, let's say X states "The sky is blue," Y is "The ocean is blue," and Z is "The sky is orange." We have ((true and true) or false), making the final result true. If we change Z to "Clouds are made up of water," then the final result will be true no matter what the values X and Y contain. Next, we look into the tag that ColdFusion uses to implement a conditional if statement.

1-Minute Drill

● What is a truth table?

● What does a conditional statement do?

ColdFusion's cfif Tag

We've examined the concept behind conditional programming logic and looked at how Boolean logic is used to make a decision. The next step is to see how to implement these features in ColdFusion. ColdFusion provides a set of tags to perform an if statement.

The cfif Tag

The tag ColdFusion uses to create a conditional statement is called *cfif*. As discussed earlier in this module, ColdFusion also has cfelse and cfelseif statements to allow for multiple choices or a default condition. This section reviews the cfif tags and some uses for them in ColdFusion development.

● A truth table is a way to get all possible outcomes of a condition.
● A conditional statement enables you to make decisions in your code

The format of the cfif statement is this:

```
<cfif Expression>
  Actions
</cfif>
```

The cfif is a tag that has an open and close tag. There are no attributes to discuss in this tag, only an expression after the cfif. The expression must result in a Boolean value.

Hint

If your expression doesn't result in a Boolean value, but is an Integer value, ColdFusion will accept a 0 as false, and anything else as true.

ColdFusion also provides tags to do else-if and else statements. The tags, as you might guess, are cfelseif and cfelse, respectively. This is the format:

```
<cfif Expression1>
  Action1
<cfelseif Expression2>
  Action2
<cfelse>
  Action3
</cfif>
```

The cfelseif tag is similar to a cfif tag. After the tag name comes an expression. These expressions can be simple or complex as long as they result in a Boolean value.

Tip

Remember, the expression in a cfif or cfelseif statement can be a complex expression.

In web development, there are many reasons to use conditional statements. In secure applications, checking to see if users are logged in before showing them the page they're trying to load is common. On a form processing page, we want to make sure the form variables are defined before processing the page. Or, perhaps you'll want to verify the data type of a form or a URL variable before processing the data. All these things can be done with the cfif statement. ColdFusion provides some specific functions for a variable's value.

Ask the Expert

Question: While reviewing the truth tables in this section, I realized if we're comparing two expressions using the AND operator, if the first condition is false, there's no need to look at the second condition because the answer will definitely be false. Am I correct in my assessment? How does ColdFusion handle situations like this?

Answer: You're correct in your assessment of the AND operator. You can say something similar about the OR operator. Once you find a single true condition, the whole expression will return a true result. You'll find you can make similar assumptions with all the Boolean operators. Earlier versions of ColdFusion would inefficiently calculate all expressions before deciding what course to take. Starting in ColdFusion 4.01, ColdFusion started to use something called *short-circuit evaluation,* which takes note of these specific Boolean conditions. If short-circuit evaluation finds something that will give it a concrete result for the expression, it won't evaluate the remainder of its expressions.

8

The first function we should look at is to check whether a variable exists. ColdFusion will produce errors if you try to access variables that don't exist. We can use the IsDefined function to check for a variable's existence. The one attribute this function takes is the name of the variable, in a string. Its use is like this:

```
<cfif IsDefined("variables.MyVar1")>
 <cfoutput>#variables.MyVar1#</cfoutput>
<cfelse>
 Warning, the variable was undefined.
</cfif>
```

This cfif statement checks for the existence of the MyVar1 variable in the local variable scope. If this is found, it outputs the variable's value. If the MyVar1 variable isn't found, it outputs an undefined variable warning. This is a common implementation for which you'll find many uses throughout your application.

ColdFusion also provides a handful of functions for checking the data type of a variable. These functions are used much in the same way the IsDefined function is used. All of them accept some value. You'll usually be testing against a variable name. Here's a partial list of the relevant data-checking functions:

- **IsBoolean**   The *IsBoolean* function tests whether the value you give it as an argument can convert into a Boolean value.

- **IsDate**   The *IsDate* function tests whether the argument is a valid date format.

- **IsNumeric**   The *IsNumeric* function is used to test if a value is a valid number value.

- **IsSimpleValue**   The *IsSimpleValue* function checks whether the variable you give it is a complex or a simple data type.

ColdFusion also provides functions for checking if a variable is a complex data type. It's important to know functions like these exist, so you can use them when the need arises during your development.

Comparison Operators

We learned about arithmetic operators and string operators in Module 6 and explored ColdFusion's Boolean operators earlier in this module, so the only operators we haven't examined yet are the comparison operators available for use in ColdFusion expressions. You can see the list of comparison operators in Table 8-1.

Operator	Shorthand/Alternates	Description
IS	EQUAL, EQ	Compares two values and returns true if the values are identical.
IS NOT	NOT EQUAL, NEQ	Compares two values and returns true if the values aren't identical.

Table 8-1   ColdFusion's Comparison Operators

Operator	Shorthand/Alternates	Description
CONTAINS	N/A	Checks to see if the value on the left is contained in the value on the right. If it is, it returns true.
DOES NOT CONTAIN	N/A	Checks to see if the value on the left is contained in the value on the right. If it is, it returns false.
GREATER THAN	GT	Checks to see if the value on the left is larger than the value on the right. If it is, it returns true.
LESS THAN	LT	Checks to see if the value on the left is smaller than the value on the right. If it is, it returns true.
GREATER THAN OR EQUAL TO	GTE, GE	Checks to see if the value on the left is greater than or equal to the value on the right. If it is, it returns true.
LESS THAN OR EQUAL TO	LTE, LE	Checks to see if the value on the left is less than or equal to the value on the right. If it is, it returns true.

Table 8-1   ColdFusion's Comparison Operators (*continued*)

You can test for equality using the IS operators. IS NOT can test for two values not being equal. You can compare numbers using GREATER THAN, LESS THAN GREATER THAN OR EQUAL TO, or LESS THAN OR EQUAL TO. CONTAINS is used to see if one value is contained in the other. DOES NOT CONTAIN is used to see if one value is not contained in the other. As shown in Table 8–1, some shorthand versions exist of many of these operators.

1-Minute Drill

● What tag does ColdFusion use to perform conditional logic?

● What is ColdFusion's equality operator?

● ColdFusion uses the cfif tag to perform conditional logic.
● IS, EQ, or EQUAL are all equality operators.

At this point you've learned about all four types of operators in ColdFusion: arithmetic, string, Boolean, and comparison. The order of operations was discussed in the section on math functions, but we need to revisit that order of operations list now that we have more operators in the mix. In ColdFusion, we can mix and match operators of the different types.

The arithmetic operators come first, and then the string operator, followed by the comparison operators, followed by the Boolean operators. This is the order:

- **Unary +, Unary –**   To show the sign of a number

- **^**   To perform exponents

- ***, /**   To multiply or divide, respectively

- ****   To perform a div function

- **MOD**   To perform modulus operation

- **+, -**   To perform addition or subtraction

- **&**   To perform string concatenation

- **EQ, NEQ, LT, LTE, GT, GTE, CONTAINS, DOES NOT CONTAIN** To perform decision operators

- **NOT**   To reverse Boolean conditions

- **AND**   To perform the Boolean and operator

- **OR**   To perform the Boolean or operator

- **XOR**   To compare using an exclusive or

- **EQV**   To compare using equivalence

- **IMP**   To compare using the implication operator

Remember, parentheses can be used in your expressions and can be used to have an effect on the order of operations. The order of operations is important to understand when we're creating conditions to command the flow of logic in your ColdFusion application.

Application.cfm

Project 8-1: Revisit Application.cfm

In Module 7, we created a sample Application.cfm. This project revisits that Application.cfm to see how we can improve the efficiency of our code by using the cfif statement. Most noticeably, our application and session variables needn't be reset if they already exist. This is where you use your conditional logic.

Step-by-Step

1. We want to look at our existing Application.cfm from Project 7-1 in Module 7. You can download this file and our updated Application.cfm from the web site.

```
<!---
Description: A Sample Application.cfm

Entering: N/A
Exiting: N/A

Dependencies: N/A
Expecting: N/A

Modification History
Date     Modifier          Modification
*********************************************************
11/09/2001 Jeff Houser, DotComIt Created
--->

<cfapplication name="SampApp"
 applicationtimeout=#CreateTimeSpan(0,1,0,0)#
 setclientcookies="Yes" clientmanagement="Yes"
 sessiontimeout=#CreateTimeSpan(0, 1, 0, 0)#
 sessionmanagement="Yes">

<!-- define the application variables -->
<cflock scope="application" type="exclusive"
    timeout="30">
 <cfset application.WebServerRoot =
                "C:\Projects\htdocs">
 <cfset application.ImageDir = "/image/">
</cflock>

<!-- define the session variables -->
<cflock scope="session" type="exclusive"
```

8

```
     timeout="30">
 <cfset session.IsLoggedIn = "False">
</cflock>

<!-- copy the session scope into the request scope -->
<cflock scope="session" type="readonly" timeout="30">
 <cfset request.TempSession = Duplicate(session)>
</cflock>
```

Notice we set the session and application variables every time the Application.cfm is executed, which is every time for every page. Let's look at the Application variables, and then we can look at the session variables.

2. The first, and perhaps most important, change we want to make is to add some modification history to your documentation header. The following file shows the results:

```
<!---
Description: A Sample Application.cfm

Entering: N/A
Exiting: N/A

Dependencies: N/A
Expecting: N/A

Modification History
Date      Modifier        Modification
*********************************************************
11/09/2001 Jeff Houser, DotComIt Created
11/13/2001 Jeff Houser, DotComIt Added checking for
            setting of app and session
            variables

--->
```

Modification history

```
<cfapplication name="SampApp"
 applicationtimeout="#CreateTimeSpan(0,1,0,0)#"
 setclientcookies="Yes" clientmanagement="Yes"
 sessiontimeout="#CreateTimeSpan(0, 1, 0, 0)#"
 sessionmanagement="Yes">

<!-- define the application variables -->
<cflock scope="application" type="exclusive"
```

```
      timeout="30">
 <cfif not IsDefined("application.WebServerRoot")>
  <cfset application.WebServerRoot =
             "C:\Projects\htdocs">
  <cfset application.ImageDir = "/image/">
 </cfif>
</cflock>

<!-- define the session variables -->
<cflock scope="session" type="exclusive"
    timeout="30">
 <cfset session.IsLoggedIn = "False">
</cflock>

<!-- copy the session scope into the request scope -->
<cflock scope="session" type="readonly" timeout="30">
 <cfset request.TempSession = Duplicate(session)>
</cflock>
```

cfif around application variables

The previous code segment adds in our modification history. Let's move down deeper into the document to examine the lock around the application variables. This code makes the assumption that if one application variable isn't defined, then all of them must not be defined. I checked the WebServerRoot variable. If it isn't defined, we go ahead and define all application variables. If it is defined, we do nothing.

The cfif and cfset all reside in an exclusive cflock block. Even though the cfif is only read access to the application scope, if we have to write the variables, we'll need an exclusive lock.

3. The last step in our code is to add our cfif statement around the session variables.

```
<!---
Description: A Sample Application.cfm

Entering: N/A
Exiting: N/A

Dependencies: N/A
Expecting: N/A

Modification History
Date    Modifier        Modification
```

8

```
*********************************************************
11/09/2001 Jeff Houser, DotComIt Created
11/13/2001 Jeff Houser, DotComIt Added checking for
           setting of app and session
           variables
--->

<cfapplication name="SampApp"
 applicationtimeout="#CreateTimeSpan(0,1,0,0)#"
 setclientcookies="Yes" clientmanagement="Yes"
 sessiontimeout="#CreateTimeSpan(0, 1, 0, 0)#"
 sessionmanagement="Yes">

<!-- define the application variables -->
<cflock scope="application" type="exclusive"
    timeout="30">
 <cfif not IsDefined("application.WebServerRoot")>
  <cfset application.WebServerRoot =
                "C:\Projects\htdocs">
  <cfset application.ImageDir = "/image/">
 </cfif>
</cflock>

<!-- define the session variables -->
<cflock scope="session" type="exclusive"
    timeout="30">
 <cfif not IsDefined("session.IsLoggedIn")>
  <cfset session.IsLoggedIn = "False">
 </cfif>
</cflock>

<!-- copy the session scope into the request scope -->
<cflock scope="session" type="readonly" timeout="30">
 <cfset request.TempSession = Duplicate(session)>
</cflock>
```

cfif around session variables

Similar to what we did with our application variables, we check for the definition of a session variable. If it doesn't exist, we create it. If it does exist, we do nothing.

The reason we don't use a cfparam around the session and application variables is this: the cfparam performs a check on all variables while we examine a single variable and the cfparam uses that check to make the decision for all variables.

Project Summary

Session and application variables are persistent variables that exist between page requests, but there's no reason to try to set the variables if they already exist. The techniques discussed here are a common solution to the problem.

Genrep.cfm

Project 8-2: Revisit Form Submission

If you remember back to Module 6, we created a form for creating a new genre in our product database. We used some string processing functions to truncate a user's entry if it was too long. This project reexamines that code and provides a better way to create a new genre. Instead of automatically truncating the information without warning the user, we use conditional logic to warn him that his entry was too long and he should modify it.

Step-by-Step

1. Open the original page, Genrep.cfm, from Project 6-1. The original code follows.

```
<!---
Description: The processing page for creating a new
             genre

Entering: Genrei.cfm
Exiting: N/A

Dependencies: N/A
Expecting: form.Genre

Modification History
Date     Modifier           Modification
************************************************************
11/06/2001 Jeff Houser, DotComIt Created
--->

<!-- insert query -->
<cfquery datasource="Chapter6" name="InsertGenre">
 INSERT INTO Genre (Genre)
 VALUES ('#Left(Genre,25)#' )
</cfquery>

<!-- output the info -->                [Left function]
<cfoutput>
 Your new genre <b>#Left(Genre,25)#</b> was created. <br>
</cfoutput>
```

This is a form processing page and we get here by submitting the Genrei.cfm template. The code first inputs the user entry into the database, and then outputs a thank you message. We use the Left function to trim unnecessary characters automatically from the user input. We want to remove the Trim function.

2. The first two things we do in this project are remove the Left function and update the modification history of our documentation.

```
<!---
Description: The processing page for creating a new genre

Entering: Genrei.cfm
Exiting: N/A

Dependencies: N/A
Expecting: form.Genre

Modification History
Date     Modifier          Modification
****************************************************
11/06/2001 Jeff Houser, DotComIt Created

11/13/2001 Jeff Houser, DotComIt Added conditional
            check to check the length
            of the form.Genre variable
--->
```

Added modification history

```
<!-- insert query -->
<cfquery datasource="Chapter6" name="InsertGenre">
 INSERT INTO Genre (Genre)
 VALUES ('#Genre#' )
</cfquery>

<!-- output the info -->
<cfoutput>
 Your new genre <b>#Genre#</b> was created. <br>
</cfoutput>
```

Removal of left function

Making these two modifications is the first step in your change. Next, we want to add our conditional.

3. The final step in our process is to add a conditional statement to check to see if the variable meets our specified length. The following shows the code in our updated Genrep.cfm template:

```
<!---
Description: The processing page for creating a new genre

Entering: Genrei.cfm
Exiting: N/A

Dependencies: N/A
Expecting: form.Genre

Modification History
Date      Modifier          Modification
***********************************************************
11/06/2001 Jeff Houser, DotComIt Created

11/13/2001 Jeff Houser, DotComIt Added conditional
                check to check the length
                of the form.Genre variable
--->
<cfif Len(form.Genre) GT 25>     ◄——————  [Check length of variable]
 Warning, the name for the genre that you were trying
 to create was too long. Please shorten it. <br>
 <A HREF="Genrei.cfm">Back to the Input Page</a>
<CFELSE>
 <!-- insert query -->
 <cfquery datasource="Chapter6" name="InsertGenre">
  INSERT INTO Genre (Genre)
  VALUES ('#Genre#' )
 </cfquery>

 <!-- output the info -->
 <cfoutput>
  Your new genre <b>#Genre#</b> was created. <br>
 </cfoutput>
</cfif>
```

8

In our cfif tag, we use the Len function against our form.Genre variable. The len function will return the length of the string. If the value is greater than 25, then we will give the user a warning message, like so:

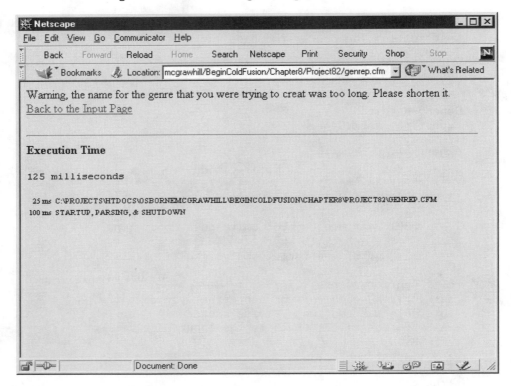

If the length of our new genre string is less than 25, we will continue to process the code normally, by inserting it into the database and displaying a thank you message to the user.

Project Summary

This project stepped you through some simple form validation you can use when you're out in the web development world. Incorrect data could cause database errors or unexpected results in your application. Verifying the data's type and value or other attributes is an important concept.

When You Have More Options

The cfif statement is an important statement to make decisions in ColdFusion. If you have many options, though, the code can become inefficient and hard to maintain because it will have to cycle through, for example, five different paths before coming to the correct path. ColdFusion provides a tag, called *cfswitch,* to help optimize performance and readability when you're working with code that necessitates numerous conditions.

cfswitch and cfcase

Coldfusion's cfswitch tag is used in situations where you have many conditions. It offers increased performance and readability over a group of cfif/cfelseif tags. The switch statements have two parts: the first part is the *switch,* which is an expression that defines how to choose the result. The second part is the *case,* which displays a list of specific values the switch might result in. Based on the switch, the case's actions are performed.

The cfswitch tag contains a single attribute: expression. It accepts the expression that will result in our condition. The cfcase tag has two attributes: value and delimiters. The *value* attribute is the value of our expression. If the result of the expression in the cfswitch is equal to the value of the value attribute in the cfcase statement, then that cfcase code is executed. Multiple values can be attributed to a single cfcase. The second attribute to the cfcase statement is the *delimiter* attribute. If you are applying multiple values to a cfcase, the delimiter attribute will specify the separator. The default value is a comma.

Both cfswitch and cfcase contain a start and end tag. Here's the format for the cfswitch and cfcase tags:

```
<cfswitch expression="Expression">

 <cfcase value="Value1">
   Actions1
   </cfcase>

 <cfcase value="Value2">
   Actions2
   </cfcase>

</cfswitch>
```

8

The cfcase tags are placed inside the cfswitch block. When ColdFusion comes up to this code, it evaluates the expression in the cfswitch. Then it checks through each cfcase tag and examines the value attribute. If the value is equal to the result of the expression, it executes the specific action in the cfcase block, and then continues template execution after the end of the cfswitch. Otherwise, it checks the next cfcase tag and checks its value. The corresponding cfif statement would be the following:

```
<cfif Expression is Value1>
 Actions1
<cfelseif Expression is Value2>
 Actions2
</cfif>
```

As your actions become more complex, the cfcase is much easier to read and more efficient.

1-Minute Drill

- What ColdFusion tag is used for advanced conditional logic?
- What is the attribute for a cfswitch tag?

Switches are great in cases where you compare the value of many variables. Perhaps you're in a secure sight. Whenever people's logins time out, you redirect them back to a login page. After they successfully login, you might want to give users a link back to the place they were. You can do this by passing a URL variable to the login page. On the processing page of the login, you can use the switch statement to compare the URL variable and send the users back to the page they were viewing.

cfdefaultcase

As with the cfif group of tags, the cfswitch provides a way to create a default action if none of the cases are valid values. The name of the tag used to accomplish this is *cfdefaultcase* and it accepts no attributes. Let's look at the format of a cfswitch that uses cfdefaultcase.

- The cfswitch and cfcase ColdFusion tags are used for advanced conditional logic.
- Expression is the attribute for a cfswitch tag.

Hint

Cfcase tags after a cfdefaultcase tag will be ignored. Cfdefaultcase must be the last command in your switch statement.

```
<cfswitch expression="Expression">

 <cfcase value="Value1">
   Actions1
 </cfcase>

 <cfdefaultcase>
   ActionsDefault
 </cfdefaultcase>
</cfswitch>
```

This code performs the first set of actions if the expression is equal to Value1. If the expression isn't equal to Value1, then it performs the default actions defined in the cfdefaultcase tag. Good to note is that our examples of the cfswitch tag have been simplified. In the real world, you usually won't want to use a cfswitch if you only have one or two options.

SongList.cfm
DiscList.cfm

Project 8-3: Choosing Different Product Layouts

In Module 5, we used Project 5-1 to create a drill-down interface for displaying products. We started out by listing the genres, and then all the songs in that genre. Finally, based on the song selected, we displayed all the songs on a disc. This project revisits the past project. We use the cfswitch tag to create separate page layouts for the discs, based on the genre.

Step-by-Step

1. Our original drill-down interface started with a list of all genres. Selecting the genre, we displayed a list of all songs. Selecting the song, we displayed all the info from the disc on which the song was located. We want to modify two templates from Project 5-1 to accomplish our new task: change the SongList.cfm and DiscList.cfm. You can download both the original and new versions of these templates from the InstantColdFusion.com web site. First, look at SongList.cfm:

```
<!---
Description: A page to list all the songs in a genre

Entering: GenreList.cfm
Exiting: DiscList.cfm

Dependencies: N/A
Expecting: GenreID

Modification History
Date      Modifier         Modification
************************************************************
10/23/2001 Jeff Houser, DotComIt Created
--->

<!-- a query to get all the songs for the
    specific genre -->
<cfquery datasource="Chapter5" name="GetSongs">
 SELECT Song.*, Artist.Artist
 FROM Song, Artist, SongGenre
 WHERE SongGenre.GenreID = #url.GenreID# AND
   SongGenre.SongID = Song.SongID AND
   Song.ArtistID = Artist.ArtistID
</cfquery>

<!-- html header -->
<html>
<head>
 <title>Song List</title>
</head>
<!-- end HTML header -->


<!-- Start Main Content-->
<body>

<table>
 <!-- cfoutput over the query -->
 <cfoutput query="getSongs">
 <tr>
 <td>
```

```
 <a href="DiscList.cfm?DiscID=#getSongs.discID#">
  #GetSongs.Song#
  </a>
 </td>
 <td>
  #GetSongs.Artist#
 </td>
 </tr>
 </cfoutput>
 <!-- end cfoutput -->
</table>
<!-- end the content table -->

</body>
</html>
```

No GenreID

Because we're planning on displaying the disc information based on the genre it's located in, we need the GenreID once we get to the DiscList.cfm page. As noted in the code, our DiscList.cfm page doesn't currently get the GenreID passed on to it. We need to add it.

2. We made two code changes to our SongList.cfm page. First, we added an entry into the modification history, and then we added the GenreID to the DiscList.cfm URL.

8

```
<!---
Description: A page to list all the songs in a genre

Entering: GenreList.cfm
Exiting: DiscList.cfm

Dependencies: N/A
Expecting: GenreID

Modification History
Date    Modifier      Modification
*********************************************************
10/23/2001 Jeff Houser, DotComIt Created
11/13/2001 Jeff Houser, DotComIT Added cfswitch
              statement for disc display
--->

<!-- a query to get all the songs for the
  specific genre -->
```

```
<cfquery datasource="Chapter5" name="GetSongs">
 SELECT Song.*, Artist.Artist
 FROM Song, Artist, SongGenre
 WHERE SongGenre.GenreID = #url.GenreID# AND
  SongGenre.SongID = Song.SongID AND
  Song.ArtistID = Artist.ArtistID
</cfquery>

<!-- html header -->
<html>
<head>
 <title>Song List</title>
</head>
<!-- end HTML header -->


<!-- Start Main Content-->
<body>

<table>
 <!-- cfoutput over the query -->
 <cfoutput query="GetSongs">
 <tr>
 <td>
  <a href="DiscList.cfm?DiscID=#GetSongs.DiscID#
           &GenreID=#url.GenreID#">
  #GetSongs.Song#
  </a>
 </td>
 <td>
  #GetSongs.Artist#
 </td>
 </tr>
 </cfoutput>
 <!-- end cfoutput -->
</table>
<!-- end the content table -->

</body>
</html>
```

Added GENREID to link

We added a modification history entry to say we were modifying the URL to pass the GenreID into the DiscList.cfm page. And when we created our links to the DistList.cfm page, we noted that the GenreID is now listed in the query string next to the DiscID.

3. The next template we want to modify is the DiscList.cfm template. You can
see our original code, as follows:

```
<!---
Description: A page to list all songs on a disc
        based on the DiscID

Entering: SongList.cfm
Exiting: N/A

Dependencies: N/A
Expecting: DiscID

Modification History
Date    Modifier        Modification
********************************************************
10/23/2001 Jeff Houser, DotComIt Created
--->

<!-- a query to get all the songs for the
   specific genre -->
<cfquery datasource="Chapter5" name="GetDisc">
 SELECT Discs.*, Song.*, Artist.Artist
 FROM Song, Artist, Discs
 WHERE Song.DiscID = #url.DiscID# AND
  Discs.DiscID = Song.DiscID AND
  Song.ArtistID = Artist.ArtistID
</cfquery>

<!-- html header -->
<html>
<head>
 <title>Disc List</title>
</head>
<!-- end HTML header -->

<!-- Start Main Content-->
<body>

<table>
 <!-- cfoutput over the query -->
 <cfoutput query="GetDisc" group="Disc">
 <tr>
  <td colspan="2">Album: #GetDisc.Disc#</td>
```

```
  </tr>
  <tr>
   <td>Song</td>
   <td>Artist</td>
  </tr>

  <cfoutput>
  <tr>
   <td>#GetDisc.Song#</td>
   <td>#GetDisc.Artist# </td>
  </tr>
  </cfoutput>
  </cfoutput>
  <!-- end cfoutput -->
</table>
<!-- end the content table -->

</body>
</html>
```

We want to make one main change to this page. We want to take the display portion of the template and modify it to display the data differently, based on the GenreID.

4. As always, we want to add an entry in the modification history:

```
<!---
Description: A page to list all songs on a disc
        based on the DiscID

Entering: SongList.cfm
Exiting: N/A

Dependencies: N/A
Expecting: DiscID

Modification History
Date    Modifier          Modification
*********************************************************
10/23/2001 Jeff Houser, DotComIt Created
11/13/2001 Jeff Houser, DotComIT Added cfswitch
            statement for disc display
--->
```

```
<!-- a query to get all the songs for the
    specific genre -->
<cfquery datasource="Chapter5" name="GetDisc">
 SELECT Discs.*, Song.*, Artist.Artist
 FROM Song, Artist, Discs
 WHERE Song.DiscID = #url.DiscID# AND
  Discs.DiscID = Song.DiscID AND
  Song.ArtistID = Artist.ArtistID
</cfquery>

<!-- html header -->
<html>
<head>
 <title>Disc List</title>
</head>
<!-- end HTML header -->

<!-- Start Main Content-->
<body>

<table>
 <!-- cfoutput over the query -->
 <cfoutput query="GetDisc" group="Disc">
 <tr>
  <td colspan="2">Album: #GetDisc.Disc#</td>
 </tr>
 <tr>
  <td>Song</td>
  <td>Artist</td>
 </tr>

 <cfoutput>
 <tr>
  <td>#GetDisc.Song#</td>
  <td>#GetDisc.Artist# </td>
 </tr>
 </cfoutput>
 </cfoutput>
 <!-- end cfoutput -->
</table>
<!-- end the content table -->

</body>
</html>
```

8

The entry simply refers to the modifications we're making, but the main bulk of our changes will reside in the cfswitch tag.

5. The next step is to change the display portion of the template to use a cfswitch statement. We'll make the current listing our default listing using the cfdefaultcase tag. Your updated code looks like this:

```
<!---
Description: A page to list all songs on a disc
        based on the DiscID

Entering: SongList.cfm
Exiting: N/A

Dependencies: N/A
Expecting: DiscID

Modification History
Date      Modifier         Modification
*********************************************************
10/23/2001 Jeff Houser, DotComIt Created
11/13/2001 Jeff Houser, DotComIT Added cfswitch
                statement for disc display
--->

<!-- a query to get all the songs for the
   specific genre -->
<cfquery datasource="Chapter5" name="GetDisc">
 SELECT Discs.*, Song.*, Artist.Artist
 FROM Song, Artist, Discs
 WHERE Song.DiscID = #url.DiscID# AND
  Discs.DiscID = Song.DiscID AND
  Song.ArtistID = Artist.ArtistID
</cfquery>

<!-- html header -->
<html>
<head>
 <title>Disc List</title>
</head>
<!-- end HTML header -->

<!-- Start Main Content-->
<body>
```

```
<table>
  <!-- cfoutput over the query -->
    <cfoutput query="GetDisc" group="Disc">
    <cfswitch expression="#url.GenreID#">

    <cfdefaultcase>
      <tr>
      <td colspan="2">Album: #getDisc.disc#</td>
      </tr>
      <tr>
      <td>Song</td>
      <td>Artist</td>
      </tr>

      <cfoutput>
      <tr>
        <td>#GetDisc.Song#</td>
        <td>#GetDisc.Artist# </td>
      </tr>
      </cfoutput>
      </cfdefaultcase>
    </cfswitch>

    </cfoutput>
  <!-- end cfoutput -->
</table><!-- end the content table -->

</body>
</html>
```

We put the GenreID variable as the expression in our cfcase statement.
ColdFusion takes the value of that variable and compares it to all the cfcase
statements. Because we have only set up cfdefaultcase at the moment, your
cfswitch isn't very useful at this point.

5. The last step in this project is to create our examples for the cfcase. I decided
to set up a few examples for the cfcase statements. The code is shown here:

```
<!---
Description: A page to list all songs on a disc
      based on the DiscID

Entering: SongList.cfm
```

8

```
Exiting: N/A

Dependencies: N/A
Expecting: DiscID

Modification History
Date     Modifier       Modification
************************************************************
10/23/2001 Jeff Houser, DotComIt Created
11/13/2001 Jeff Houser, DotComIT Added cfswitch
             statement for disc display
--->

<!-- a query to get all the songs for the
   specific genre -->
<cfquery datasource="Chapter5" name="GetDisc">
 SELECT Discs.*, Song.*, Artist.Artist
 FROM Song, Artist, Discs
 WHERE Song.DiscID = #url.DiscID# AND
  Discs.DiscID = Song.DiscID AND
  Song.ArtistID = Artist.ArtistID
</cfquery>

<!-- html header -->
<html>
<head>
 <title>Disc List</title>
</head>
<!-- end HTML header -->

<!-- Start Main Content-->
<body>

<table>
 <!-- cfoutput over the query -->
 <cfoutput query="GetDisc" group="Disc">
 <cfswitch expression="#url.GenreID#">

  <cfcase value="18">
  <!-- if the genre is TV -->
  <tr>
   <td>Album: </td>
   <td>Song</td>
   <td>Artist</td>
```

```
</tr>

<cfoutput>
<tr>
 <td>#GetDisc.disc#</td>
 <td>#GetDisc.Song#</td>
 <td>#GetDisc.Artist# </td>
</tr>
</cfoutput>
</cfcase>

<cfcase value="14">
<!-- if the genre is rap -->
<tr>
 <td colspan="2" bgcolor="##000000">
 <font color="##ffffff">
  Album: #GetDisc.Disc#
 </font>
 </td>
</tr>
<tr>
 <td bgcolor="##000000">
 <font color="##ffffff">
  Song
 </font>
 </td>
 <td bgcolor="##000000">
 <font color="##ffffff">
  Artist
 </font>
 </td>
</tr>

<cfoutput>
 <tr>
 <td bgcolor="##000000">
  <font color="##ffffff">
  #GetDisc.Song#
  </font>
 </td>
 <td bgcolor="##000000">
  <font color="##ffffff">
  #GetDisc.Artist#
  </font>
```

```
     </td>
      </tr>
     </cfoutput>
     </cfcase>

     <cfdefaultcase>
     <tr>
      <td colspan="2">Album: #GetDisc.Disc#</td>
     </tr>
     <tr>
      <td>Song</td>
      <td>Artist</td>
     </tr>

     <cfoutput>
     <tr>
      <td>#GetDisc.Song#</td>
      <td>#GetDisc.Artist# </td>
     </tr>
     </cfoutput>
     </cfdefaultcase>
    </cfswitch>

    </cfoutput>
    <!-- end cfoutput -->
    </table><!-- end the content table -->

    </body>
    </html>
```

For the TV genre, GenreID 18, I set it up so the disc title isn't separated from the song and artist name. The disc title is displayed once for every song and artist.

I set up something different for Genre 14, the rap genre. This layout is distinguished by the colors used to display the information. The background color of the table cells is set to black and the text color is shown as white using the HTML font tag. You can define numerous other layouts to suit your needs.

Project Summary

This project demonstrates how we can use the cfswitch tags as an advanced conditional statement. Examining the code in this project, you might think the final template is getting fairly large and, therefore, might be difficult to manage, especially if you were to create separate layouts for all 20 genres we have in the database. You might be right. In Module 10, we examine code modularization and ways to help simplify complicated templates like this one.

Module Summary

Conditional logic is an important programming concept. Decisions are made, whether with or without user input in all applications. Understanding how to operate with cfifs and cfswitch statements is important. The next chapter explores another important programming concept: looping constructs.

✓ *Mastery Check*

8

1. A function used to check for the existence of a variable is ___.

2. Create the truth table for this statement: ((NOT A) and
(((X and Y) or Z) EQV ((X or Y) and Z))).

_____

_____

3. Based on Project 8-3, expand your code to include additional genres layouts. You can design the layouts in any way you choose.

_____

_____

☑ Mastery Check

4. What are the primary tags used in conjunction with cfif statement?

    A. cfthen

    B. cfif

    C. cfelse

    D. cfelseif

    E. All of the above

5. A Boolean variable is one that can have only _____ values.

6. What is the tag used to create a default condition in a cfswitch statement?

    A. cfswitch

    B. cfif

    C. cfdefaultcase

    D. cfcase

7. Which are Boolean operators and which are decision operators?

    A. NOT

    B. EQUAL

    C. AND

    D. EQV

    E. GT

    F. LT

8. What is used to list all possible answers to a Boolean expression?

_____

_____

☑ Mastery Check

9. The AND operator returns a _____ value if both the conditions are true.

10. The OR operator returns a _____ value if the two conditions are opposites of each other.

8

Module 9

How to Loop in ColdFusion

The Goals of This Module

- Introduce the concept of looping and explore why loops are important to programming
- Learn how to loop in ColdFusion
- Introduce the cfloop tag
- Learn how to loop with the cfoutput tag

This module explains looping, introduces different types of loops, and shows how to implement them in ColdFusion. We'll learn about ColdFusion's two main types of loops—index loops and conditional loops—and then examine the cfloop tag, which is used to create loops in ColdFusion. We'll also see projects where looping is important.

What Is a Loop?

In programming logic, a *loop* is a way to repeat a certain section of code more than once. If you were driving and kept making right-hand turns, you would eventually end up back in the same place you started. In programming, a loop does the same thing. A loop brings you back to where the loop started and it continues execution. This section steps us through some examples where looping is used in the programming.

Say we want to perform a find and replace function in a file. Open a document in your favorite word processor. We want to replace every *A* with a *Z*. Open the Search and Replace window and input the proper data. Most word processors have a Replace All button. When you click this button, the word processor starts from the beginning of the document. It searches through the text until it finds an *A*. Then it changes that value to a *Z*. Then the word processor looks for the next *A* and it changes that value; then it looks for the next *A*, and changes that one to a *Z*. This process goes on and on, until we're at the end of the document. This is a looping example. We have some actions repeating over and over.

Let's say you know three *A*s are in a document. We could write code that changes all three *A*s to *Z*s. The code would look something like this block of pseudocode:

```
Find First A
  Change First A to Z
Find Second A
  Change Second A to Z
Find Third A
  Change Third A to Z
```

While this code would be functional, it's limited. If we have more than three *A*s in a document, this wouldn't affect anything after the third *A*. By examining the code, you'll notice we're repeating almost the same steps three times in a row. This is the ideal situation for a loop.

Two lines repeat in the previous code segment. Find the letter *A* and change that *A* to a *Z*. Instead of writing this code three separate times, we can write it once and run the same code over and over until the end of our document.

```
Begin Loop
 Find Next A
 Change A to Z
End Loop If end of document, otherwise execute again
```

Our code here is pseudocode. Later in this module, we'll see the ways to implement this functionality in ColdFusion. Now, let's look at two specific types of loops.

Index Loops

An *index loop* is designed to repeat a certain section of code a specific number of times. We'll look at some standard elements of an index loops, and then see an example.

Hint

If you're familiar with other programming languages, you might have heard of index loops referred to as for loops.

An index loop has some standard elements. Index loops iterate a specific number of times, so one of the standard attributes is the number of times we want to iterate. Many languages, including CFML, also enable you to set the starting number and the finishing number. This lets us step from one number to another. Instead of iterating your code five times—from 1 to 5—you can use an index loop to count from 2 to 6, 6 to 10, or 17 to 21.

Sometimes, you'll want to keep track of which iteration you're in within the loop. Are you running it for the first time or the second time? Sometimes you need to know for your processing. This value is stored in a variable and you define the variable name as part of your loop syntax. The variable is often called the *index*. The loop is named after this value. Finally, a common attribute is to define a step value. A *step value* is a number added to your index after the iteration is completed and before starting the next one. In most cases, the step will be 1. When you are looping from 1 to 5, you'll start at 1, and then go to 2, 3, 4, and, finally, to 5. If you set a different step value, say 2, you'll start at 1, and then go to 3, and then to 5.

9

Tip

If you want to step backward, you can assign the step value to a negative number.

Say, for example, you want to create a program to perform a factorial and display the results for each step. When you take the factorial of a number, you multiply the factorial of itself minus one. The factorial of 1 is 1. The factorial of 2 is 2 times the factorial of 1. The factorial of 3 is 3 times the factorial of 2, or 3 multiplied by 2 multiplied by 1. Given the number you're performing the factorial on, you can use an index loop to find the value.

Let's write some code, without a loop, to find the factorial of the number 5. This is our pseudocode:

```
X = 5
Output X
X = X * 4
Output X
X = X * 3
Output X
X = X * 2
Output X
X = X * 1
Output X
```

We take a variable, X, and set it to 5. Then we output the value. Next, we multiple the original value by 5 minus 1, or 4. We output that result. The process continues until we run out of numbers. This code would be easier to write in a loop, so here's the loop code:

```
Result = 1
Loop index X from 5 to 1 step -1
  result = result * x
  output result
end loop
```

This takes much less code to accomplish the same task. If we were to modify this code, we only have to modify one line, not five. With the use of variables, the code can also easily be expanded to work with numbers greater than five. In this case, our loop is stepping from 5 to 1, with a step of negative 1. The loop counts down. The code is then implemented with X equal to 5. Our result will be 5. Then X is equal to 4 and our result is 20. Then X is equal to 3 and our result is 60. Then *X* is equal to 2 and our result is 120. Finally, *X* is equal to 1 and the result is 120. Now that we've finished our loop, the code ends.

Note

Index loops are great for processing arrays. Arrays are complex data structures discussed in Module 13.

Conditional Loops

Conditional loops are different than index loops. An index loop has a set number of times the loop will iterate, while code in a *conditional loop* continues to execute until a certain condition is met. Two types of conditional loops usually exist: while loops and repeat loops. *While loops* check the condition at the beginning of the loop. This is before any of the loop code started executing. *Repeat loops* check the condition at the end of the loop, after the code has executed. A repeat loop also executes the loop code at least once.

Caution

ColdFusion's tag syntax doesn't support repeat loops. You can accomplish this in ColdFusion's script language, CFScript, which is discussed in Module 12.

The find and replace example used earlier in this module was an example of a conditional loop. In that case, we were looping until we got to the end of the document. If we hadn't reached the end of the document yet, the loop would continue to execute.

Tip

Many situations that require a loop can be accomplished successfully using different kinds of loops.

Here's another situation where you might want to use a conditional loop. Think about your web browser. A web browser asks a server out on the Internet for a web page. The server processes the page request and returns the results to the web browser. In many cases, this is only a matter of sending an HTML request to the end user. What happens when the web server is down? Your web browser will hang for a bit and, eventually, pops up an error message saying the server timed out. This is an example of conditional logic.

9

Let's examine a general algorithm our browser might use when it loads a page. The browser either has a built-in or a user-defined value for page timeout. We simply have to check the timeout value against the length of time we've been waiting for the page to be returned. This is the algorithm:

```
Request Page
WaitingForPage = 0
While (WaitingforPage < PageTimeout) or
   (Page not received)
 Increment WaitingforPage
EndWhile

If We got the Page
 Display it
Else
 Display timeout error
Endif
```

The algorithm begins with a page request. Then, we set a default value to a variable to keep track of how long we've been waiting for the page. Next, we enter into a conditional loop. If the WaitingForPage variable is less than the PageTimeout variable and we haven't received the page we requested yet, we want to enter the loop. The loop code increments the variable that holds the amount of time we've been waiting for the page. The loop terminates if one of two conditions occurs: we receive the page we requested or we have been waiting too long. We complete the algorithm with an if statement. If we got the page, display it, or else display the timeout error.

1-Minute Drill

- What is a loop?
- What are the two types of loops in ColdFusion?

- A loop is a way to repeat certain sections of code over and over.
- The two types of loops in ColdFusion are index loops and conditional loops.

Looping in ColdFusion with cfloop

Now we need to examine how to implement the two main types of loop within ColdFusion. ColdFusion provides a tag, cfloop, which enables us to accomplish both those tasks. Although the tag is the same, the setup is different, depending on the type of loop you want to implement. Each type of loop is examined first, and then we see some examples of each one.

Index Loops

Remember, index loops enable you to repeat a certain block of code for a set number of intervals. ColdFusion's cfloop tag lets us perform these types of loops. We'll look at the attributes the cfloop tag accepts to create an index loop, and then we'll turn the factorial algorithm into real ColdFusion code.

To create an index loop, the cfloop tag accepts four attributes:

- **Index** The *index* attribute accepts a text value. This is the name of the variable that holds the number of the current iteration. This value starts at the from value and increments to the to value. The index attribute is a required attribute.

- **From** The *from* attribute is a required attribute that accepts an integer value. The integer is the initial value of the index attribute.

- **To** The *to* attribute is an integer value that's the final value of the index. When the index is greater than this value, the loop is finished. This is a required attribute.

- **Step** The *step* attribute is the only optional attribute for an index loop. It defines the amount the index will increment each time through the loop. The default value is 1.

Let's review the factorial algorithm and implement it with ColdFusion code.

```
Result = 1
Loop index X from 5 to 1 step -1
 result = result * x
 output result
end loop
```

9

We need to set a result variable to a default value. We can do this with the cfset tag, and then we enter our loop. We can use cfloop for the loop. To change the result variable, we can use a cfset again. To output the current value, use a ColdFusion expression around a cfoutput.

Here's the ColdFusion code:

```
<cfset Result = 1>
<cfset From = 5>
<cfloop index="X" from="#From#" to="1" step="-1">
 <cfset Result = Result * X>
 <cfoutput>#Result#<br></cfoutput>
</cfloop>
```

I set up the From value as a variable. This allows more flexibility in the application, in case we want to expand it to allow for user input. The output of this code can be seen here:

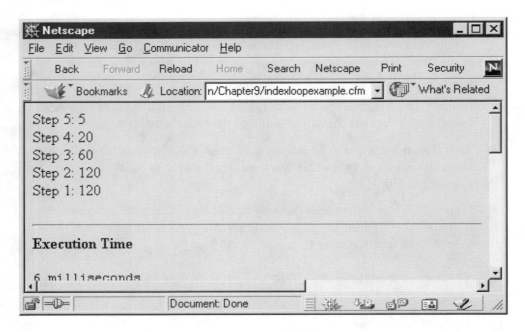

We output the step of the variable for execution of the loop and the current value of our result. The fifth step is 5 * 1. We take the result, 5, and multiply it by four factorial. Four factorial is four times three factorial. We multiply 5 × 4

to get 20. Then the third step is to multiply 20 by three factorial. The process repeats until we get the final result, 120.

Conditional Loops

This section demonstrates how we can use the cfloop tag to create a conditional loop. Then we'll see some examples of where we'd want to use conditional loops.

For a conditional loop, we only need to take note of one attribute: the condition attribute. The condition attribute is a required attribute and its value is a ColdFusion expression (we learned about ColdFusion expressions in Module 6). We can use our search and replace example from the previous section and implement something similar in ColdFusion. Although we don't have documents in ColdFusion, we can perform string processing.

We can replace all the *A* characters with *Z* characters in a string. Look at this sentence:

```
And they all laughed at that joke.
```

If we change every *A* to a *Z*, your result sentence will be

```
Znd they zll lzughed zt thzt joke.
```

The resulting sentence isn't correct English, but it works fine for example purposes. We can accomplish this functionality using some of ColdFusion's string processing functions.

Let's modify our original algorithm:

```
Begin Loop until end of string
  If first character is A
    change to Z
  Else
    Leave alone
  Endif
  remove current character from string
End Loop
```

We're going to loop until the end of the string and check each character of the string. If the character is an *A*, then copy a *Z* to a resultant string. If the character isn't an *A*, we copy over the unchanged character to the resultant

9

string. Before ending the loop, remove the first character from the string we're processing.

Look at the following ColdFusion code:

```
<cfset StartSentence = "And they all laughed at
          that joke.">
<cfset Result = "">
<cfset TempSentence = "And they all laughed at
          that joke.">

<cfloop condition="Len(TempSentence) GT 0">
 <cfset Character = Left(TempSentence, 1)>
 <cfif (Character is "a")>
  <cfset Result = Result & "z">
 <cfelse>
  <cfset Result = Result & Character>
 </cfif>

 <cfif (Len(TempSentence)) GT 1>
   <cfset TempSentence = Right(TempSentence,
              Len(TempSentence)-1)>
 <cfelse>
  <cfset TempSentence = "">
 </cfif>
</cfloop>

<cfoutput>
 Original: #StartSentence# <br>
 Result:  #Result#
</cfoutput>
```

We need three separate variables to accomplish our task. The first variable is the string we start with: StartSentence. The second variable is the Result variable. The Result variable is initialized to a blank value. The third variable is a temporary variable to hold the sentence, TempSentence.

After initializing the variables, we enter the loop. Our condition checks the length of the temporary sentence variable with zero. Each cycle through the loop removes a character from our temporary sentence. When we run out of characters in the temporary variable, we want to end the loop. We check this condition by checking the length of the variable against the number zero. As long as its length is greater than zero, we still want to cycle through the loop.

Caution

When creating conditional loops, make sure the loop control variable is being set each time through the loop. If the loop control variable doesn't change, the condition will never be met and the loop will be infinite.

Now we're entering the loop. Take the first character of the temporary sentence and copy it into a separate variable. We use the left function to accomplish this. If the variable's value is *A*, copy a *Z* into the result value. Notice we use string concatenation to append the string to the end of the result value. If the character isn't *A*, we copy the character into the result set unchanged.

1-Minute Drill

● What tag is used to create loops in ColdFusion?
● What is the difference between index and conditional loops?

Finally, remove the first character from the string. We do this using the Right function and the Len function. If we give the right function the length of the string, minus one, our resultant string will be the original string, without the first character. The right function must be given a positive value for its number. If only a single character is left in the TempSentence variable, we want to set it to the empty string, thus ending the loop. The template ends with our outputting the original value and the resultant value.

Caution

The search and replace code described in this section could be replaced with ColdFusion's replace function. We could use this method for alternate string processing if necessary, though.

● The cfloop tag is used to create loops in ColdFusion.
● Index loops will loop a specific number of times. Conditional loops will loop until a certain condition becomes true.

9

Project 9-1: Finding the Factors of a Number

This project follows along the lines of the factorial example. We'll set up a form so a user can enter a number. Submitting the form will factor the number and factoring the number finds all the values that will divide evenly into the number. We'll output the numbers that factor into our original input.

Step-by-Step

1. We have to create two form pages. The input page, Factori.cfm, is what you want to look at first. You can download this page from the InstantColdFusion.com web site. Here's the code:

```
<!---
Description: Page to factor a number: input page

Entering: N/A
Exiting: Factorp.cfm

Dependencies: N/A
Expecting: N/A

Modification History
Date    Modifier        Modification
***********************************************************
11/19/2001 Jeff Houser, DotComIt Created
--->

<!-- create the form tag -->
<form action="Factorp.cfm" method="post">
 <!-- create the input for our number -->
 Insert a Number:
 <input type="text" name="NumberToFactor">
 <input type="Submit">

</form>
```

Our input page is fairly simple. We have our documentation header and, following that, the body of our template contains a simple form. We're posting information on to the Factorp.cfm template. We have one form variable, a text box, to accept our number input. As with most forms, we finish it off with a Submit button.

2. The next step in our project is to create the processing page of the template. The page, Factorp.cfm, can also be downloaded from this book's web site. We begin with our documentation header:

```
<!---
Description: Code to factor a number

Entering: Factori.cfm
Exiting: N/A

Dependencies: N/A
Expecting: form.NumberToFactor

Modification History
Date    Modifier         Modification
***********************************************************
11/19/2001 Jeff Houser, DotComIt  Created
--->
```

The header bears no surprises. We're entering from the input page, Factori.cfm, and we're expecting a single value to be defined upon entry into this page: form.NumberToFactor. This is the value of the input box on the previous page. Next, we have a loop.

3. To perform the factorization, we want to check every number between 1 and our resultant number to see if it divides evenly into the number. We can do this using an index loop:

```
<!---
Description: Code to factor a number

Entering: Factori.cfm
Exiting: N/A

Dependencies: N/A
Expecting: form.NumberToFactor

Modification History
Date    Modifier         Modification
***********************************************************
11/19/2001 Jeff Houser, DotComIt  Created
--->
```

9

```
<!-- enter into the loop -->
<cfloop index="TempNum" from="1" to="#NumberToFactor#">

</cfloop>
<!-- end loop -->
```

cfloop tag

Our index loop has four attributes and the index attributes takes a temporary variable name. The from attribute is 1, because our loop starts at 1. The to attribute accepts the value passed to us from the input page.

4. The next step is to check to see if the current index divides evenly into the current number. We do this by using the MOD operator: Take the number MOD index and compare the results with zero. If the result is zero, then no remainder exists and we have a factor:

```
<!---
Description: Code to factor a number

Entering: Factori.cfm
Exiting: N/A

Dependencies: N/A
Expecting: form.NumberToFactor

Modification History
Date     Modifier          Modification
************************************************************
11/19/2001 Jeff Houser, DotComIt  Created
--->

<!-- enter into the loop -->
<cfloop index="TempNum" from="1" to="#NumberToFactor#">

 <cfoutput>
  <!-- if there is a zero remainder then we have a
       factor, display it -->
  <cfif (NumberToFactor MOD TempNum) is 0>
    #TempNum# is a factor of #form.NumberToFactor#<br>
  </cfif>
 </cfoutput>

</cfloop>
<!-- end loop -->
```

Mod function

If the number MOD index equation returns a zero, we display output, displaying the factor. If it doesn't, we do nothing. Because every number, at the least, will have two factors, itself and the number 1, we needn't provide code for what happens if no factors are found. This finishes your project.

Project Summary

This project used looping to find the factorial of a number. Loops like these are used mainly to process complex data structures such as arrays, which is covered in more detail in Module 13. It is important to understand loops and how they can be applied to accomplish your goals.

Looping Over a Query

Some of the most common reasons we'd want to use looping constructs are to perform a loop over a query. ColdFusion provides two different ways to inherently loop over a query: using the cfoutput tag and the cfloop tag. The following section examines which tag is better and which is worse.

Using cfoutput to Loop Over a Query

You might not have known this at the time, but looping was introduced in Module 5. We used the cfoutput tag to display all the rows returned by a database query. *Cfoutput* is the most common way to loop over a query.

Various query attributes exist for use in the cfoutput tag:

9

- **Query**   The *query* attribute is an optional attribute and accepts the name of the query you want to loop over.

- **Startrows**   The *startrows* attribute defines the first record in the query where we want to start our processing. This is an optional attribute.

- **Maxrows**   The *maxrows* attribute is an optional attribute, which defines the maximum number of times we'll perform the code in the loop.

- **Group**   The *group* attribute is used in conjunction with grouping, as discussed in Module 5. It accepts a string value that's the name of a database field. The output is grouped on that field.

- **Groupcasesensitive**   The *groupcasesensitive* attribute is an optional attribute, which accepts a Boolean value, with the default value being yes. It tells us whether to group the output in a case-sensitive manner.

You can set up a cfoutput block to loop over a query with only the query attribute. The *startrows* and *maxrows* attributes are good for situations when we want to create Forward and Next buttons to cycle through your data, instead of displaying it all on one page. The *grouping* attributes are good for helping to display your data in a more organized format than you could get without them. You can't nest cfoutput tags without use of these attributes. Because we've already been using the cfoutput tag to loop over queries, we'll forego some specific examples and move on to the cfloop tag.

Looping Over a Query with cfloop

Databases and queries are at the heart of all ColdFusion development. In addition to the cfoutput tag, the *cfloop* tag can also be used to process a query. The cfloop tag is great for when you don't need to output the query data, but we're performing some other form of processing on it.

The attributes to the cfloop tag are the following:

- **Query**   The *query* attribute is a required attribute, which contains the name of the query you want to execute your loop code on.

- **Startrow**   The *startrow* attribute is an attribute that specifies the first row of the query you want to execute the loop code on. This is an optional attribute.

- **Endrow**   The *endrow* attribute is an optional attribute that specifies the last row of the query you want to execute the loop code on.

The cfloop tag provides some capabilities that cfoutput doesn't. There are no limits on nesting loops, as with the cfoutput tag. You can use as many cfloops inside one another as you need. The recommendation is that you be careful when nesting loops because it could cause performance degradation. Cfloop doesn't provide any of the grouping functionality cfoutput provides.

Most commonly, cfloop is used instead of cfoutput when you want to perform a loop inside a cfoutput block. Perhaps you're populating a form with values from a database, so your web surfer can edit it. You have the whole form in a cfoutput block. If you have a drop-down list being filled from another table, you can use the cfloop tag to populate the drop-down list. This makes cleaner code than ending the cfoutput block, starting another to populate the drop-down list, and then starting a third cfoutput block after the drop-down list is finished.

1-Minute Drill

● What are the two tags that can be used to loop over a query?

● Although cfloop tags can be nested as much as you need them, cfoutput tags can only be nested with the use of the ___ attribute.

The next step is to look at how the cfloop tag might be set up. Assume you have a database with a table called table1 and this table has two columns: TableID and TableData1. TableID is the primary key of the table and TableData1 is a number field. Say we want to round the number field up to the ones place, removing all the decimal values from it, and to insert the value back into the database. You can use ColdFusion's round function to do the rounding. This code does that:

```
<cfquery name="TestQuery" datasource="Datasource">
 SELECT * FROM Table1
</cfquery>

<cfloop query="TestQuery">
 <cfquery>
  UPDATE Table1
  SET TableData1 = Round(TableData1)
  WHERE TableID = #TestQuery.TableID#
 </cfquery>
</cfloop>
```

We start by performing a query to get data from our imaginary table. Then, we enter into the loop over the query. We perform a query inside the loop to update the information, which finishes our example.

songu.cfm

Project 9-2: Selecting Default Values in an Update Form

This project revisits the code created in Project 5-2, which enables us to edit a song in our song database. We're going to expand on the song update form,

---

● Cfloop and cfoutput are the two tags that can be used to loop over a query.
● Cfoutput tags can only be nested with the use of the group attribute.

9

using some of the looping knowledge we learned in this module. We can also apply some of the conditional logic we learned in Module 8.

Step-by-Step

1. You can download the file for the song update template Songu.cfm from InstantColdFusion.com. Start by examining the code from Project 5-2. We make one immediate modification, which is to add an entry into your modification history:

```
<!---
Description: Page to update Song Data

Entering: N/A
Exiting: Songp.cfm

Dependencies: N/A
Expecting: SongID

Modification History
Date     Modifier            Modification
*************************************************************
10/23/2001 Jeff Houser, DotComIt    Created
11/19/2001 Jeff Houser, DotComIt Modified to use
             cfloop inside cfoutput
             and check the default
             values for drop down lists
--->

<!-- get the song info -->
<cfquery datasource="Chapter9" name="GetSongInfo">
 SELECT Song.*
 FROM Song
 WHERE Song.SongID = #url.SongID#
</cfquery>

<!-- get all artists -->
<cfquery datasource="Chapter9" name="GetArtists">
 SELECT Artist.*
 FROM Artist
 ORDER BY Artist
</cfquery>
```

Modification history

```
<!-- get all discs -->
<cfquery datasource="Chapter9" name="GetDiscs">
 SELECT Discs.*
 FROM Discs
 ORDER BY Disc
</cfquery>

<!-- the form -->
<form action="Songp.cfm" method="post">
 <table>
  <cfoutput>
   <!-- pass the hidden songID -->
   <input type="Hidden" name="SongID"
       value="#TetSongInfo.SongID#">

   <!-- The Song Name -->
   <tr>
    <td>Song Name: </td>
    <td>
     <input type="Text" name="Song"
         value="#GetSongInfo.Song#">
    </td>
   </tr>
  </cfoutput>

  <!-- Select the Artist -->
  <tr>
   <td>Artist:</td>
   <td>
    <select name="ArtistID">
     <cfoutput query="GetArtists">
      <option value="#GetArtists.ArtistID#">
      #GetArtists.Artist#
     </cfoutput>
    </select>
   </td>
  </tr>

  <!-- Select the Disc -->
  <tr>
   <td>Disc:</td>
```

```
<td>
 <select name="DiscID">
  <cfoutput query="GetDiscs">
   <option value="#GetDiscs.DiscID#">
    #GetDiscs.Disc#
  </cfoutput>
 </select><br>
</td>
</tr>

<tr>
<td colspan="2"><input type="Submit"></td>
</tr>

</table>
</form>
```

2. The next step is to put the whole form in a single cfoutput. We'll also change the cfoutput tags to cfloop tags. The updated code is like this:

```
<!---
Description: Page to update Song Data

Entering: N/A
Exiting: Songp.cfm

Dependencies: N/A
Expecting: SongID

Modification History
Date    Modifier          Modification
********************************************************
10/23/2001 Jeff Houser, DotComIt    Created
11/19/2001 Jeff Houser, DotComIt Modified to use
           cfloop inside cfoutput
           and check the default
           values for drop down lists

--->

<!-- get the song info -->
```

```
<cfquery datasource="Chapter9" name="GetSongInfo">
 SELECT Song.*
 FROM Song
 WHERE Song.SongID = #url.SongID#
</cfquery>

<!-- get all artists -->
<cfquery datasource="Chapter9" name="GetArtists">
 SELECT Artist.*
 FROM Artist
 ORDER BY Artist
</cfquery>

<!-- get all discs -->
<cfquery datasource="Chapter9" name="GetDiscs">
 SELECT Discs.*
 FROM Discs
 ORDER BY Disc
</cfquery>

<!-- the form -->
<cfoutput>
 <form action="Songp.cfm" method="post">
  <table>
   <!-- pass the hidden songID -->
   <input type="Hidden" name="SongID"
     value="#GetSongInfo.SongID#">

   <!-- The Song Name -->
   <tr>
    <td>Song Name: </td>
    <td>
     <input type="Text" name="Song"
       value="#GetSongInfo.Song#">
    </td>
   </tr>

   <!-- Select the Artist -->
   <tr>
    <td>Artist:</td>
    <td>
```

cfoutput surrounding the form

9

```
      <select name="ArtistID">
<cfloop query="GetArtists">
      <option value="#GetArtists.ArtistID#">
      #GetArtists.Artist#
     </cfloop>
     </select>
    </td>
   </tr>

   <!-- Select the Disc -->
   <tr>
    <td>Disc:</td>
    <td>
     <select name="DiscID">
      <cfloop query="GetDiscs">
       <option value="#GetDiscs.DiscID#">
       #GetDiscs.Disc#
      </cfloop>
     </select><br>
    </td>
   </tr>

   <tr>
    <td colspan="2"><input type="Submit"></td>
   </tr>

  </table>
 </form>
<cfoutput>
```

cfloop

cfoutput surrounding the form

This step removed the original cfoutput tags. We put the new cfoutput tags around the form tag: one before the open form tag and one after the close form tag. Instead of using cfoutput to create the artist and disc drop-down lists, I changed the tags to cfloop. Cfloop can be used within a cfoutput, but cfoutputs can't be nested.

3. The final step we need to take to modify the code in this template is to modify the select lists. We want to default the select value to the currently selected value in the database. We can do this using conditional logic:

```
<!---
Description: Page to update Song Data

Entering: N/A
Exiting: Songp.cfm
```

```
Dependencies: N/A
Expecting: SongID

Modification History
Date      Modifier              Modification
*************************************************
10/23/2001 Jeff Houser, DotComIt      Created
11/19/2001 Jeff Houser, DotComIt Modified to use
              cfloop inside cfoutput
              and check the default
              values for drop down lists
--->

<!-- get the song info -->
<cfquery datasource="Chapter9" name="GetSongInfo">
 SELECT Song.*
 FROM Song
 WHERE Song.SongID = #url.SongID#
</cfquery>

<!-- get all artists -->
<cfquery datasource="Chapter9" name="GetArtists">
 SELECT Artist.*
 FROM Artist
 ORDER BY Artist
</cfquery>

<!-- get all discs -->
<cfquery datasource="Chapter9" name="GetDiscs">
 SELECT Discs.*
 FROM Discs
 ORDER BY Disc
</cfquery>

<!-- the form -->
<cfoutput>
 <form action="Songp.cfm" method="post">
  <table>
   <!-- pass the hidden songID -->
   <input type="Hidden" name="SongID"
     value="#GetSongInfo.SongID#">

   <!-- The Song Name -->
   <tr>
    <td>Song Name: </td>
    <td>
```

9

```
      <input type="Text" name="Song"
          value="#GetSongInfo.Song#">
    </td>
  </tr>

  <!-- Select the Artist -->
  <tr>
    <td>Artist:</td>
    <td>
      <select name="ArtistID">
        <cfloop query="GetArtists">
          <option value="#GetArtists.ArtistID#"
            <cfif GetArtists.ArtistID is
                GetSongInfo.ArtistID>selected
            </cfif>
          >
          #GetArtists.Artist#
        </cfloop>
      </select>
    </td>
  </tr>

  <!-- Select the Disc -->
  <tr>
    <td>Disc:</td>
    <td>
      <select name="DiscID">
        <cfloop query="GetDiscs">
          <option value="#GetDiscs.DiscID#"
            <cfif GetDiscs.DiscID is GetSongInfo.DiscID>
            selected
            </cfif>
          >
          #GetDiscs.Disc#
        </cfloop>
      </select><br>
    </td>
  </tr>

  <tr>
    <td colspan="2"><input type="Submit"></td>
  </tr>

  </table>
 </form>
<cfoutput>
```

Conditionals

Conditionals

To find the current artist associated with the song selection, we use a cfif statement. It checks if the value of the current ArtistID is equal to the value of the selected ArtistID. We perform the disc comparison in a similar way.

Project Summary

The bulk of all ColdFusion code you write will be used to display or edit data. This project taught us to use loops and conditional logic to set HTML drop down lists to their current value. The easier that your interface is to use, the fewer problems your users will have.

Module Summary

This module taught us the concept of loops. We learned about conditional and index loops, and how to implement those loops in ColdFusion. The next module delves into another important programming concept: code modularization.

9

✓ Mastery Check

1. A loop is designed to _____ a certain section of code.

2. Another name for an index loop is

   A. Normal loop

   B. For loop

   C. Iteration loop

   D. Repeat loop

3. In an index loop, what is a step?

   _____

   _____

4. Conditional loops in ColdFusion are created with one attribute, the condition attribute. What is the value for this attribute?

   _____

   _____

5. The cfoutput tag can use the _____ and _____ attributes to process only part of a query.

6. What will the output be for this code?

```
<cfloop index="temp" from="1" to="100" step="5">
 <cfoutput>#temp#, </cfoutput>
</cfloop>
```

7. The cfoutput tag can be used to loop over a _____.

8. When looping over a query, what are the differences between cfoutput and cfloop?

   A. Cfloop can be used to group query output, but cfoutput can't.

   B. Cfloop can be used to output query information, but cfoutput can't.

   C. Cfoutput can be used to group query output, but cfloop can't.

   D. Cfoutput can be used to output query information, but cfloop can't.

☑ Mastery Check

9. The cfloop tag can be used to create all types of loops, except _____

A. Query loops

B.   Index loops

C. For loops

D. Repeat loops

10. Conditional loop execution is controlled by a ColdFusion expression. The execution of the loop will cease when the expression result is _____.

9

Module 10

Reusing Your Code

The Goals of This Module

- Explore the benefits of code modularization
- Learn about the cfinclude tag
- Learn about custom tags
- Create your own custom tag

This module explains some of the benefits of code modularization and teaches you how to write your code in modular form. We'll learn how you can implement code modularization in ColdFusion.

The Benefits of Code Modularization

This section explains what modularizing your code means. We see some examples of where you might want to use code modularization. Finally, we learn how to create code modularization using the cfinclude tag.

An Overview of Code Modularization

Let's pretend you're sitting down to create a document editor from scratch. You're moving through your code and you come to a point where you're creating the capability to save documents. You decide you have two options: to save the current document or to save the document under a different name. Let's examine the algorithm for each of these scenarios.

If we wanted to save the current document, the algorithm would look like:

```
If filename is not known
 get filename
end If
Save Document
```

We have two main operations to perform in our algorithm. First, we get the filename to which we're saving the document. Then we perform the actions to save the document. If we were going to save the document under a different name, the algorithm would look like this:

```
Get Filename
Save Document
```

When we examine the two algorithms, we'll notice they're similar. Both of the actions accomplished in the second algorithm exist in the first algorithm.

Up until this module, we only had enough knowledge to use identical blocks of code in two separate spots. *Code modularization* enables us to write the code in a single spot, but to execute the code in different spots.

Benefits of Code Modularization

The use of code modularization has many benefits:

- **Code Reuse** When you can write your code in one spot and call it from many places, you're reusing your code. This is the main purpose and the primary benefit of code modularization. You can write your code once and use it everywhere it's needed.

- **Quicker Coding** As you code more, you develop a library of actions or procedures that you use on a common basis. Each addition to your library increases your efficiency in coding because you won't have to code it again and again.

- **Parallel Development** When you can break up your code into separate chunks, you can write the code segments separate from each other. In teams of multiple developers, this enables you to develop two, or more, separate chunks of code at the same time and you can put them back together later.

- **Less Debugging** After you write a code segment, you can test its function separate from the rest of your code. Once you test or debug your code, you can rest in peace, knowing the code works fine. You needn't go through the debugging process every time you use the code.

- **Easier to Make Changes** If something in your block of code needs to be changed, you can change it in one place, instead of making the change in many spots. This can be a big time saver.

Now, you'll find out how we can accomplish code modularization in ColdFusion.

10

The cfinclude Tag

We can achieve code modularization in ColdFusion in two ways: custom tags and includes. This section looks at includes and the cfinclude tag. Custom tags are discussed in the section "What Is a Custom Tag?" in this module.

The cfinclude tag enables us to include the content from one ColdFusion template in to another, separate, ColdFusion template. The cfinclude tag has only one attribute—the template attribute—which accepts a string value that's the name of the template we're going to include in the current template. The template attribute accepts a value relative to the current directory, similar to creating an HTML link. An example follows, and then we'll see how it works.

We need two templates. This file is named Template1.cfm:

```
This is the first line of Template 1<br>
This is the last line of Template 1<br>
```

And this file is named Template2.cfm:

```
This is the first line of Template 2<br>
This is the last line of Template 2<br>
```

If we were to execute either template, ColdFusion would merely output the text without any processing.

1-Minute Drill

● What is code modularization?

● One method of code modularization in ColdFusion is through the use of an ____.

Suppose we want to place the Template2.cfm text in between the first and last line of template 1. This is where we can use the cfinclude tag:

```
This is the first line of Template 1<br>
<cfinclude template="Template2.cfm">
This is the last line of Template 1<br>
```

ColdFusion will process this page in this manner:

1. Stream the This is the first line of Template 1
 string to the browser.

2. Find the cfinclude tag. ColdFusion will find the template name, Template2.cfm, and then process it.

3. ColdFusion will stream the template 2 text to the browser: This is the first line of Template 2
 This is the last line of Template 2
.

4. When it finishes executing the cfinclude tag, the template will continue on and streams the last line to the browser: This is the last line of Template 1
.

● Code modularization is a way to write code once and use it in many places.
● One method of code modularization in ColdFusion is through the use of an include.

The resulting browser text is the following:

```
This is the first line of Template 1<br>
This is the first line of Template 2<br>
This is the last line of Template 2<br>
This is the last line of Template 1<br>
```

Although this example is simple, it demonstrates how the cfinclude tag works.

Hint

The Application.cfm and OnRequestEnd.cfm files are known as *implicit includes*. If ColdFusion finds the files, it will execute them on every page request.

Many uses exist for the cfinclude tag in web development. Most commonly, I use this tag to add a standard header and footer to every page in my site. Navigation bars are also good uses for an include. Includes can be used to separate business logic from your display code, as well. When we develop our code, if you have a chunk of code you want to use across multiple templates, you'll probably want to make that code an include.

DiscList.cfm
DefaultTemplate.cfm
FolkTemplate.cfm
RapTemplate.cfm
TVTemplate.cfm

Project 10-1: Creating Display Templates with an Include

This project revisits Project 8-1 in Module 8. We were working on our drill-down interface, stepping through the list of genres to the list of songs and, finally, to the disc information. Project 8-1 used a cfcase statement to create different ways to display the information. And, now, we'll rework this code to use includes.

10

Step-by-Step

1. Look at your original DiscList.cfm template. The code follows.

```
<!---
Description: A page to list all songs on a disc based
    on the DiscID

Entering: SongList.cfm
Exiting: N/A

Dependencies: N/A
Expecting: DiscID
```

```
 GenreID

Modification History
Date  Modifier     Modification
*******************************************************
10/23/2001 Jeff Houser, DotComIt Created
11/13/2001 Jeff Houser, DotComIT Added cfswitch
      statement for disc display
--->

<!-- a query to get all the songs for the
  specific genre -->
<cfquery datasource="Chapter10" name="GetDisc">
 SELECT Discs.*, Song.*, Artist.Artist
 FROM Song, Artist, Discs
 WHERE Song.DiscID = #url.DiscID# AND
 Discs.DiscID = Song.DiscID AND
 Song.ArtistID = Artist.ArtistID
</cfquery>

<!-- html header -->
<html>
<head>
 <title>Disc List</title>
</head>
<!-- end HTML header -->

<!-- Start Main Content-->
<body>

<table>
 <!-- cfoutput over the query -->
 <cfoutput query="GetDisc" group="Disc">
  <cfswitch expression="#url.GenreID#">

   <cfcase value="18">
    <!-- if the genre is TV -->
    <tr>
     <td>Album: </td>
     <td>Song</td>
     <td>Artist</td>
    </tr>

    <cfoutput>
```

```
    <tr>
      <td>#GetDisc.Disc#</td>
      <td>#GetDisc.Song#</td>
      <td>#GetDisc.Artist# </td>
    </tr>
  </cfoutput>
</cfcase>

<cfcase value="14">
  <!-- if the genre is rap -->
  <tr>
    <td colspan="2" bgcolor="##000000">
    <font color="##ffffff">
     Album: #getDisc.disc#
    </font>
    </td>
  </tr>

  <tr>
    <td bgcolor="##000000">
    <font color="##ffffff">
    Song
    </font>
    </td>
    <td bgcolor="##000000">
    <font color="##ffffff">
    Artist
    </font>
    </td>
  </tr>

  <cfoutput>
    <tr>
     <td bgcolor="##000000">
      <font color="##ffffff">
       #GetDisc.Song#
      </font>
     </td>
     <td bgcolor="##000000">
      <font color="##ffffff">
       #GetDisc.Artist#
      </font>
     </td>
    </tr>
```

10

```
    </cfoutput>
  </cfcase>

  <cfcase value="2">
  <!-- if the genre is Folk -->
  <tr>
   <td colspan="2" bgcolor="##00ffff">
    <font color="##000000">
     Album: #GetDisc.Disc#
    </font>
   </td>
  </tr>
  <tr>
   <td bgcolor="##00ffff">
    <font color="##000000">
     Song
    </font>
   </td>
   <td bgcolor="##00ffff">
    <font color="##000000">
     Artist
    </font>
   </td>
  </tr>

  <cfoutput>
   <tr>
    <td bgcolor="##00ffff">
     <font color="##000000">
      #GetDisc.Song#
     </font>
    </td>
    <td bgcolor="##00ffff">
     <font color="##000000">
      #GetDisc.Artist#
     </font>
    </td>
   </tr>
  </cfoutput>

  </cfcase>

  <cfdefaultcase>
   <tr>
```

```
      <td colspan="2">Album: #GetDisc.Disc#</td>
    </tr>
    <tr>
     <td>Song</td>
     <td>Artist</td>
    </tr>

    <cfoutput>
     <tr>
      <td>#GetDisc.Song#</td>
      <td>#GetDisc.Artist# </td>
     </tr>
    </cfoutput>
   </cfdefaultcase>
  </cfswitch>

 </cfoutput>
 <!-- end cfoutput -->
 </table>
 <!-- end the content table -->

 </body>
 </html>
```

What we want to do is remove the specific display code segment inside the cfswitch statement and create each segment individually as its own template. Then, you can modify the cfswitch statement in this template to reference the includes.

2. We want to create our new templates to use as includes. Let's start with the default template:

```
<!---
Description: The default disc display template

Entering: N/A
Exiting: N/A

Dependencies: N/A
Expecting: GetDisc query

Modification History
Date   Modifier    Modification
************************************************************
```

10

```
11/26/2001 Jeff Houser, DotComIt Created
--->

<!-- this is displayed if no other specific genre
  is defined -->

<!-- cfoutput over the query -->
<cfoutput query="GetDisc" group="Disc">
 <tr>
  <td colspan="2">Album: #GetDisc.Disc#</td>
 </tr>
 <tr>
  <td>Song</td>
  <td>Artist</td>
 </tr>

 <cfoutput>
  <tr>
   <td>#GetDisc.Song#</td>
   <td>#GetDisc.Artist# </td>
  </tr>
 </cfoutput>
</cfoutput>
```

This file has its own documentation header. Make a note that the GetDisc query needs to be defined before calling this template. The body text is a straight copy-and-paste from our original DiscList.cfm file.

3. Repeat Step 2 for each genre that has a special listing. Create the files FolkTemplate.cfm, RapTemplate.cfm, and TVTemplate.cfm.

4. Modify the DiscList.cfm file, so we remove the display code from within the cfswitch statement and place it the cfinclude lines:

```
<!---
Description: A page to list all songs on a disc based
    on the DiscID

Entering: SongList.cfm
Exiting: N/A

Dependencies: N/A
Expecting: DiscID
 GenreID
```

```
Modification History
Date  Modifier    Modification
*********************************************************
10/23/2001 Jeff Houser, DotComIt Created
11/13/2001 Jeff Houser, DotComIT Added cfswitch
       statement for disc display
11/26/2001    Jeff Houser, DotComIt Modified cfswitch
        to use cfincludes
--->

<!-- a query to get all the songs for the
  specific genre -->
<cfquery datasource="Module5" name="GetDisc">
 SELECT Discs.*, Song.*, Artist.Artist
 FROM Song, Artist, Discs
 WHERE Song.DiscID = #url.DiscID# AND
 Discs.DiscID = Song.DiscID AND
 Song.ArtistID = Artist.ArtistID
</cfquery>

<!-- html header -->
<html>
<head>
 <title>Disc List</title>
</head>
<!-- end HTML header -->

<!-- Start Main Content-->
<body>

<table>

 <cfswitch expression="#url.GenreID#">

 <cfcase value="18">
  <!-- if the genre is TV -->
  <cfinclude template="TVTemplate.cfm">
 </cfcase>

 <cfcase value="14">
  <!-- if the genre is Rap -->
  <cfinclude template="RapTemplate.cfm">
 </cfcase>
```

cfincludes

10

```
<cfcase value="2">
 <!-- if the genre is Folk -->
 <cfinclude template="FolkTemplate.cfm">
</cfcase>

<cfdefaultcase>
 <!-- if no genre defined -->
 <cfinclude template="DefaultTemplate.cfm">
</cfdefaultcase>
</cfswitch>

<!-- end cfoutput -->
</table>
<!-- end the content table -->

</body>
</html>
```

cfincludes

We added a new entry into our modification history to make note of the change we made to this template. Further down in the template is our updated cfswitch statement. You'll notice the changes are as discussed. When surfing the web site, a user won't experience any difference between this and the final code but, from a coding perspective, it's much easier to make changes.

Project Summary

This project demonstrated a practical application of an include. It improves the readability of DiscList.cfm template and makes it easier for us to create new templates for the display of the data. It also makes using the same display method simple for multiple genres.

Custom Tags

This section examines custom tags. We'll start by looking at custom tags, and then discuss the shortfalls of includes and how custom tags deal with these shortfalls. Finally, we learn about the different ways to implement custom tags in ColdFusion.

What Is a Custom Tag?

The use of includes in your code is a great way to organize your code and prepare it for reuse. Includes do have drawbacks, though. An include has access to variables that exist in the current document, if they were created before the include. The calling template has access to any variables created in the include, as long as they're accessed after the include. However, no formal way exists to send values to, or from, an include.

If you create an include that's contingent on preexisting values, then the code becomes less modular. If you write code that's contingent on a value returned from an include, then your code might fail if that value isn't defined in the included code. ColdFusion uses custom tags to deal with this information.

If you have experience in traditional programming languages, you'll recognize that custom tags are similar to procedures or methods from the object-oriented world. When you call a procedure or method, you send it specific variables or values. The language performs some kind of processing on those values and returns the results. A custom tag operates in much the same way.

Writing Custom Tags

Two types of custom tags exist—cfx custom tags and CFML custom tags. Discussion of cfx custom tags is beyond the scope of this book, so let's concentrate on how to write CFML custom tags. This section shows us how to write a custom tag in CFML.

CFML custom tags are no different than normal CFML templates. You can use any of the CFML constructs you want, as well as any HTML elements or any additional text that needs to be executed. Two relevant templates exist when discussing custom tags: the first is the custom tag itself and the second is the calling template, which is the template that calls the custom tag.

Inside a custom tag, ColdFusion provides a scope that contains all variables passed into the custom tag. This scope is called the *attributes scope*. Custom tags are a good place for the use of the cfparam tag. Remember, cfparam is an assignment tag, which first checks for the value's existence before assigning it a value. If you need to access variables from the calling template, ColdFusion offers something called the callers scope. The *callers scope* enables you to create variables that can be accessed by the template that called the custom tag or to access variables created in the custom tag.

When the tag is called, a special variable scope is used to define specific variables to the execution of the tag. The name of the scope is *thistag*. These are the variables that exist in the scope:

● **ExecutionMode** If your tag has an open and close tag, the valid values of the *ExecutionMode* variable are start and end, depending on whether the code is executing for the start or the end of the tag. You can use this attribute in a conditional statement to run different code for the beginning and the end of the tag.

10

- **HasEndTag**   The *HasEndTag* variable can be used to distinguish between custom tags that have an end tag and custom tags that don't have an end tag.

- **GeneratedContent**   The *GeneratedContent* variable contains all the output the custom tag will generate. This variable is always empty when processing a start tag.

- **AssocAttribs**   If you're dealing with nested tags, the *AssocAttribs* variable is used in conjunction with the cfassociate tag. The variable will hold all attributes of all the nested tags. Discussion of this method is beyond the scope of this book.

You can access any of these variables by using the `thistag.VariableName` syntax. This special scope enables you to have greater flexibility in creating your custom tags than you would have without it.

Note

Variables in the request scope are available to the custom tag, the caller, and all includes.

Calling Custom Tags

After creating your custom tag, you need to know how to call it. ColdFusion provides a few different ways to do that, including a naming syntax for ColdFusion custom tags and a tag designed strictly for the purpose of calling custom tags. Let's look at the naming convention used to call custom tags.

When you want to call a custom tag, you can use the syntax cf_*filename*. You use the letters cf, followed by an underscore. The final piece of the custom tag name is the filename you're calling. If you create a custom tag called MyCustomTag.cfm, you can call this using the syntax cf_MyCustomTag. When you call a custom tag like this, ColdFusion will look for the file in two places. The first is in the current directory and, if ColdFusion doesn't find it there, then it will look in the customtags subdirectory of your ColdFusion installation directory. The file better be in both spots.

Ask the Expert

Question: I heard you can extend ColdFusion's functionality using other programming languages. Is this true? How can you do that?

Answer: ColdFusion provides additional extensibility using a special kind of custom tag: cfx tags. You can write custom tags for Java, C++, or Delphi programming languages. Because of the functionality available in these languages, you can use cfx custom tags to accomplish actions that wouldn't normally be doable in ColdFusion alone. Once created and compiled, a cfx tag must be registered in the ColdFusion administrator before it can be used on a site. Functionality created in cfx custom tags ranges from maintaining Windows NT user accounts to integration with credit-card processing services to advanced XML parsers. Creation of cfx custom tags is beyond the scope of this book, but you can check out the list of custom tags available at Macromedia's developer's exchange at http://devex.macromedia.com/developer/gallery.

You can pass parameters to your custom tag by listing name value pairs after the tag name. Say the MyCustomTag.cfm custom tag accepts two variables: TempVariable1 and TempVariable2. We could call the custom tag like this:

```
<cf_mycustomtag TempVariable1="My Var"
    TempVariable2="My Var 2">
```

This code will perform exactly as we want.

The second way to call on a custom tag is through the use of cfmodule. We'll examine the three attributes of cfmodule:

- **Template** The *template* attribute contains the location of the file you're calling as your custom tag. This is a required attribute.

10

● **Name** The *name* attribute is used to call custom tags residing in the server's customtag directory. It uses the syntax *directory1.directory2.directory3.filename*. The previous example will look for the FileName.cfm file in the directory3 subdirectory of directory2, which is also a subdirectory of directory1.

● **Attribute_Name** The *attribute_name* attribute is a list of name value pairs listed after the template attribute. The number, names, and values of each attribute is defined, depending on the tag.

● **Attributecollection** This value accepts a complex data type called a *structure*. Structures are discussed in Module 13. We use the attributecollection attribute to pass many parameters into a custom tag using a single variable.

Cfmodule has some advantages over the cf_ syntax. First, with cfmodule, you specify the location of your custom tag, so ColdFusion won't have to search for it because the location is already given to you. Second, using this tag enables you to call custom tags that are neither in the current directory nor in the server's custom tag directory. If you're storing your custom tags in a directory below or above your current directory, this can be helpful. This is also good when you're sharing custom tags across multiple directories, yet still want to organize them in your file structure.

1-Minute Drill

● What is the ColdFusion tag that can be used to call a custom tag?

● A custom tag is akin to what in a traditional programming language?

● The ColdFusion tag that can be used to call a custom tag is a cfmodule.
● A custom tag is akin to a procedure or a method in a traditional programming language.

Project 10-2: Writing Your Own Custom Tag

This project views an alternate way to accomplish the functionality described in Project 10-1. Based on the GenreID, we want to view the code in a specific format. We can write a custom tag to choose the template to display. This effect will further simplify our DiscList.cfm template.

Step-by-Step

1. We want to create a custom tag that will choose a template to return its value to the calling template. We start by creating our documentation header for the custom tag:

```
<!---
Description: Custom Tag to choose which
    template to display

Entering: N/A
Exiting: N/A

Dependencies: N/A
Expecting: url.GenreID

Modification History
Date  Modifier    Modification
***********************************************************
11/26/2001 Jeff Houser, DotComIt Created
--->
```

This tag will expect that the url.GenreID variable is defined. It will return the template for which we want to display your data.

2. Moving right along, we want to add our cfswitch statement. This cfswitch will be similar to the one in our DiscList.cfm template.

```
<!---
Description: Custom Tag to choose which
    template to display
```

10

```
Entering: N/A
Exiting: N/A

Dependencies: N/A
Expecting: url.GenreID

Modification History
Date  Modifier     Modification
**********************************************************
11/26/2001 Jeff Houser, DotComIt Created
--->

<cfswitch expression="#url.GenreID#">

 <cfcase value="18">
  <!-- if the genre is TV -->
 </cfcase>

 <cfcase value="14">
  <!-- if the genre is Rap -->
 </cfcase>

 <cfcase value="2">
  <!-- if the genre is Folk -->
 </cfcase>

 <cfdefaultcase>
  <!-- if no genre defined -->
 </cfdefaultcase>
</cfswitch>
```

This step just outlined our cfswitch statement. Check for each of the genres and perform a certain action if a genre matches. We haven't discussed what action we want to perform yet, though.

Hint

Because the GenreID is in the URL scope, we won't have to pass it into the custom tag.

3. Now we fill in the action we perform when we find the specific genre chosen. We set the name of the template to a local variable. This is the code:

```
<!---
Description: Custom Tag to choose which
    template to display

Entering: N/A
Exiting: N/A

Dependencies: N/A
Expecting: url.GenreID

Modification History
Date  Modifier      Modification
*********************************************************
11/26/2001 Jeff Houser, DotComIt Created
--->

<cfswitch expression="#url.GenreID#">

 <cfcase value="18">
  <!-- if the genre is TV -->
  <cfset variables.DisplayTemplate = "TVTemplate">
 </cfcase>

 <cfcase value="14">
  <!-- if the genre is Rap -->
  <cfset variables.DisplayTemplate = "RapTemplate">
 </cfcase>

 <cfcase value="2">
  <!-- if the genre is Folk -->
  <cfset variables.DisplayTemplate = "FolkTemplate">
 </cfcase>

 <cfdefaultcase>
  <!-- if no genre defined -->
  <cfset variables.DisplayTemplate ="DefaultTemplate">
 </cfdefaultcase>
</cfswitch>
```

cfsets

10

4. We return our DisplayTemplate variable to the calling template and we use a cfset to do this, creating the variable in the caller scope. This is the code:

```
<!---
Description: Custom Tag to choose which
    template to display

Entering: N/A
Exiting: N/A

Dependencies: N/A
Expecting: url.GenreID

Modification History
Date  Modifier    Modification
*******************************************************
11/26/2001 Jeff Houser, DotComIt Created
--->

<cfswitch expression="#url.GenreID#">

 <cfcase value="18">
  <!-- if the genre is TV -->
  <cfset variables.DisplayTemplate = "TVTemplate">
 </cfcase>

 <cfcase value="14">
  <!-- if the genre is Rap -->
  <cfset variables.DisplayTemplate = "RapTemplate">
 </cfcase>

 <cfcase value="2">
  <!-- if the genre is Folk -->
  <cfset variables.DisplayTemplate = "FolkTemplate">
 </cfcase>

 <cfdefaultcase>
  <!-- if no genre defined -->
  <cfset variables.DisplayTemplate ="DefaultTemplate">
 </cfdefaultcase>
</cfswitch>

<cfset caller.DisplayTemplate =
       variables.DisplayTemplate>
```

cfset in calling template

The final line creates the DisplayTemplate variable in the calling template and finishes the custom tag.

5. The final step is to modify our DiscList.cfm template to use the custom tag. This is the code:

```
<!---
Description: A page to list all songs on a disc based
    on the DiscID

Entering: SongList.cfm
Exiting: N/A

Dependencies: ChooseTemplate.cfm custom tag
Expecting: DiscID
 GenreID

Modification History
Date  Modifier    Modification
***********************************************************
10/23/2001 Jeff Houser, DotComIt Created
11/13/2001 Jeff Houser, DotComIT Added cfswitch
        statement for disc display
11/26/2001 Jeff Houser, DotComIt Modified cfswitch
        to use cfincludes
11/26/2001 Jeff Houser, DotComIt Modified added use
        of custom tag
--->

<!-- a query to get all the songs for the
  specific genre -->
<cfquery datasource="Chapter10" name="GetDisc">
 SELECT Discs.*, Song.*, Artist.Artist
 FROM Song, Artist, Discs
 WHERE Song.DiscID = #url.DiscID# AND
 Discs.DiscID = Song.DiscID AND
 Song.ArtistID = Artist.ArtistID
</cfquery>

<!-- html header -->
<html>
<head>
 <title>Disc List</title>
</head>
<!-- end HTML header -->
```

10

```
<!-- Start Main Content-->
<body>

<table>

 <cfmodule template="ChooseTemplate.cfm">          ◀──── Call custom tag
 <cfinclude template="#DisplayTemplate#.cfm">

</table>
<!-- end the content table -->

</body>
</html>
```

We use the cfmodule tag to call our custom tag. The custom tag chooses which template we want to display. Then, we use a cfinclude to display that template. We automatically append the .cfm text to the end of our template name, which completes our DiscList.cfm template.

Project Summary

This project shows how you might use a custom tag to simplify your code even further. Although we needn't pass any values into the tag because URL variables are available inherently to the custom tag, we do return a value. Understanding how custom tags can be used to perform tasks such as this is important.

Module Summary

This module taught you the important concepts of code modularization. The main purpose of coding things in a modular format is to emphasize code reuse. This is perhaps one of the most important concepts you can learn when coding web sites. The next module examines error-handling procedures in ColdFusion.

✓ *Mastery Check*

1. The two forms of code modularization in ColdFusion are _____ and _____ .

2. How are CFML custom tags different than normal ColdFusion templates?

   _____

   _____

3. What are some of the benefits of code modularization?

   A. Quicker coding

   B. Easier debugging

   C. Faster program execution

   D. Parallel development

4. What is the one parameter to the cfinclude tag?

   _____

   _____

5. Why does code modularization make for less debugging?

   _____

   _____

6. Custom tags can be called using:

   A. The cfmodule tag

   B. The cfinclude tag

   C. The syntax cf_*tagname*

   D. The cfexecute tag

10

☑ Mastery Check

7. In Project 10-1, we only showed the code for the include that displayed the default template. Create the includes for the other genres with special display types.

   _____

   _____

8. Where can custom tags reside?

   A. The customtag directory of your ColdFusion server

   B. Another web server

   C. The current directory

   D. Your web site's parent directory

   E. All of the above

9. What is parallel development?

   _____

   _____

10. In what languages can custom tags be written?

    _____

    _____

Module 11

Handling Errors
in ColdFusion

The Goals of This Module

- Provide an overview of error handling
- Introduce the cferror tag
- Learn about run-time exception handling

This module examines the important concepts of error handling. Like it or not, we aren't perfect. We can't develop bug-free applications every time and we aren't able to anticipate every action the end user might take to break the system. Barring the old baseball bat through monitor trick, we can identify some common areas or situations where errors might be introduced into our application. Once we identify those areas, we can also write some code to handle those errors when they occur.

An Overview of Errors

No matter how much time you spend debugging your application, problems can occur. We'll examine why errors happen and look at the types of errors that can occur in your ColdFusion development.

Mistakes Happen and It Isn't Always Your Fault

If you don't already know, an *error* in your software application is an unexpected occurrence in that application. Errors are often called *bugs* in software development. The term "bug" is an early one, referring to the time a moth was found dead in a switch, thus preventing the switch from making its connection. From then on, looking for problems with software code became known as "looking for bugs."

Two types of bugs exist: *fatal* and *nonfatal*. *Fatal bugs*, or errors, force a program to stop. Say you're installing a program on your computer. Halfway through the install, the disk drive runs out of space. What happens now? The install program is trying to write to a full hard drive. This will, obviously, cause problems. Another fatal error could be caused by invalid memory access. From a programmer's perspective, you can't do much to control the system's memory use outside your program. Excessive memory use from outside programs could reduce the amount of memory available to your program, forcing your program not to work. Hardware errors are also something you cannot account for, but that could force your program to stop or the computer to shut down.

Nonfatal errors are much more common. These are the errors that can usually be caught or fixed during the execution of a program. For example, say you were trying to save a file, but typed in *123 instead of 123. On the Windows operating system (OS), the asterisk can't be used in filenames. Trying to create this file will cause an error. With this type of error, however, you can easily prevent it from being fatal. Instead of trying to create the file and causing an error, you can tell the user why the filename is wrong and ask for another one.

This module focuses on nonfatal errors that can be anticipated and addressed without causing fatal flaws. The next section looks at the different types of errors you might come across in the web development world.

Types of Errors in ColdFusion

There are errors that you will come across in web development, which you might not experience in other areas of programming. Some errors you may have no control over. If your database server crashes, your web server will not be able to access it. Nothing you do in ColdFusion will cause the user's browser to crash, yet doing so will definitely terminate your application for that user. This section concentrates on the different types of errors you'll come across in your web applications and examines some of the ways to approach them but, first, you should know some common definitions in error handling.

The following are some of the words and definitions that are pertinent to error-handling procedures:

- **Exception**   An *exception* is simply another name for an error.

- **Throw**   When an error occurs, the system performs an operation to let the program know that an error has occurred. This is known as *throwing an error* or *throwing an exception*.

- **Catch**   When the program tries to address the error, this is known as *catching an error*.

The reason for the throw and catch baseball analogy is this: When an error occurs, it interrupts the normal flow of the program. The code automatically moves from where it is to the error-handling portion of the code. Instead of walking in an iterative manner, the code jumps around, much like a baseball is thrown. Here's a list of different types of errors:

- **Code Errors**   *Code errors* are errors in your code that cause ColdFusion to stop processing a page and show you an error similar to that shown in Figure 11-1. Common causes of these errors could be mismatched open and close tags, a missing number sign when trying to display a variable, or trying to access a variable that wasn't yet created. Your end user should

11

never see these types of errors. You should catch them all in the development stages while you're testing your pages.

- **Missing Page Errors**   *Missing page errors* are, as you might have guessed, the result of requesting a page that isn't there. These errors are usually because of HTML links pointing to the wrong directory. If a cfinclude tries to include a nonexistent file, the same type of error will also result. These types of errors are most common when you're linking to a site separate from your own or someone is linking back to your site. Because you have no control over the other site, you might not be notified when it changes and your link becomes outdated. The same is true when people link to you.

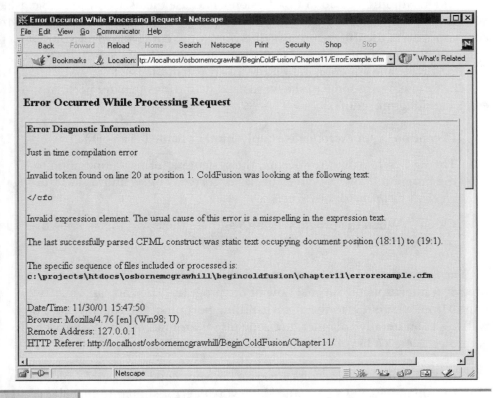

Figure 11-1   A page containing code errors

● **User Input Errors** Whenever you ask the user for information, you never know what you'll get. The recommendation is that you verify the information you were just given before you try to process it. If you were looking for a number, but were given text, trying to perform mathematical functions on the data will cause strange results at best or display error messages at worst.

● **Security Errors** *Security errors* happen when a user tries to access something to which she isn't allowed access. The most common resolution in application-based security is to redirect the user to a login page. If using server-side security, the server automatically prompts for authentication before opening access to the restricted area.

● **Database Errors** *Database errors* usually occur because of failed database operations. The potential kinks in your code, such as a malformed insert statement, will be ironed out as you debug your application in the development stage. When the application is rolled out, the usual cause for database problems is a break in the connection between your web server and your database server. Invalid input, as previously described, could cause additional problems if you use that invalid input in your SQL statements.

These are the different types of errors you'll probably come across as you develop web sites. Try to anticipate these errors and build in some code to handle them because errors can frustrate your users and make them leave your site.

1-Minute Drill

● Another name for an error in a software program is a _____.

● What are the types of errors you should catch when you're debugging?

● A bug is another name for an error in a software program.
● You should catch code errors when you're debugging.

Generic Error Handlers

This section discusses a way to set up generic error handlers. You first learn what a generic error handler is, and then you examine ColdFusion's cferror tag. Then you learn about all the error types that can exist in ColdFusion.

The cferror Tag

ColdFusion provides a way to create general error handlers. A *general error handler* doesn't try to correct the error—it's only a way to provide a pretty message to your end user if an error occurs and isn't handled. ColdFusion does provide tags to try to catch and fix the error before the application breaks. Those tags are discussed in the Specific Error Handlers section of this module.

The tag ColdFusion uses for error handling is called cferror. The following are the attributes to the cferror tag:

- **Type**   The *type* attribute is a required attribute. This tells the tag the type of error to watch for. Valid values for this type are exception, request, validation, and monitor.

- **Template**   The *template* attribute is a required attribute that defines the page to be executed if the specific type of error occurs.

- **Mailto**   The *mailto* attribute is an optional attribute. It contains an e-mail address that will be accessible from the error template.

- **Exception**   The *exception* attribute is a required attribute if the type attribute contains a monitor or exception. It defines the specific exception that this error handler will watch for. All the different types of exceptions will be discussed in the Types of Errors section of this module.

Next, we examine the four types of errors (Exception, Request, Monitor, and Validation) in more detail. Then you'll see what happens when the error handler springs into action and executes the template page.

Hint

The mailto attribute can be a bit confusing because it doesn't send off an e-mail to the specified e-mail address.

The valid values for the type attribute to the cferror tag are the following:

- **Exception**   When an error happens, which is specified in the exception attribute, the template will be evoked. In the resulting template, you can use the full range of ColdFusion tags. This type of exception handling can also be set up in the ColdFusion administrator.

- **Request**   When a request error occurs, such as a file isn't found, this type of cferror template is executed. This includes some special error variables, which are discussed momentarily, but it doesn't allow for access to the full range of CFML tags.

- **Validation**   When you're using a cfform tag, a validation error template is executed when form data isn't properly validated. You can check Module 4 or your ColdFusion documentation for more information on cfform and its built-in validation characteristics. Many advanced ColdFusion programmers don't use the tag.

- **Monitor**   Monitor templates are dynamically invoked when the error occurs that's specified in the exception template. This happens before any attempt at correcting the error. This is used primarily for keeping an eye on complex applications.

Now that your error occurred, what happens next? ColdFusion creates a special error variable, with certain values. Then it executes a monitor template for that type of exception, if it exists. If no monitor exception template exists, then it tries to correct the error. If it's unable to fix the error on-the-fly, it executes the other template defined in cferror tag. What happens in this template? The short answer is this: anything you want. Most commonly, you'll want to display some form of error message apologizing to the user for the error.

11

Let's look at the special variables created for access in the error template. Unless specified, all variables are available in exception, request, or monitor templates only.

- **Error.Diagnostic**   The *Diagnostic* variable contains the detailed diagnostic messages from the ColdFusion server. You use this variable to debug the error.

- **Error.MailTo**   The *MailTo* variable contains the value specified in the mailto attribute of the cferror tag. You can use this variable to send off an e-mail to the developer, probably you, notifying yourself of the exception.

- **Error.DateTime**   The *DateTime* variable contains the date and time the error occurred. You can use this date and time information to determine if any extraneous circumstances existed at the time of the error, such as a server problem.

- **Error.Browser**   The *Browser* variable contains the name of the browser where the error occurred. You can use the browser information for further testing.

- **Error.GeneratedContent**   The *GeneratedContent* variable contains the content generated by the failed request—before it failed, of course. You can use this to determine what portion of the code executed properly before failure.

- **Error.RemoteAddress**   The *RemoteAddress* variable contains the Internet Protocol (IP) address where the error template was executed.

- **Error.HTTPReferrer**   The *HTTPReferrer* variable contains the page that sent the browser to the template that caused the error. You can use this in conjunction with the Template variable to trace the flow of the application that caused the error.

- **Error.Template**   The *Template* variable contains the filename of the template where the error occurred. You can use this in conjunction with the HTTPReferrer template to trace the flow of the application that caused the error.

- **Error.QueryString**   The *QueryString* variable contains the portion of the URL that resides after the question mark. You can use this to help discern the state the application was in when the error was executed.

- **Error.ValidationHeader**   The *ValidationHeader* variable is the header text for the validation message. This variable is only accessible for validation errors.

- **Error.InvalidFields**   The *InvalidFields* variable shows the list of fields that weren't validated. This variable is only accessible for validation errors.

- **Error.ValidationFooter**   The *ValidationFooter* variable displays the text to be used for the footer of the validation error. It isn't accessible by request, exception, or monitor errors.

In your template, you use these variables to make the error message pretty for your user. You'll usually want to add site navigation, and standard header and footer links to the site.

Types of Errors

Although we already discussed different classes of errors in the previous section, we haven't yet learned the specific types of errors ColdFusion will look for. The error classes are validation, request, monitor, and exception. We could make an argument that monitor exceptions don't count because they react to any error we specify. Exception errors could also be under suspicion because we must further define the error type we're trying to watch out for with the exception attribute of the cferror tag. This section lists and explains the potential values for the cferror tag.

This is the list of exception names you can put in the exception attribute of the cferror tag:

11

- **Database**   *Database* errors are errors with the database. This could be caused by invalid SQL code or ODBC problems.

- **Template**   *Template* errors are caused by cfinclude, cfmodule, and cferror. It's ironic that a cferror tag could cause an error, but if the directory structures are improper, this can be the case.

- **Missinginclude**   The cfinclude tag causes the *missinginclude* error, which is caused by trying to reference a file that isn't there.

- **Object**   The *object* error is raised by problems with the cfobject tag. Examination of the cfobject tag is beyond the scope of this book.

- **Security**   *Security* errors are caused when problems exist with the ColdFusion security tags, such as CFLDAP or the isauthenticated function. Discussion of security topics is beyond the scope of this book.

- **Expression**   The *expression* error happens when ColdFusion has a problem evaluating an exception. You can read more about ColdFusion expressions in Module 6.

- **Lock**   The *lock* error occurs when a cflock tag times out and doesn't achieve the relevant lock. You can read more information about locking in Module 7.

- **Application**   *Application* errors are those raised by the cfthrow tag, which is discussed in the Specific Error Handlers section.

- **Custom_exception_type**   We can create our own custom error types with the cfthrow tag. This is commonly done in custom tags, discussed in Creating Custom Exceptions, although its use isn't limited to that.

- **Any**   The *any* type of exception handler is a failsafe. If everything else fails to catch the error, then the any template is executed.

1-Minute Drill

- ColdFusion's cferror tag is used to create _____ error handlers.
- What error type catches any type of error?

Even though we needn't memorize every type of error, getting a general concept of what types of errors can exist in ColdFusion and what to watch for is a good idea. Now we tackle a project that shows you how to set up site-wide error handlers.

- ColdFusion's cferror tag is used to create generic error handlers.
- Any is the error type that catches any type of error.

Project 11-1: Creating an Application-Wide Error Handler

The best place to implement the cferror tag is in the Application.cfm. This way, you can write it once and have it work for all files of your web site. You'll remember the Application.cfm from Module 7. The Application.cfm is an implicit include that's executed before the template that was requested. This project develops an exception error handler to handle all errors.

Step-by-Step

1. The first step in this project is to create our template to handle the exceptions. You can download this template—Error.cfm—from InstantColdFusion.com. This template is going to have two portions. The first portion will e-mail the error message and the second will display information to the user about the error. This is the beginning of your error template:

```
<!---
Description: This page will be displayed if there is
    an error.

Entering: N/A
Exiting: N/A

Dependencies: N/A
Expecting: N/A

Modification History
Date  Modifier    Modification
*********************************************************
11/29/2001 Jeff Houser, DotComIt Created
--->

<cfmail to="#error.MailTo#" from=error@farcryfly.com
  subject="There was an Error">
Warning there was a database error in #error.Template#
on #error.DateTime#

Browser: #error.Browser#
Query String: #error.QueryString#
Remote Address: #error.RemoteAddress#
HTTP Referrer: #error.HTTPReferer#
```

```
This was the error message:

#error.Diagnostics#

</cfmail>
```

We have our documentation header, as always. Then we enter into a tag we haven't discussed yet: cfmail. The cfmail tag is used in ColdFusion to send an e-mail message. We use three pertinent attributes:

- **To**   The *to* attribute accepts the name of the e-mail address to which we're sending our e-mail.
- **From**   The *from* attribute defines the e-mail address from which the mail is being sent.
- **Subject**   The *subject* attribute defines the subject header of the e-mail message.

We're e-mailing the error message to the person defined in the mailto attribute of the cfmail tag. The from address will be errors@yourdomain. Our subject is, quite simply, an error has occurred on the site. The body of the e-mail message reiterates the error variables to help debug the application.

Caution

For the cfmail tag to work, the SMTP mail server must be set up in the ColdFusion administrator.

2. The next step in our template is to display the information to the user. We can display as much or as little information to the user as we want. In a full-fledged application, we would probably want to include the navigation elements of the site, at the least. For our sample project, we'll strictly redisplay most of the relevant error information sent in the e-mail:

```
<!---
Description: This page will be displayed if there is
    an error.
```

```
Entering: N/A
Exiting: N/A

Dependencies: N/A
Expecting: N/A

Modification History
Date  Modifier     Modification
***********************************************************
11/29/2001 Jeff Houser, DotComIt Created
--->

<cfmail to="#error.MailTo#" from=error@farcryfly.com
  subject="There was an Error">
Warning there was a database error in #error.Template#
on #error.DateTime#

Browser: #error.Browser#
Query String: #error.QueryString#
Remote Address: #error.RemoteAddress#
HTTP Referrer: #error.HTTPReferer#

This was the error message:

#error.Diagnostics#

</cfmail>

<cfoutput>
Warning there was a database error in #error.Template#
on #error.DateTime#<br><br>

<b>Browser</b>: #error.Browser#<br>
<b>Query String</b>: #error.QueryString# <br>
<b>Remote Address</b>: #error.RemoteAddress#<br>
<b>HTTP Referrer</b>: #error.HTTPReferer#<br><br>

<b>This was the error message:</b><br>
#error.Diagnostics#<br>

</cfoutput>
```

We display the template and date the error occurred. Then we display the browser info, query string, remote address, and the HTTP referrer. Finally, we display the diagnostic message, which contains the error itself. When executed because of an error, the result looks like this:

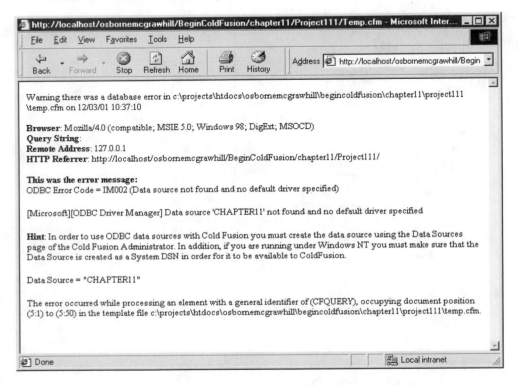

3. The final step in setting up our error handler is to add our cferror tag to the Application.cfm file. This is the code:

```
<!---
Description: A Sample Application.cfm

Entering: N/A
Exiting: N/A

Dependencies: N/A
Expecting: N/A
```

```
Modification History
Date  Modifier    Modification
****************************************************
11/09/2001 Jeff Houser, DotComIt Created
11/13/2001 Jeff Houser, DotComIt Added checking for
    setting of app and session variables
--->

<cfapplication name="SampApp"
 applicationtimeout=#createtimespan(0,1,0,0)#
 setclientcookies="Yes" clientmanagement="Yes"
 sessiontimeout=#CreateTimeSpan(0, 1, 0, 0)#
 sessionmanagement="Yes">

<!-- define the application variables -->
<cflock scope="APPLICATION" type="exclusive"
  timeout="30">
 <cfif NOT IsDefined("application.WebServerRoot")>
  <cfset application.WebServerRoot =
          "C:\Projects\htdocs">
  <cfset application.ImageDir = "/image/">
 </cfif>
</cflock>

<!-- define the session variables -->
<cflock scope="session" type="exclusive" timeout="30">
 <cfif not IsDefined("session.IsLoggedIn")>
  <cfset session.IsLoggedIn = "False">
 </cfif>
</cflock>

<!-- copy the session scope into the request scope -->
<cflock scope="session" type="readonly" timeout="30">
 <cfset request.TempSession = Duplicate(session)>
</cflock>

<cferror mailto="jeff@instantcoldfusion.com"
    type="exception" exception="any"
    template="Error.cfm">
```

cferror tag

11

The cferror tag at the end of the file sets up my e-mail address in the mailto field. The tag states that if any sort of exception error occurs, the Error.cfm template will be executed.

Project Summary

As you can see from this project, exception handling is fairly simple to set up. Despite its importance, when all is said and done, this aspect of application development often falls by the wayside. A few short minutes near the end of a project could save you considerable time in problems that you might not have otherwise discerned.

Specific Error Handlers

In the previous section, we learned about general error handlers. In addition to general error handlers, ColdFusion also provides a way to create specific error handlers. These *specific error handlers* target certain blocks of code and watch it for any potential errors in that code. I'll show you how to watch for these errors, and then we learn how to throw our own errors.

cftry and cfcatch

ColdFusion uses two tags to deal with exceptions: cftry and cfcatch. Both of these tags must be used in conjunction with each other. The cfcatch tag must be used inside a cftry block, so we'll look at the cftry first.

The *cftry* tag is the tag with no attributes: it contains both a start and end tag. Inside a cftry block, you put the code you think might cause an error and the code to handle the error handler. When you use a cftry statement, you're saying try to run this code and, if it throws an exception, catch it; otherwise, continue. Here's an example.

Say we're performing an insert into a database and we want to watch for any database errors. We can use a cfquery tag to perform the database insert. The cftry tag will watch for errors:

```
<cftry>
 <cfquery name="TestQuery" datasource="MyDB">
  INSERT INTO MyTable(MyData1, MyData2)
  VALUES('mydata1', 'mydata2')
 </cfquery>
</cftry>
```

This code will try to execute the insert query. We do have a missing piece, though. We don't yet have any code to try to resolve the error. The cfcatch tag is designed for this.

The *cfcatch* tag contains one attribute: type. The *type* attribute contains the name of the exception type the catch block will try to resolve. The valid values for the type attribute are application, database, template, security, object, missinginclude, expression, lock, custom_type, and any, all of which were discussed previously. The any type is the default value. The cfcatch has both a start and an end tag.

Let's revisit the previous example:

```
<cftry>
 <cfquery name="TestQuery" datasource="MyDB">
 INSERT INTO MyTable(MyData1, MyData2)
 VALUES ('mydata1', 'mydata2')
 </cfquery>

 <cfcatch type="database">  ←————    cfcatch block
 [Insert code here to fix problem]
 </cfcatch>
</cftry>
```

The cfcatch block resides inside the cftry block. We try to execute the query and, if an error occurs, ColdFusion starts looking for the cfcatch block to handle the type of error that occurred. We're catching for database errors. The code you want to use to fix the problem depends on the type of error that occurred.

Tip

You can use more than one cfcatch tag inside a cftry block.

Just as with general error handler templates, variables are accessible within a cfcatch block. The following is a list of the variables you can access.

- **Cfcatch.Type**   The *Type* variable contains the type of exception we just caught.

- **Cfcatch.Message**   The *Message* variable contains the diagnostic message, if available, or an empty string if no diagnostic message was provided.

- **Cfcatch.Detail**   The *Detail* variable provides the detailed message from the ColdFusion interpreter.

- **Cfcatch.TagContext**   The *TagContext* variable contains the tag stack, which is the name and position of each tag, and the full pathnames of the files in the stack. The tag stack's main use is when you're using custom tags.

11

- **Cfcatch.NativeErrorCode**   The *NativeErrorCode* variable is available only for database errors. It contains the error code returned from the database or ODBC drivers.

- **Cfcatch.SQLState**   The *SQLState* variable is also available only from a database perspective. If the database doesn't provide this, the default value is negative 1.

- **Cfcatch.ErrNumber**   The *ErrNumber* variable is valid only for expression errors. It contains a ColdFusion internal error number.

- **Cfcatch.MissingFileName**   The *MissingFilename* variable contains the name of the missing file if the exception type is missinginclude.

- **Cfcatch.LockName**   The *LockName* variable contains the name of the variable that caused the problems. If the lock wasn't named, which is common when locking session, application, or server variables, the name will be set to anonymous.

- **Cfcatch.LockOperation**   The *LockOperation* variable contains the type of operation that failed: timeout, Create Mutex, or unknown.

Note

When the LockOperation fails with Create Mutex as the reason, it means it couldn't get a handle on a Mutex object. A *Mutex* is an object that will allow for multiple threads to access it, but not at the same time.

- **Cfcatch.ErrorCode**   If the error type is a custom type, then the *ErrorCode* variable contains the error code specified in the cfthrow tag.

- **Cfcatch.ExtendedInfo**   The *ExtendedInfo* variable is available only to application and custom errors. It contains the custom error message specified in the cfthrow tag, if any.

We could revisit our previous code segment with some of this new information:

```
<cftry>
 <cfquery name="TestQuery" datasource="MyDB">
  INSERT INTO MyTable(MyData1, MyData2)
  VALUES ('mydata1', 'mydata2')
```

```
</cfquery>

<cfcatch type="database">
 <cfif cfcatch.NativeErrorCode = 1>
   <cfoutput>
    The database is broken.
    The Error Code: #cfcatch.NativeErrorCode#
    The SQL State: #cfcatch.SQLState#
   </cfoutput>
 </cfif>
 </cfcatch>
</cftry>
```

This code checks the error code and, if it's equal to 1, it will output the variables. The specific actions you want to take depend on what your code is doing.

Caution

I don't know of a database that has an error code of 1. The previous code segment is strictly for demonstration purposes.

Creating Custom Exceptions

During your course of development, you might need to create custom exceptions. This probably will happen in custom tags, although its use isn't limited to that. Say you were creating a custom tag to register a user on a web site. You want the custom tag to require a user name, a password, a first name, and a last name. What happens if someone tries to call on the custom tag without passing in one of those variables? Well, you could set up the tag to define a default value for the missing variable. Or, you could throw an error and have the calling application deal with it in whatever manner it sees fit.

ColdFusion provides the cfthrow tag to let you create custom exceptions. These are the attributes to the cfthrow tag:

11

- **Type** The *type* attribute is an optional attribute that defines the type of error you're throwing. It's the default type application.

- **Message** The *message* attribute is used to describe the error. It can be accessed in the cfcatch block by the message attribute.

- **Detail**   The *detail* attribute is an optional attribute that provides a detailed description of the event that caused the error. You can put whatever information you want in here. ColdFusion will append the position of the error to the end of your text. The cfcatch block accesses this variable.

- **Errorcode**   The *errorcode* attribute is an optional attribute that contains any information you wish to place in it. The cfcatch block can access this variable.

- **Extendedinfo**   The *extendedinfo* attribute contains information you supply. This variable can contain anything you want. The cfcatch block can access the value in this variable.

Next, let's look at some sample code that will throw an exception.

Hint

The cfthrow tag must be used inside a cftry block.

Let's explore the user registration example referenced previously. We're writing a custom tag and four of the parameters must be required: First Name, Last Name, User Name, and Password. We can check for their existence using a cfif block and throw an exception if they aren't defined:

```
<cfif NOT IsDefined("FirstName") AND
  NOT IsDefined("LastName") AND
  NOT IsDefined("Username") AND
  NOT IsDefined("Password")>
 <cfthrow type="undefinederror"
   Message="required variables were undefined"
   ErrorCode = "711">
</cfif>
```

In a real-world application, we might want to expand the previous code and let the user know what variables weren't defined, but I'll leave that for a Mastery Check question at the end of the module. We can catch the error in a similar way to this:

```
<!-cftry block -->
<cftry>
 <!-- call the custom tag to register -->
 <cf_register>

 <!-- catch the error if necessary -->
 <cfcatch type="undefinederror">
  <cfoutput>
   Warning, there was an error #cfcatch.ErrorCode#
  </cfoutput>
 </cfcatch>
</cftry>
```

The only remedy to the situation we prescribe in this case is to display the error code. In a real-world situation, though, we would probably want to expand this to send the user back to a place where they can reenter the relevant information.

1-Minute Drill

- If an exception handler is unable to catch an exception, what tag can be used to send it to another exception handler?

- The cfcatch tag is used to catch an error. It must reside between the open and close ___ tag.

What happens if a cfcatch block is unable to fix the error? You can rethrow the error with ColdFusion's cfrethrow tag, which has no attributes. The *cfrethrow* tag is used to tell ColdFusion to look for another error handler because the one that caught the exception is unable to handle the error. This tag is most useful in any error handlers. If the error is the type that any exception won't catch, we'll want to rethrow it. When we rethrow it, though, we lose the type and relevant details of the original exception.

11

- If an exception handler is unable to catch an exception, the cfrethrow tag can be used to send it to another exception handler.
- The cfcatch tag must reside between the open and close cftry tag.

Project 11-2: Adding Error Handling to Product Display Pages

This project revisits the code created in Project 10-1. Project 10-1 had added the use of includes to show different discs of different genres in different layouts. But what happens if an include is somehow missing? You can use cftry and cfcatch to handle this error.

Step-by-Step

1. The first step in this project is to add the cftry block around the code that might potentially create an error. That code is the cfswitch statement. You can see the template in the following:

```
<!---
Description: A page to list all songs on a disc based
    on the DiscID

Entering: SongList.cfm
Exiting: N/A

Dependencies: N/A
Expecting: DiscID
 GenreID

Modification History
Date  Modifier     Modification
************************************************************
10/23/2001 Jeff Houser, DotComIt Created
11/13/2001 Jeff Houser, DotComIT Added cfswitch
        statement for disc display
11/26/2001 Jeff Houser, DotComIt Modified cfswitch
        to use cfincludes
12/02/2001 Jeff Houser, DotComIt Modified to add
        error handling
--->

<!-- a query to get all the songs for the
  specific genre -->
<cfquery datasource="Chapter10" name="GetDisc">
 SELECT Discs.*, Song.*, Artist.Artist
 FROM Song, Artist, Discs
 WHERE Song.DiscID = #url.DiscID# AND
 Discs.DiscID = Song.DiscID AND
 Song.ArtistID = Artist.ArtistID
```

```
</cfquery>

<!-- html header -->
<html>
<head>
 <title>Disc List</title>
</head>
<!-- end HTML header -->

<!-- Start Main Content-->
<body>

<table>

 <cftry>
  <cfswitch expression="#url.GenreID#">

  <cfcase value="18">
    <!-- if the genre is TV -->
    <cfinclude template="TVTemplate.cfm">
  </cfcase>

  <cfcase value="14">
   <!-- if the genre is Rap -->
   <cfinclude template="RapTemplate.cfm">
  </cfcase>

  <cfcase value="2">
   <!-- if the genre is Folk -->
   <cfinclude template="FolkTemplate.cfm">
  </cfcase>

  <cfdefaultcase>
   <!-- if no genre defined -->
   <cfinclude template="DefaultTemplate.cfm">
  </cfdefaultcase>
  </cfswitch>
 </cftry>

 <!-- end cfoutput -->
</table>
<!-- end the content table -->

</body>
</html>
```

cftry block

11

We added our cftry block around the cfswitch statement.

2. A cftry block isn't useful without a cfcatch block. Our next step is to decide what the cfcatch block will do. We could make it display a default template or we could display an error message, letting the user know a problem occurred displaying the template. I decided to display the error message:

```
<!---
Description: A page to list all songs on a disc based
    on the DiscID

Entering: SongList.cfm
Exiting: N/A

Dependencies: N/A
Expecting: DiscID
 GenreID

Modification History
Date  Modifier    Modification
*************************************************************
10/23/2001 Jeff Houser, DotComIt Created
11/13/2001 Jeff Houser, DotComIT Added cfswitch
        statement for disc display
11/26/2001 Jeff Houser, DotComIt Modified cfswitch
         to use cfincludes
12/02/2001 Jeff Houser, DotComIt Modified to add
         error handling
--->

<!-- a query to get all the songs for the
  specific genre -->
<cfquery datasource="Chapter10" name="GetDisc">
 SELECT Discs.*, Song.*, Artist.Artist
 FROM Song, Artist, Discs
 WHERE Song.DiscID = #url.DiscID# AND
 Discs.DiscID = Song.DiscID AND
 Song.ArtistID = Artist.ArtistID
</cfquery>

<!-- html header -->
<html>
<head>
 <title>Disc List</title>
```

```
</head>
<!-- end HTML header -->

<!-- Start Main Content-->
<body>

<table>

 <cftry>
  <cfswitch expression="#url.GenreID#">

   <cfcase value="18">
    <!-- if the genre is TV -->
    <cfinclude template="TVTemplate.cfm">
   </cfcase>

   <cfcase value="14">
    <!-- if the genre is Rap -->
    <cfinclude template="RapTemplate.cfm">
   </cfcase>

   <cfcase value="2">
    <!-- if the genre is Folk -->
    <cfinclude template="FolkTemplate.cfm">
   </cfcase>

   <cfdefaultcase>
    <!-- if no genre defined -->
    <cfinclude template="DefaultTemplate.cfm">
   </cfdefaultcase>
  </cfswitch>

  <cfcatch type="missinginclude">
   Warning, this disc could not be displayed. <br>      cfcatch block
  </cfcatch>

 </cftry>

 <!-- end cfoutput -->
</table>
<!-- end the content table -->

</body>
</html>
```

11

We added the cfcatch block before the close cftry, but after the close cfswitch tag. This will catch every missinginclude error that occurs. If the error occurs, we will see a display like this:

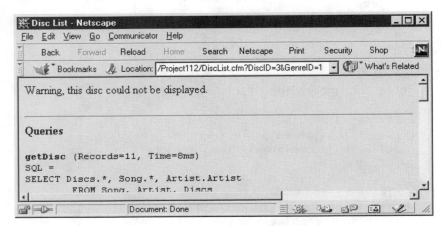

Project Summary

This project showed you how to set up the catching of specific errors. The example used was a missing include file, but the theory can be applied to any sort of errors. It is important to pay attention to these things.

Module Summary

This module explored the important concepts of error handling. Error handling is one of the most underused areas of web development. The next module moves into a topic completely unrelated, cfscript, which is a scripting language included in ColdFusion, similar to JavaScript. Cfscript provides an alternate way to perform many ColdFusion development tasks.

☑️ *Mastery Check*

1. When an error occurs, the program is known to be _____ an error. The error handle that tries to address the error is said to be _____ an error.

2. What are some common types of errors you might come across in web development?

    A. Database errors

    B. Data input errors

    C. Connection errors

    D. Miscellaneous errors

    E. File errors

3. Generic error handlers are usually defined with the _____ tag in the _____ file.

4. What are the types of generic error handlers you can create?

    A. Database

    C. Monitor

    D. Exception

    E. Custom

5. When an error occurs, ColdFusion creates a special variable object called _____. This variable is available to the template called by the cferror tag.

6. If you think some code might throw an error, what might you surround the code in?

    _____

    _____

7. If a cfcatch error handler is unable to handle a specific error, you can use _____ to throw the error again.

11

✓ Mastery Check

8. If you're creating a custom tag and need to create your own error type, what tag would you use?

_____

9. What tag can be used to send an e-mail message?

A. Cfcheckemail

B. Cfmail

C. Cfcatch

D. cfget

10. Take the example from the text, shown in the following, and rewrite it so the extendedinfo attribute of the cfthrow tag tells you what variables are undefined.

```
<cfif not IsDefined("FirstName") and
  not IsDefined("LastName") and
  not IsDefined("Username") and
  not IsDefined("Password")>
 <cfthrow type="undefinederror"
   Message="required variables were undefined"
   errorCode = "711">
</cfif>
```

Module 12

CFScript

The Goals of This Module

- Introduce CFScript
- Compare CFScript and CFML
- Learn how to implement computer programming concepts in CFScript
- Introduce user-defined functions

In addition to CFML, a scripting language called CFScript is built into ColdFusion. This module shows us how to program in CFScript. We learn how to implement programming logic, such as conditional and looping logic, using CFScript. Along the way, we learn some of the strengths and weaknesses of CFScript but, first, we learn something about CFScript.

What Is CFScript?

This section explores what CFScript is and why it was created. We learn the syntax of CFScript and compare it to CFML.

A CFML Scripting Language

CFScript is a scripting language built into ColdFusion and it's based on the JavaScript language. *JavaScript* is a scripting language built into web browsers and is commonly used for form validation and manipulation. CFScript was designed to give JavaScript users a starting point into learning how to code with ColdFusion.

Although CFScript uses the JavaScript syntax, JavaScript and CFScript are two different languages with different purposes. JavaScript is a client-side language, a concept we touched upon in Module 1. The client-side language will run in the browser on the user's machine. ColdFusion, including CFScript, is a server-side language. By the time the page is transferred to the browser, it's already too late for ColdFusion to perform any additional processing on the data in the page.

CFScript is, sadly, one of the most poorly documented features of ColdFusion. Macromedia, the company that makes ColdFusion, recommends reading up on JavaScript to understand CFScript. While this could be a start to learning about CFScript, we need to remember some important aspects of the CFScript language and how those aspects relate to JavaScript:

- CFScript uses ColdFusion expressions and JavaScript doesn't. ColdFusion expressions are completely independent of JavaScript, being neither a limited nor expanded version of them.

- CFScript isn't case-sensitive. If you have experience with JavaScript, you know the variables myname and MyName will be treated as two completely different entities. JavaScript will be unable to find any correlation between the two.

● All statements end in a semicolon; in JavaScript, this isn't always the case. Using a strict delimiter between statements makes telling where one statement ends and the next one starts easier for ColdFusion. That said, ColdFusion will ignore extraneous white space or carriage returns inside a single CFScript statement.

● Assignment in CFScript is handled as a statement; in JavaScript, assignment is handled as an expression. This is most easily explained with an example. If we were creating an if statement, the condition is an expression, returning a true or false value. In JavaScript, you can create or change variables in the middle of the if statement. CFScript won't allow this.

● Some implicitly available JavaScript objects, such as Window and Document, aren't available in CFScript. These objects simply don't apply to CFScript. These objects are part of the Document Object Model (DOM) and exist so JavaScript can access the current page with which it's interacting. ColdFusion is a server-side language and, once the page is sent to the web browser, it can no longer access the page.

● When grouping together blocks of code, you surround the code with curly brackets { }. This is identical to JavaScript. Although the use of curly brackets is most commonly used in conditional or looping statements, it can be used anywhere.

● CFML tags aren't available for use in CFScript. The wide array of ColdFusion functions is available to CFScript. This means CFScript can perform data manipulation, as we learned in Module 6. CFScript can't perform database queries, however, as we learned in Module 5. JavaScript can access neither CFML tags nor ColdFusion functions.

● CFScript has access to ColdFusion variables created in a template before the CFScript code. CFScript can access variables in any scopes. By the same token, variables created in a CFScript block are accessible to ColdFusion code that falls after the block.

12

The remainder of this module is devoted to writing CFScript in ColdFusion. We learn about variable assignment, conditional logic, and looping logic. If you needed a refresher course on ColdFusion expressions, you might want to turn back to Module 6.

Coding in CFScript

This section looks at how to set up your CFScript. We learn how to create comments within CFScript, how to output information using CFScript, and, finally, you see some simple examples that mix CFML with CFScript.

ColdFusion provides a tag that's strictly for creating CFScript blocks. The tag, aptly named cfscript, has both an open and close tag. A block of CFScript code looks like the following:

```
<cfscript>
 CFScript Code Here
</cfscript>
```

CFScript blocks can be as complicated or as simple as you choose.

We learned earlier that CFScript is made up of statements. ColdFusion statements can be grouped together using the open and close curly brackets. Semicolons are used to separate CFScript statements. We can rewrite the previous CFScript block like this:

```
<cfscript>
 statement1;
 statement2;
 statement3;
 . . .
 statement n;
</cfscript>
```

This will perform all the CFScript statements, one after the other, until the end of the CFScript block.

Most of this module is devoted to exploring the different types of statements that can be used within CFScript. If necessary or relevant, we can block off different sets of CFScript code:

```
<cfscript>
 {
  statement1;
  statement2;
 }
 {
  statement3;
  . . .
  statement n;
```

```
   }
</cfscript>
```

This can be used to group together multiple conditional statements or loops. It can also be done to improve the readability of your code, by grouping together related statements.

As previously discussed, an important aspect of writing code is the documentation of the code. CFScript includes a way to document your code in exactly the same way JavaScript does. You can create a single line of documentation using two forward slashes //. Multiple lines of documentation can be enclosed between /* and */. The following is a documented piece of CFScript:

```
<cfscript>
 // This is the first documented line
 {
   statement1;
   statement2;
 }
 /* This is a multiline
     documented portion
 */
 {
   statement3;
     . . .
   statement n;
 }
</cfscript>
```

As with JavaScript, ColdFusion, or any other programming language, you can have as many, or as few, lines of documented code as you need.

Before moving on to some simple examples of CFScript, we should learn the output function: WriteOutput. This function can be used anywhere that a function can be used, but it's most useful in CFScript. The value of the *WriteOutput* function is an expression. Say we want to output some text within CFScript:

```
<cfscript>
 // Output a Value
 WriteOutput("My Value");
</cfscript>
```

12

This is a simple way to output a value. We can also use more complicated expressions, such as:

```
<cfscript>
 // Output a Value
 WriteOutput(1 + 1);
</cfscript>
```

This performs the math, 1 + 1, and outputs the result, 2.

At this point, we only know how to do two things with CFScript. We can create a comment and output an expression. You'll remember that an expression can be the name of a variable. This example creates a ColdFusion variable, using cfset, and outputs its value via CFScript.

```
<!--- Create a ColdFusion variable --->
<cfset MyVariable = "Test Var 1">

<!--- output the variable via CFScript --->
<cfscript>
 // Output a Value
 WriteOutput(MyVariable);
</cfscript>
```

The output you get from this will be the text Test Var 1 on a blank HTML page. While we wouldn't want to do this in a real-world situation, it does demonstrate what we know about CFScript to date. As we learn more about CFScript, we can perform more complex actions within it.

1-Minute Drill

● CFScript is a scripting language similar to _____.

● CFScript is written using what ColdFusion tag?

● Which character separates statements in CFScript?

● CFScript is a scripting language similar to JavaScript.
● CFScript is written using ColdFusion's cfscript tag.
● The semicolon separates statements in CFScript.

Assignment in CFScript

After having discussed how to output expressions using CFScript, the next step is to examine how to perform assignment. CFML has two tags for assignment: cfparam and cfset. We used cfset in an example in the previous section. Now, we'll rewrite that example to use the assignment functionality of CFScript.

Assignment in CFScript is similar to a cfset tag. The main difference is that the tag name is left out:

```
VariableName = Expression;
```

You define the variable name, followed by an equal sign, followed by a ColdFusion expression. Variable names in CFScript follow all the naming conventions you need to follow in CFML. You can revisit variable naming conventions in Module 2.

Ask the Expert

Question: If everything that can be done in CFScript can be done in CFML, why do we need both methods? How can we decide which one to use? Is one more efficient than the other?

Answer: CFScript was developed to try to ease developers in other languages into ColdFusion development. This is why its syntax is drawn from JavaScript, which in itself is similar to Java, which is similar to C. CFML is used to draw in the people who have HTML knowledge, but no programming background. In many cases, using one or the other can be a matter of personal preference.

CFScript is believed to be quicker and more efficient than some. This is because CFScript is only one ColdFusion tag, versus the many ColdFusion tags it would take to achieve functionality similar to a single CFScript block. Every time the ColdFusion application server comes across a ColdFusion tag, it calls a DLL file, sitting out there on the server hard drive. ColdFusion takes time to call this DLL, while a CFScript block only has to call this DLL once and it will process the code. This is why some believe CFScript is quicker. Macromedia has never made an official announcement, to my knowledge.

From a practical point of view, if you have at least three assignments, CFScript seems quicker for assignment, but cfset is the way to go if you

> have under three assignments. If you use cfoutput with the query attribute
> or a cfloop tag, looping is generally faster than using CFScript's looping
> capabilities. Because no one—barring Macromedia programmers or
> employees—knows the inner workings of the ColdFusion server, you'll
> have to experiment with your specific application to see which works best.

In the previous section, we created an example, where we created a value
in CFML, and then output that value using CFScript. Let's revisit that example
and modify it so it's coded completely in CFScript.

```
<!--- CFScript to create and output a variable --->
<cfscript>

 // create a variable
 MyVariable = "Test Var 1"

 // Output a Value
 WriteOutput(MyVariable);
</cfscript>
```

The first two lines of your CFScript block create the variable and document its
creation.

Name the variable MyVariable. After that follows an equal sign, and then
our string value for the variable. The following two lines output the value. The
first line documents our output statement, of course. The second line uses the
WriteOutput function to output the value.

Note

Because CFScript will handle ColdFusion expressions, you can perform math and
string-processing operations in much the same way as you do in CFML.

Conditional Logic

This section examines conditional logic in CFScript. As with CFML, two types
of conditional statements are available in CFScript. You can create simple if

statements, as well as the more advanced switch and case statements. We'll start by looking at if statements.

If Statements

CFScript contains an if statement to perform conditional logic. Module 8 originally introduced conditional logic. An if statement enables you to check a condition. If the condition is true, then you perform the actions described; otherwise, you don't. Let's begin by examining the format of an if statement.

The CFScript if statement is modeled much like a CFML if statement. This is the code:

```
If (Expression) {
  statement1;
}
```

If the expression returns a true result, then statement1 is executed; otherwise, the code will continue after the end of the code block.

As discussed earlier, the open and close curly brackets distinguish the start and end of a CFScript code block. The expression must be enclosed in parentheses.

Tip

If there's only one statement to your condition, you needn't include the open and close curly brackets specifying a block of code. I like to include them for readability.

As with CFML conditionals, there's a way to create a default condition using an else keyword. If the expression is true, we do one thing or else we do something completely different. This is the format:

```
If (Expression) {
  statement1;
} Else {
  statement2;
}
```

The statements can be any valid statements in CFScript.

12

The else statement, as with the if statement, is surrounded by curly brackets, specifying the potential for a block of code. All the statements end with a semicolon. An example follows.

One of the most useful ColdFusion functions is the IsDefined function. You can use IsDefined to check for the existence of a variable. It returns a Boolean value, indicating whether the variable in question exists. This is some code:

```
<cfscript>
  If (IsDefined("Test")) {
    WriteOutput("The Test Variable was Defined");
  } else {
    WriteOutput("The Test Variable was Not Defined");
  }
</cfscript>
```

This code checks to see if the test variable is defined. If it is, we display a message saying the variable is defined. Otherwise, we display a message saying the variable isn't defined.

One thing that exists in CFML, but isn't a feature of CFScript is a way to perform an elseif. It's easy enough to get the else if functionality if you need it, however. You can use an if statement in the else condition of your original if statement, like this:

```
<cfscript>
  If (IsDefined("Test")) {
    WriteOutput("The Test Variable was Defined");
  } else if (Not IsDefined("Test")){
    WriteOutput("The Test Variable was Not Defined");
  }
</cfscript>
```

We begin with our initial if condition. Instead of an inherent elseif command, such as cfelseif, we use the else keyword, and then have a space. After the space, we start our second if tag.

Switch-Case Statements

In addition to the if statement, CFScript also has a way to create switch-case statements (remember from Module 8 that a switch statement is best used when you're checking a single variable for multiple values). CFML uses the cfswitch and cfcase tags to create a switch statement. There's also a way to perform these statements in CFScript, using the keywords switch and case.

Let's start by looking at the syntax of a switch statement:

```
<cfscript>
 switch (Expression) {

  case Value1 : {
   statement1;
   break;
  }

  case Value2 : {
   statement2;
   break;
  }
 }
</cfscript>
```

We begin with the switch keyword, followed by an expression, and then you start a block of code.

The first entry into our code block is the case keyword. Following that, we have a value. CFScript checks the result of the expression to see if it's equal to the value. If it is equal, we execute the statement; otherwise, we move on to the next case block.

Before moving on, let's examine the first case block, which begins with a statement or list of statements. We end it with the break statement. *Break* is a reserved word, which tells CFScript you're finished with the switch statement because you found your proper value. CFScript continues execution at the end of the switch block when it comes across the break command. If you don't use the break command, then CFScript will continue to execute conditions. Other than the performance degradation for checking conditions, which you already know won't satisfy the condition, there's another reason you want to use the break command: the default condition.

CFML contained a tag called cfdefaultcase. In a switch-case statement, the cfdefaultcase statement was used to define the default behavior if your expression didn't evaluate to a valid value. CFScript provides a keyword called *default* for this purpose, which is set up like the following:

```
<cfscript>
 switch (Expression) {
```

12

```
case Value1 : {
 statement1;
 break;
}

case Value2 : {
 statement2;
 break;
}

default: {
 statementdefault;
 break;
 }
 }
</cfscript>
```

Default
block

After our case statements, we have a new block, called the *default block*. The ColdFusion interpreter will execute the default block if none of the other case values are true.

If you don't use the break tag in your case blocks, the default condition will be executed, even if we find a block of case code that meets the condition. This is usually undesirable. Once the default block is executed, the switch is finished and execution moves to the code that resides after the end of the switch block.

Here's an example. Suppose the user just entered the name of her car into a form and submitted it. On the processing page of the form, we're using CFScript to process the user's input:

```
<cfscript>
 // check the value of the car
 switch(form.Car) {

  // Grand Caravan
  case "Dodge Grand Caravan":{
   Type = "Minivan";
   Seats = 6;
   break;
  }
```

```
// Durango
case "Dodge Durango":{
 Type = "Sport Utility";
 Seats = 8;
 break;
}

// Unknown default condition
default:{
 Type = "Unknown";
 Seats = 0;
 break;
 }
 }
</cfscript>
```

Assuming the variable is already defined on entry into the page, we jump right into our CFScript block.

The switch statement makes reference to the form variable, Car. We first check its value to see if it's set to "Dodge Grand Caravan." If it is, we define some other variables: type and seats. If it isn't, we move on to the next case. If the car value is set to Dodge Durango, we set the Seats and Type variables for that type of car. Whatever we want to do to these variables goes beyond the scope of this example.

1-Minute Drill

● What are two ways to implement conditional logic in CFScript?

● A CFScript if statement doesn't provide a parallel to CFML's _____ tag.

● Conditional logic can be implemented in CFScript with an if statement or a switch / case statement.
● A CFScript if statement doesn't provide a parallel to CFML's cfelseif tag, but you can easily create the else-if functionality by combining CFScripts else command with an additional if command.

Looping Logic

This section explores looping logic in CFScript. CFScript has more variations on looping than you can achieve with normal CFML. We learn about for loops, while loops, and do-while loops.

For Loops

A for loop in CFScript is similar, in concept, to an index loop using the cfloop tag (index loops were discussed in Module 9). A for loop will iterate a specific section of code a set number of times. For loops in CFScript are different in implementation than index loops in CFML, but those of you with JavaScript experience, will recognize the syntax.

```
for (Initialize Expression ;
     Condition ;
     Increment Expression) {
 statement;
}
```

The loop begins with the keyword for. Then we have an open parenthesis. Three different entities are in the parenthesis. First, we have an expression used to initialize your variable. This is usually something like LoopControl = 1. Then, there's a semicolon. After the semicolon, we have an expression used as the condition. For example, if we want to loop while LoopControl is less than five, you would put LoopControl LT 5 in this spot. Once the LoopControl variable becomes greater than or equal to five, the execution will stop. After the condition, we have another semicolon and a final expression. The last expression between the parentheses is the increment expression. We use this to increment the LoopControl variable. If we were creating a standard loop, where we increment our LoopControl variable by one each time, we would make this value something like this: LoopControl = LoopControl + 1.

Note

The break keyword used in switch-case conditionals can also be used to stop the execution of a loop. If we want to stop the current execution of a loop, but not stop it completely, we can use the continue keyword.

After the for keyword and list of expressions, you put the code you're going to execute inside the block. The for loop can execute as many statements as necessary. Based on the discussion in the previous paragraph, let's write some code to perform the loop that cycles from one to five:

```
<cfscript>
// Start for Loop
for (LoopControl = 1;
     LoopControl LT 5 ;
     LoopControl = LoopControl + 1) {
// Output the Loop Control variable
 WriteOutput(LoopControl);
}

</cfscript>
```

ColdFusion is processing the code and it comes across this loop.

ColdFusion is going to create a variable called LoopControl and set its initial value to one. Then, it will perform the block of code and output the LoopControl variable, giving it a value of one. Next, ColdFusion will execute the increment statement, changing the value of LoopControl from one to two. Next, ColdFusion checks the condition. Is LoopControl less than five? Is the number two less than the number five? Yes, it is.

Execute the body of the loop again. It outputs the number two. This process repeats: increment LoopControl from two to three, check the condition, output the value. Increment LoopControl from three to four, check the condition, output the value. Increment LoopControl from four to five and check the condition. At this point, the condition is no longer met. The value won't be output and the execution of the loop will end. This is the nature of a for loop.

Hint

CFScript also provides a for-in loop for dealing with advanced data types, such as structures or lists. Complex data types are discussed in Module 14.

12

While Loops

While loops in CFScript are similar to conditional loops in CFML. A while loop checks for a condition, first. Then it performs a statement or statements. At the end, a while loop goes back and checks the condition again. The process repeats until the condition evaluates to false.

Let's begin by looking at the format of a while loop:

```
while (Expression) {
 statement;
}
```

The text reads much like it's executed. While the expression is true, execute the statement or block of statements. The loop repeats until the expression is no longer true.

To show an example of a while loop, we can use the same example we used in our for loop. We'll loop from the number one to the number five. This is the code:

```
<cfscript>
 // Initialize Loop Control Variable
 LoopControl = 1;

 // Enter While Loop
 While (LoopControl LT 5) {

 // Write Output
  WriteOutput(LoopControl);

 // Increment variable
  LoopControl = LoopControl + 1;
 }
</cfscript>
```

Although this loop will perform the same thing as your previous for loop, it's set up differently.

For starters, before entering the loop, we must make sure we set our LoopControl variable to an initial value, one. Then you enter into our loop. We start with the while keyword. Then we have the condition, surrounded by parentheses. We're looping while LoopControl is less than five. Then, we enter into your code block.

We're performing two operations inside the code block. The first one will output the value of the variable. The second will increment the LoopControl value by one. The resulting output, 1234, is the same as we would achieve from the for loop we created in the previous example. Usually, you won't want to use while loops to increment numbers in an iterative fashion. You would use them for more complex conditions, such as looping over a query.

Caution

Loop control variables in a while loop don't automatically increment or change as they do in a for loop. If you forget to change this value during each iteration, it causes an infinite loop on the server, wasting precious resources and, perhaps, even bringing it down.

Do-While Loops

We can implement one more type of loop in CFScript and this is a do-while loop. There's no direct way to accomplish a do-while loop in CFML. Do-while loops are similar to while loops with one major difference. In a *while* loop, the condition is checked before we execute the loop code. In a *do-while* loop, we will execute the loop code before checking the condition.

Look at the format for a do-while loop:

```
do {
 statement1
} while (expression) ;
```

It starts out with the keyword do, and then we enter into the loop block.

As with all CFScript, the block is specified using the open and close curly brackets. The block code includes a list of statements, dictating the loop's behavior. At the end of the loop, after the close curly bracket, we put the while clause, which uses the keyword while, followed by an expression. A do-while loops reads much like how it executes. Do these statements while this condition is true.

Following along with while loops and for loops, we'll implement your greater than five example:

```
<cfscript>
 // Initialize Loop Control Variable
 LoopControl = 1;

 // Enter Do-While Loop
 do {
 // Write Output
  WriteOutput(LoopControl);

 // Increment variable
  LoopControl = LoopControl + 1;
```

12

```
} while (LoopControl LT 5);

</cfscript>
```

This loop starts out by setting the LoopControl variable to its default value, 1. Next, we enter into the loop.

We begin with the do keyword, followed by an open curly bracket. Then, we enter the loop. The LoopControl variable's value is output., and then we increment it by one. Next, we check its value with our condition. Is it less than five? It is, so we execute the loop one more time. Output the value two, and increment the LoopControl to three. Three is still less than five, so do it again. Output the three and add one to the LoopControl variable. Is four less than five? It is, so we do it again, resulting in the LoopControl being equal to five. Is five less than five? No, it isn't; it's equal. The execution of the loop stops.

1-Minute Drill

● How many types of loops exist in CFScript?

● For loops are called ___ loops in CFML.

User-Defined Functions

One of the most eagerly anticipated features of ColdFusion's fifth release was the capability to create user-defined functions. This section explores user-defined functions by explaining what they are, as well as how to implement and use them in ColdFusion.

What Are User Defined Functions?

Using CFScript, you can create a user-defined function (UDF). A *UDF* is a way to achieve code modularization, as discussed in Module 10. UDFs are akin to custom tags in CFML. They enable you to write a certain series of commands once and use them in many places.

● Three types of loops are in CFScript.
● For loops are called index loops in CFML.

Some differences exist between custom tags and user-defined functions:

- User-defined functions are written in CFScript; custom tags are written in CFML.

- The code that defines a UDF must be defined on the page that calls it. Custom tags code is located in a separate file and called from the page.

- UDFs must return a value, while custom tags don't.

- UDFs can be used anywhere a ColdFusion expression can be used, including between pound signs and in tag attributes. Custom tags must be called using the normal tag use.

- Because UDFs are written in CFScript, they have access to all CFScript capabilities, but cannot execute CFML tags. Custom tags have access to the full range of CFML tags and ColdFusion functions.

- UDFs are generally faster than custom tags, although you can't achieve all the functionality in a UDF that could be created using a custom tag.

UDFs are great for operations such as string manipulation and mathematical functions that aren't already built in to ColdFusion. Custom tags are better for operations like credit card processing or where you are creating lots of output.

Tip

Check out the common function library project at cflib.org. This site was designed to help share open source user-defined functions for ColdFusion.

Creating a User-Defined Function

This section demonstrates the format of a user-defined function and shows you some examples. UDFs are set up in CFScript, just as a function is set up in JavaScript:

12

```
function FunctionName ( ParameterList )
{
 variable declarations
 statements;
 return expression;
}
```

The function name follows most of the same rules as naming a ColdFusion variable.

This can be a mix of letters and number, but it must not start with a number. Periods can't be used within a function name and you can't use the name of a function that already exists, whether it's one built into ColdFusion or one you created yourself.

After the function name, comes the parameter list, surrounded by parentheses. You can have as many parameters as needed. All the parameters are required when calling the function. Arguments passed into the function must either exceed or equal the number of arguments defined in the parameter list. A way does exist to have optional arguments in a UDF. All the arguments passed into a function are put into a complex variable called Arguments. The Arguments variable is an array, as is discussed in more detail in Module 13, but I'll cover it briefly here.

You can define a function like this:

```
Function MyFunction (Variable1, Variable2)
{
 statements;
 return;
}
```

You can call MyFunction using any of these commands:

```
MyFunction(Value1, value2)
MyFunction(Value1, Value2, Value3)
MyFunction(Value1, Value2, Value3, Value4)
```

When the function is called, the Arguments variable is created. You can access arguments one and two using the names Variable1 and Variable2, respectively.

But, arguments three and four aren't explicitly defined in the argument list of the function and, therefore, aren't required arguments. You can access them using the syntax of Arguments[3] or Arguments[4]. Arrays are discussed in more depth in Module 14.

The following is an important concept: You can pass variables in two different ways in most programming languages. These two ways are called pass by reference and pass by value. If the variables are *passed by reference,* then a pointer to the data is passed into the function. If the variables are *passed by value,* then a copy of the variable is made and that copy is passed into the function. If variables passed by reference are modified in the function, then the values are also modified in the code that calls the function and will remain permanently changed. If the variables are passed by value, then any changes made to those variables are made to copies. The copies cease to exist when the function is finished executing.

ColdFusion doesn't let you choose which method you want to send your variables. Simple data types such as integers, strings, Booleans, and time date values are passed by values. Arrays are a complex data type passed by value, but other complex data types, such as structures and queries, are passed by reference.

After the function declaration and argument list, the next portion of our function defines local variable. Local variable definitions must be defined at the top of the function before any other processing code. They won't be accessible anywhere else in your ColdFusion template and they only exist during the execution of the function. You define local function variables using syntax similar to defining a JavaScript variable:

```
var VariableName = InitialValue;
```

You begin with the var keyword. Then you have the name of the variable.

The variable name should follow the normal naming ColdFusion variable naming conventions. Then we have an equal sign and the initial value of the variable. The initial value can be any valid ColdFusion expression. Our custom function will also have access to any existing variable defined in the calling page.

Hint

When calling a function, you can use a function as an argument to another function.

After our local variable declarations, we have the body of the function. The body must include at least one valid CFScript statement, but it can have as many as you need. Following the body, every UDF must include a return statement. The return statement contains the value returned by the function. You can return any valid expression. Based on the function's execution, you can return different return statements.

12

Tip

Every function must include a return statement. Any code located after the return statement won't be executed.

Here's a simple example. You can write a function, with no arguments, that will output a value:

```
<cfscript>
 function OutputText (){
  WriteOutput("Test Function");
  return true;
 }
</cfscript>
```

We created a simple function called output text. This uses the WriteOutput function to output some test text.

The function has an empty parameter list. It contains two statements: the first outputs your text and the second returns a value, true. The function is that simple. Next, look at an example that will accept some parameters.

1-Minute Drill

● User-defined functions in CFScript are akin to ____ in CFML.

● To return a value from a UDF, what keyword must you use?

This example expands on the previous example. We'll create a function that will output the value of the variable passed into it:

```
<cfscript>
 function OutputText (MyVariable){
  WriteOutput(MyVariable);
  return true;
 }
</cfscript>
```

● User-defined functions in CFScript are akin to custom tags in CFML.
● You must use the return keyword to return a value from a UDF.

After the function name, we have an argument list of a single variable, MyVariable. In the body of the function, we have two statements: the first statement outputs the variable's value and the second returns the value true. That ends the function.

ProperCase.cfm
GenreList.cfm

Project 12-1: Creating a ProperCase Function

A *ProperCase* function is one that properly formats a person's name. The proper case of a person's name means the first letter of each word is capitalized and all others are in lowercase. The proper case for my name would be Jeffry Houser. Incorrect case might be JEffry HouSer. A function like this would be used primarily for formatting data for output.

Step-by-Step

1. The first thing we need to do is create your function. Later in this project, we'll see some uses of the function. The function will be created in its own file: ProperCase.cfm. We can use this file to include it anywhere we want to use it. You can download the file from the book's web site. Let's begin by creating an empty file with the documentation header:

```
<!---
Description: Function to display a username
             in proper case

Entering: N/A
Exiting: N/A

Dependencies: N/A
Expecting: N/A

Modification History
Date      Modifier                Modification
************************************************************
12/10/2001 Jeff Houser, DotComIt   Created
--->

<cfscript>

</cfscript>
```

12

Because the file is only going to contain a custom tag, the entering and exiting entries are left blank.

We aren't expecting anything to be passed into this template and no file dependencies exist. In addition to the header commentary, I added the cfscript open and close tags. The UDF must be defined inside a CFScript block.

2. The next step is to create the outline of the function. We're going to name the function ProperCase. It will accept a single value, the string we want to put into proper case. Here's the updated code segment:

```
<!---
Description: Function to display a username
             in proper case

Entering: N/A
Exiting: N/A

Dependencies: N/A
Expecting: N/A

Modification History
Date       Modifier                Modification
*************************************************************
12/10/2001 Jeff Houser, DotComIt   Created
--->

<cfscript>

  //function to put a name in proper case
  // that means the first letter of each word,
  // before the space is capitalized

  function ProperCase(S)  ◄————————    Function
  {                                     declaration
  }
</cfscript>
```

Because ColdFusion is a loosely typed language, we needn't define the type of variable being passed into the function. Variable type was discussed in Module 2.

3. To make our function work, we have to examine each character of the string individually. If the previous character was a space, we want to make sure the current character is made into a capital letter. We need to keep track, then, of the current character and the previous character. You also want to create a resultant string.

```
<!---
Description: Function to display a username
              in proper case

Entering: N/A
Exiting: N/A

Dependencies: N/A
Expecting: N/A

Modification History
Date        Modifier                Modification
*********************************************************
12/10/2001 Jeff Houser, DotComIt    Created
--->

<cfscript>

  //function to put a name in proper case
  // that means the first letter of each word,
  // before the space is capitalized

  function ProperCase(S)
  {
    // our return string
    var Returns = "";          ◄────────────┐

    // the current character                 │
    var Current = "";          ◄────── Local variable
                                        declarations
    // the last character we looked at       │
    var Previous = "";         ◄────────────┘

  }
</cfscript>
```

As discussed, we defined three local variables in the previous code: a Current variable is used to keep track of the current character we're looking at; a Previous variable is used to compare the current character to the previous character; and a return string variable, Returns, to keep track of the string that we will return at the end of the function. Notice we're documenting each line of code as we write this function.

4. The next step in our code is to create the loop. We need two additional variables for the loop processing. We'll use a temporary string—TempS— that we'll use to grab the current character we're looking at. We also create

12

a NumCharacter variable to keep track of the number of characters in our loop. This is the code:

```
<!---
Description: Function to display a username
             in proper case

Entering: N/A
Exiting: N/A

Dependencies: N/A
Expecting: N/A

Modification History
Date        Modifier                Modification
****************************************************************
12/10/2001 Jeff Houser, DotComIt   Created
--->

<cfscript>

  //function to put a name in proper case
  // that means the first letter of each word,
  // before the space is capitalized

  function ProperCase(S)
  {
   // our return string
   var Returns = "";

   // the current character
   var Current = "";

   // the last character we looked at
   var Previous = "";

   // a temporary variable, that contains our original
   // string, with all leading/trailing spaces removed
   var Temps = trim(S);

   // the length of the string, for use in the loop
   NumCharacters = len(Temps);
```

```
for(Counter=1;
    Counter LTE NumCharacters;
    Counter=Counter+1){              ─┐
                                      ├─ Loop
}
}
</cfscript>
```

We set up the loop as a for loop. It initializes a counter, starting at one.

The loop is to execute until the counter is less than or equal to the NumCharacters variable. The increment condition of the loop adds one to the Counter variable. Now, we're prepared to examine the loop code.

5. The first thing we do in the loop is set the Current and Previous variables. We set Previous to the value of Current. Then, we use the Left function to change the Current variable to the leftmost character of the string we're processing. The code is shown in the following:

```
<!---
Description: Function to display a username
             in proper case

Entering: N/A
Exiting: N/A

Dependencies: N/A
Expecting: N/A

Modification History
Date        Modifier               Modification
*********************************************************
12/10/2001 Jeff Houser, DotComIt   Created
--->

<cfscript>

 //function to put a name in proper case
 // that means the first letter of each word,
 // before the space is capitalized

 function ProperCase(S)
 {
  // our return string
  var Returns = "";
```

```
// the current character
var Current = "";

// the last character we looked at
var Previous = "";

// a temporary variable, that contains our original
// string, with all leading/trailing spaces removed
var Temps = Trim(S);

// the length of the string, for use in the loop
NumCharacters = Len(Temps);

for(Counter=1;
    Counter LTE NumCharacters;
    Counter=Counter+1){

 // initialize the previous character we looked
 // at and the current character we are looking at
 Previous = Current;
 Current = Left(Temps,1);

 // if our temp string has more than 1 character
 // in it, remove that character from the string
 if (Len(Temps)-1 IS NOT 0){
  Temps = Right(Temps,Len(Temps)-1);
 }

 }
}
</cfscript>
```

The last bit of code added here is an if statement. The next iteration through the loop will return the same character if we don't remove the character.

We can remove the character using a combination of ColdFusion's string-processing functions. The Len function, minus one, gives us the length of the current string. Subtract one from that value to get the new length. Then we use the Right function to return all the characters, except the one we're looking at currently. We put this in an if statement because if only one character is left in the string, then we'll be trying to take zero characters from the string, which would cause an error.

6. The next section of code will put the current character in the proper case. If the previous character is blank or an empty string, we want to put the current character in uppercase. We do this by using ColdFusion's UCase function. The UCase function puts a letter into uppercase.

```
<!---
Description: Function to display a username
              in proper case

Entering: N/A
Exiting: N/A

Dependencies: N/A
Expecting: N/A

Modification History
Date       Modifier                Modification
**************************************************************
12/10/2001 Jeff Houser, DotComIt    Created
--->

<cfscript>

 //function to put a name in proper case
 // that means the first letter of each word,
 // before the space is capitalized

 function ProperCase(S)
 {
  // our return string
  var Returns = "";

  // the current character
  var Current = "";

  // the last character we looked at
  var Previous = "";

  // a temporary variable, that contains our original
  // string, with all leading/trailing spaces removed
  var Temps = Trim(S);

  // the length of the string, for use in the loop
```

12

```
NumCharacters = Len(Temps);

for(Counter=1;
    Counter LTE NumCharacters;
    Counter=Counter+1){

 // initialize the previous character we looked
 // at and the current character we are looking at
 Previous = Current;
 Current = Left(Temps,1);

 // if our temp string has more than 1 character
 // in it, remove that character from the string
 if (Len(Temps)-1 IS NOT 0){
  Temps = Right(Temps,Len(Temps)-1);
 }

 // if our previous character was a space or blank,
 // upper case the current character
 // otherwise force the character into lowercase
 if (Previous IS " " or Previous IS "") {
  if (Current IS NOT " " or Current IS NOT ""){
   Returns = Returns & UCase(Current);
  }
 }
 else{
  Returns = Returns & LCase(Current);
 }
 }

 }
</cfscript>
```

If the previous character isn't a space or empty string, we set the current character to lowercase using the LCase function.

As you'll notice, as we add these characters, we're appending them to the end of our Returns value. This is how we string together our resultant string, character by character. One character is processed for every iteration of the loop.

7. The final step in the creation of the function is to add our return value. The value we're returning is the resultant string, ReturnS. The return command is followed by a close curly bracket, ending the function.

```
<!---
Description: Function to display a username
             in proper case

Entering: N/A
Exiting: N/A

Dependencies: N/A
Expecting: N/A

Modification History
Date        Modifier                Modification
*********************************************************
12/10/2001 Jeff Houser, DotComIt    Created
--->

<cfscript>

 //function to put a name in proper case
 // that means the first letter of each word,
 // before the space is capitalized

 function ProperCase(S)
 {
  // our return string
  var Returns = "";

  // the current character
  var Current = "";

  // the last character we looked at
  var Previous = "";

  // a temporary variable, that contains our original
  // string, with all leading/trailing spaces removed
  var Temps = Trim(S);

  // the length of the string, for use in the loop
  NumCharacters = Len(Temps);

  for(Counter=1;
      Counter LTE NumCharacters;
      Counter=Counter+1){
```

```
// initialize the previous character we looked
// at and the current character we are looking at
Previous = Current;
Current = Left(Temps,1);

// if our temp string has more than one character
// in it, remove that character from the string
if (Len(Temps)-1 IS NOT 0){
  Temps = Right(Temps,Len(Temps)-1);
}

// if our previous character was a space or blank,
// uppercase the current character
// otherwise force the character into lowercase
if (Previous IS " " OR Previous IS "") {
  if (Current IS NOT " " OR Current IS NOT ""){
    Returns = Returns & UCase(Current);
  }
}
else{
  Returns = Returns & LCase(Current);             Returns
}
}

  return Returns;
}
/cfscript>
```

8. We need to look at one more thing: how the function works. We can fall back on the drill-down interface, which we've been using throughout this book. We'll implement the ProperCase function in the GenreList.cfm template. This is the code:

```
<!---
Description: A page to list all the genres

Entering: N/A
Exiting: SongList.cfm

Dependencies: N/A
Expecting: N/A

Modification History
```

```
Date         Modifier              Modification
*********************************************************
10/23/2001   Jeff Houser, DotComIt   Created
12/09/2001   Jeff Houser, DotComIt   Modified to add
                                     ProperCase Function
--->

<cfinclude template="ProperCase.cfm">          ProperCase
                                                include

<!--- a query to get the list of all Genres --->
<cfquery datasource="Chapter12" name="GetGenre">
 SELECT *
 FROM Genre
 ORDER BY Genre
</cfquery>

<!-- HTML header -->
<html>
<head>
 <title>Genre Page</title>
</head>
<!-- end HTML header -->

<!-- Start Main Content-->
<body>

<table>
 <tr>
  <td>Genre</td>
 </tr>
 <!-- cfoutput over the query -->
 <cfoutput query="GetGenre">
  <tr>
   <td>
    <a href="SongList.cfm?GenreID=#GetGenre.GenreID#">
    #ProperCase(GetGenre.Genre)#
    </a><br>                      ProperCase
   </td>                          function
  </tr>
 </cfoutput>
 <!-- end cfoutput -->
</table>
<!-- end the content table -->

</body>
</html>
```

12

In the beginning of the template, we used the cfinclude tag to add the function on to the page. Then, we called the function lower in the page, when we're looping over the GetGenre query.

Figure 12-1 shows what the output from this page looks like:

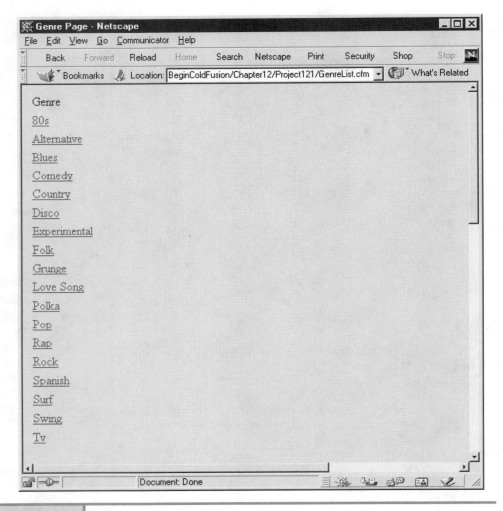

Figure 12-1 The GetGenre page

Project Summary

When a user is entering data, you never know what you're going to get. Checking the data to make sure it's in a format you're expecting is important. The ProperCase function demonstrates the capability to parse a string and verify its data. This function could primarily be used for guaranteeing that data will be displayed in a format the user expects.

Module Summary

This module examined CFScript, the scripting language in ColdFusion. CFScript can be a powerful tool in your developer's toolbox, providing you with an alternate way to accomplish many tasks. The next module examines complex variable types, such as structures and arrays.

12

☑ Mastery Check

1. As with index loops in CFML, for loops in CFScript can also be used to count down. Write a for loop that will execute from five to one.

_____

_____

2. What's the difference between a while loop and a do-while loop?

_____

_____

3. Groups of code in CFScript are enclosed between what two characters?

   A. { }

   B. [ ]

   C. < >

   D. ( )

4. What can you use to output the result of an expression in CFScript?

_____

_____

5. If you want to stop the execution of a switch-case statement, what command would you use?

   A. Stop

   B. Continue

   C. Break

   D. Cease

   E. None of the above

6. How are local variables created in a user-defined function?

_____

_____

✓ *Mastery Check*

7. Write some CFScript to create a variable named Module12. Give it the default value of Question 7.

_____

_____

8. You can define the default case in a switch-case statement by using which keyword?

   A. Default

   B. Value

   C. Last

   D. Failed

9. If you want to check for the existence of a variable, what type of statement would you use?

_____

_____

10. CFScript has access to the full range of CFML. True or false?

_____

_____

12

Module 13

Lists

The Goals of This Module

- Introduce lists in ColdFusion
- Learn about ColdFusion's list functions
- Create some code to process a form checkbox

This module introduces lists and discusses how lists can be used within ColdFusion. Lists are slightly more advanced than a simple data type, such as an integer or string, but they don't reach the full level of complexity an array or structure would. Arrays and structures are discussed in Module 14.

What Is a List?

This section introduces you to lists. A *list* is a group of elements, separated by a delimiter, usually a comma. As you will see in a minute, lists aren't true complex data types, but they are a good way to bridge the gap between simple data types and true complex data types. Let's start by examining what a list is.

Different Types of Lists

Lists are a group of multiple values that reside under a single variable name. Unlike other complex data types, lists are stored internally as strings in ColdFusion. All operations performed on a list are implemented as string processing. This can make lists less efficient than structures or arrays, but it's still important to understand what lists are and how they can be used.

A *delimiter* is a character that separates the elements of a list. This delimiter is usually a comma, but it can be any character you choose. Here's an example of a list:

```
"1,2,3,4,5,6,7,8,9,10"
```

This list is one that contains ten elements, all of them integers. The list starts at one and counts up to ten. The delimiter for this list is a comma. Lists don't have to stick with the comma as a delimiter. You could use a URL as a list if you look at the / as a delimiter. Here's an example:

```
"www.macromedia.com/software/coldfusion/"
```

Using the / as a delimiter, this URL is a list with three elements. The first element is "www.macromedia.com." The second is "software," and the third is "coldfusion." We could also look at this list differently, as if it had a period as a delimiter. If this were the case, the three elements of this list would be "www," "macromedia," and "com/software/coldfusion/."

The final list example we'll look at is a sentence:

```
"The Quick Brown Fox Jumped Over The Lazy Dogs"
```

A sentence could be a list if the space character is the delimiter. This sentence has nine items, when used as a space. Each word is a list element. These examples should show you the potential power you can have in lists.

Note

A list can have more than one delimiter, for example a comma and a semicolon. When specifying a delimiter for a list with multiple delimiters, you use a list.

You need to know these important points about lists:

- White space isn't inherently considered a delimiter; it must be explicitly defined in your list-processing function. This is best explained with the previous sentence example. Without specifying the space as a delimiter, the list would only have a length of one.

- Extraneous delimiters after the last element or before the first element are ignored. Let's use this list as an example:

```
",,1,2,3,4,5,6,7,8,9,10,,"
```

This list still has ten values.

- Perhaps as an extension to the previous point, empty elements aren't counted as list items. We can add empty elements to the middle of this list, like so:

```
"1,2,3,4,,5,6,7,,8,9,10"
```

The additional commas between elements four and five, and seven and eight don't add elements to the list. ColdFusion ignores them when it processes the list.

- An empty list is equivalent to an empty string.

With some of these concepts behind us, let's look at how to create and use lists in ColdFusion.

13

List Creation and Maintenance

The first issue we need to examine is list creation. How do we create lists in ColdFusion? Because lists are stored as strings, we can create them just like we can create any other string. Strings can be created using the assignment operators cfset or cfparam.

Tip

If you create a form input page that uses check boxes, the form's submission will create a comma-delimited list of all the checked items.

Let's look at an example of list creation:

```
<cfset MyList = "1,2,3,4,5,6,7,8,9,10">
```

This creates a ten-element list of numerical elements, 1–10. It's that easy.

In addition to using cfset or cfparam to create a list, ColdFusion provides several built-in functions for updating the values in a list. You can see them in Table 13-1.

Say we want to add a zero to the beginning of the list. We can use the ListPrepend function to accomplish this:

```
<cfset MyList = ListPrepend(MyList, 0)>
```

The prepend function adds a value to the beginning of the list. This function has two required values: the list and the value.

If you're using a list that doesn't use the comma as a delimiter, you can also specify which delimiter you're using as a third parameter. The delimiter attribute defaults to a comma on all list functions if it is left out. The resulting list from the previous function would be 0,1,2,3,4,5,6,7,8,9,10.

Hint

Because lists are stored internally as strings, all of ColdFusion's string functions can be used on lists and all of ColdFusion's list functions can be used on strings.

Function Name	Parameters	Usage
ListAppend	**List**: The List **Value**: The value you want to add to the end of the list **Delimiters**: An optional attribute that specifies the delimiter for the list	Adds a value to the end of the list.
ListPrepend	**List**: The List **Value**: The value you want to add to the beginning of the list **Delimiters**: An optional attribute that specifies the delimiter for the list	Adds a value to the beginning of a list.
ListDeleteAt	**List**: The List **Position**: The position of the value you are deleting **Delimiters**: An optional attribute that specifies the delimiter for the list	Removes the value at the location of the list. All values after that value will change their list location, which will be down one location.
ListInsertAt	**List**: The List **Position**: The position where you're inserting a value **Delimiters**: An optional attribute that specifies the delimiter for the list	Adds a value to the list at the specified location. All values after the new location will change their positions.
ListSetAt	**List**: The List **Position**: The position where you're changing a value **Delimiters**: An optional attribute that specifies the delimiter for the list	Changes a value in the list, at the specified location. This function has no effect on the other elements of the list.

Table 13-1   Functions to Update a List

ColdFusion also provides a similar function to enable us to add a value to the end of the list. This function, called *ListAppend*, accepts the same parameters as ListPrepend. This is the function:

```
<cfset MyList = ListAppend(MyList, 11)>
```

Our resulting list would be 0,1,2,3,4,5,6,7,8,9,10,11.

13

What happens if we want to insert a value into the middle of the list? Thankfully, the ColdFusion gods thought of that, too. They provided us with a *ListInsertAt* function, which accepts four separate attributes in this order: the list, the position where we want to add a value, the value we want to add, and the delimiters for the list. Let's add the number 5.5 to the middle of the list:

```
<cfset MyList = ListInsertAt(MyList, 7, 5.5)>
```

This will add our value to the seventh position of the list, which is between the numbers five and six. Your resulting list is 0,1,2,3,4,5,5.5,6,7,8,9,10,11.

1-Minute Drill

- ColdFusion treats a list as a _____.
- How can you create lists in ColdFusion?

Now, suppose we want to replace a specific value in the list. Similar to the ListInsertAt function, ColdFusion has a *ListSetAt* function, which, instead of inserting a value, changes a specific value in the list. Let's change the 5.5 value to 5.8:

```
<cfset MyList = ListSetAt(MyList, 7, 5.8)>
```

The resulting list would be 0,1,2,3,4,5,5.8,6,7,8,9,10,11.

Caution

When using the ListSetAt or ListInsertAt functions, make sure the position attribute isn't greater than the size of the list. If it's greater, ColdFusion will throw an error.

Now, suppose you suddenly woke up and realized you only want integers in your list and no decimals. ColdFusion provides the *ListDeleteAt* function to delete an element from the middle of a list. The ListDeleteAt function has three

---

- ColdFusion treats a list as a string.
- Lists can be created in ColdFusion using the cfset or cfparam tags.

arguments: the list, the position we're removing the element from, and the delimiters for the list. This would be our function:

```
<cfset MyList = ListDeleteAt(MyList, 7)>
```

The resulting list would be 0,1,2,3,4,5,6,7,8,9,10,11.

Note

None of the list functions will modify the list variable passed into it; they only return the modified list value.

Other List Operations

This section explores some advanced list functionality that can be performed in ColdFusion. We'll learn how to loop over a list, how to find and retrieve specific elements in a list, and some of the miscellaneous list functions in ColdFusion.

Looping Over a List

ColdFusion provides a way to loop over the values in a list, so you can process each one individually and the cfloop tag provides this functionality. You'll remember the cfloop tag from Module 9. To loop over a list, you can use three separate attributes with the cfloop tag:

- **Index**   The *index* attribute is used much as it's used for index loops. This attribute is a variable that will contain the value of the current list element and it is required.

- **List**   The *list* attribute is a required attribute. It contains the list we're going to loop over.

- **Delimiters**   The *delimiters* attribute is an optional attribute that defines the delimiter for the list. The default value for this attribute is a comma.

Here's your list from the previous section:

```
1,2,3,4,5,6,7,8,9,10
```

13

This list uses a comma as the delimiter and contains ten elements, all integers. Let's set up a loop:

```
<cfloop index="Temp" list="1,2,3,4,5,6,7,8,9,10">
 <cfoutput>#Temp#</cfoutput><br>
</cfloop>
```

This loop will output the numbers one after the other, as in Figure 13-1.

Looping over lists can be used for multiple purposes. We explore looping over a list's elements in Project 13-1.

Finding Values in a List

This section examines some of the functions used to process list values. We concentrate on functions that can be used to find the location of specific values in the list and retrieve those values. You can see Table 13-2 for a complete list of variables you'll use in this section.

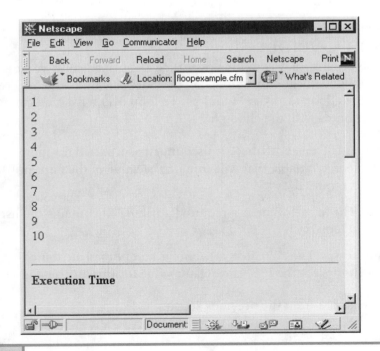

Figure 13-1 Loop output page

Function Name	**Parameters**	**Usage**
ListFirst	**List**: The List **Delimiters**: An optional attribute that specifies the delimiter for the list	Returns the first element of a list.
ListLast	**List**: The List **Delimiters**: An optional attribute that specifies the delimiter for the list	Returns the last element of a list.
ListRest	**List**: The List **Delimiters**: An optional attribute that specifies the delimiter for the list	Returns the list without the first element.
ListGetAt	**List**: The List **Position**: The position where you're retrieving the value. **Delimiters**: An optional attribute that specifies the delimiter for the list	Returns the element at the given position.
ListContains	**List**: The List **Substring**: The value you're searching for. **Delimiters**: An optional attribute that specifies the delimiter for the list	Returns the list index of the first list element that contains the specified substring. Similar to ListFind, except partial matches will be returned as true. Returns 0 if not found.
ListContainsNoCase	**List**: The List **Substring**: The value you're searching for **Delimiters**: An optional attribute that specifies the delimiter for the list	Same as ListContains, except not case-sensitive. Returns 0 if not found.
ListFind	**List**: The List **Value**: The value you're searching for **Delimiters**: An optional attribute that specifies the delimiter for the list	Returns the list index of the first occurrence of the value you're searching for. Similar to ListContains, except it must be an exact match. Returns 0 if not found.
ListFindNoCase	**List**: The List **Value**: The value you're searching for **Delimiters**: An optional attribute that specifies the delimiter for the list	Same as list find, except not case-sensitive. Returns 0 if not found.

Table 13-2 Functions to Retrieve List Values

13

Let's look at some of the simplest functions: ListFirst and ListLast. They are, respectively, used to getting the first and last elements from a list. Using the same list as earlier in this module, here are some examples. This is the list as we initially created it:

```
<cfset MyList = "1,2,3,4,5,6,7,8,9,10">
```

If we want to get the first element from the list, we could use the ListFirst function, like so:

```
<cfset FirstElement = ListFirst(MyList)>
```

The MyList variable remains unchanged, but now the FirstElement variable contains the value of one. If we want the last value from the list, we would use the ListLast function:

```
<cfset LastElement = ListLast(MyList)>
```

As with the ListFirst function, our list remains unchanged. The LastElement variable will now contain the value of ten, which is the last element of the list.

In addition to the ListFirst and ListLast functions, ColdFusion provides a ListRest function. This returns a list with its first element removed and the following is its format:

```
<cfset MyList = ListRest(MyList)>
```

This MyList variable contains this value 2,3,4,5,6,7,8,9,10.

You might be wondering how you can get a value that resides in the middle of a list. The answer is in the ListGetAt function. The ListGetAt function is similar to the ListLast and ListFirst functions, except you can specify the position of the element you want to get. Let's look.

```
<cfset MiddleElement = ListGetAt(MyList,5)>
```

The previous example will get the fifth element of the MyList variable and that element is five. The MiddleElement variable now has that value.

If you want to use the ListGetAt function, you need a way to determine which element to get. ColdFusion provides some functions strictly for that purpose: ListContains and ListFind. Each of these functions is case-sensitive by default, but each has noncase-sensitive alternatives in the form of ListContainsNoCase and ListFindNoCase. The *ListContains* function searches for a substring within a list, while the *ListFind* function searches for a list element that's an exact match. Let's look at some examples.

To examine the differences between ListFind and ListContains, we want to use a list with more complex values than integers. We can move on to this sentence:

```
<cfset MyList = "The,Quick,Brown,Fox,
        Jumped,Over,The,Lazy,Dogs">
```

For simplicity and consistency with other examples, instead of spaces, I separated each list element by a comma. This list contains nine elements. Let's start with an example of ListFind because that's the easier to understand function.

```
<cfset BrownIndex = ListFind(MyList,"Brown")>
```

Looking at our list, we can see Brown is the third element of our list, so the BrownIndex variable will now contain a three. You can use this result for additional list processing, if necessary.

We can implement the same example as the previous one using the ListContains function:

```
<cfset BrownIndex = ListContains(MyList,"Brown")>
```

The results are exactly the same as if we'd used the ListFind function. So, what are the differences between the two functions? ListContains searches for a substring. Say, for example, we want to search for the letter *o*. These are two examples:

```
<cfset OIndexFind = ListFind(MyList,"o")>
<cfset OIndexContains = ListContains(MyList,"o")>
```

The first example, using ListFind, won't return anything. No list element is equal to the letter *o*. There are, however, list elements that contain the letter *o*. The ListContains function will return the index of the first of them. This index is the third list element, number three.

13

Miscellaneous List Functions

This last look at lists examines some of the other list-processing functions that exist in ColdFusion. These functions provide functionality that moves beyond adding, deleting, or finding values in our list. (See Table 13-3 on the following page.) Let's look at a function to find out how many items are in a list.

The function to find out how many items are in a list is called the *ListLen* function. The ListLen function accepts two attributes: the list and the delimiter of the list. The delimiter, as always, is an optional attribute that defaults to a comma. All these examples will use our number list from the previous section:

```
<cfset MyList = "1,2,3,4,5,6,7,8,9,10">
```

Using our number list from the previous section, we could determine the length of the list like this:

```
<cfset MyListLen = ListLen(MyList)>
```

This statement set the value of the MyListLen function to ten because ten elements are in the list.

If you want to change the delimiters of a list, you could use the *ListChangeDelims* function, whose attributes are the list value and the new delimiter. You can also specify the old delimiter, if this is different from a comma. If we want to change all our commas to semicolons, we would use this function:

```
<cfset MyListNewDelim = ListChangeDelims(MyList,";")>
```

The resulting list would be 1;2;3;4;5;6;7;8;9;10.

ColdFusion also gives you the option to qualify each element of the list. This means you take a specific character and put it before and after each element. If we want to surround each element of our list in double quotes, we would use the ListQualify function to do this. The two required parameters to the *ListQualify* function are the list and the qualifier. The third parameter is the delimiter parameter. The fourth parameter is a constant value that accepts the values of CHAR or ALL. ALL is the default and it will qualify all elements of the

Function Name	Parameters	Usage
ListLen	**List**: The List	Returns the length of the list.
	Delimiters: an optional attribute that specifies the delimiter for the list	
ListChangeDelims	**List**: The List	Changes the delimiters on the list.
	NewDelimiter: The character to which you want to change the current delimiter	
	Delimiters: An optional attribute that specifies the current delimiter for the list. The default is a comma.	
ListQualify	**List**: The List	Returns a list with each element surrounded by the qualifier character. Places a character, or characters, around each element of a list. If the element attribute is set to CHAR, only list elements comprised of characters are qualified; otherwise, all elements are qualified.
	Qualifier: The value you want to place at the beginning or end of each list element	
	Delimiters: An optional attribute that specifies the delimiter for the list	
	Elements: The keyword ALL or CHAR. The default is All.	
ListSort	**List**: The List	Returns a sorted list.
	SortType: The sort of type you want to perform: Numeric, Text, or TextNoCase	
	SortOrder: An optional attribute that defines the sort order. Values are Asc, for ascending, or Desc for descending	
	Delimiters: An optional attribute that specifies the delimiter for the list	
ListToArray	**List**: The List	Returns an array with the list values. The opposite of this function is ArrayToList.
	Delimiters: An optional attribute that specifies the delimiter for the list	
ListValueCount	**List**: The List	Returns the number of instances of a specific value in the list.
	Value: The value you're checking against	
	Delimiters: An optional attribute that specifies the delimiter for the list	
ListValueCountNoCase	**List**: The List	The same as ListValueCount, except with a case-sensitive search.
	Value: The value you're checking against	
	Delimiters: An optional attribute that specifies the delimiter for the list	

Table 13-3   Miscellaneous List Functions

13

list. CHAR will only qualify elements comprised of alphanumeric characters. The following is an example of the function:

```
<cfset MyListQualified =
    ListQualify(MyList, "'",",","ALL")>
```

Our resulting list is '1','2','3','4','5','6','7','8','9','10'. In the previous section, we used functions like ListContains and ListFind to find values in a list. A limitation of these functions is they only return the index of the first value. What happens if you want to get more than the first value? If you know the number of incidents of your intended value, you could enter into a loop to process all of them. The ListValueCount and ListValueCountNoCase provide this functionality. They return the number of list values that is equal to the value you specify. If we want to find the number of 1's in our string, we would set up this function:

```
<cfset NumOf1s = ListValueCount(MyList,1)>
```

The NumOf1s variable would now be equal to one because only a single one is in your list.

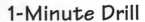

1-Minute Drill

● What tag can be used to loop over a list?

● If you want to sort a list, what function would you use?

ColdFusion provides two functions that can easily be used to change a list into an array and back. These functions are ListToArray and ArrayToList. Arrays are discussed in more detail in Module 14. The *ListToArray* function has two parameters: the list, and the delimiters of the list. Each element of the list will be turned into an element from the array. To execute the conversion:

```
<cfset ArrayFromList = ListToArray(MyList)>
```

This code will create an array from the MyList variable.

Finally, ColdFusion also offers a function that will sort a list. The name of the function is *ListSort*: the first parameter is the list and the second parameter

---

● The cfloop tag can be used to loop over a list.
● ListSort is the function that sorts a list.

is the type of sort. You can set up this function to sort either alphabetically or numerically. The values of the ListSort function are numeric, text, and textnocase. *Textnocase* sorts it alphabetically without any consideration to the letter's casing in the list elements. The next parameter is the order of the sort and it's an optional parameter. Its valid values are either asc or desc, stemming from the sort types in SQL. The final parameter is the delimiter parameter. Let's sort out the list:

```
<cfset MyListSorted =
    ListSort(MyList,"Numeric","Desc")>
```

The MyListSorted variable would now contain `10,9,8,7,6,5,4,3,2,1`.

Songu.cfm
Songp.cfm

Project 13-1: Processing Check Boxes as Lists

This module revisits Project 9-2. In Project 9-2, we created an interface for editing our song data. One thing we didn't include is a way to edit the genre of a song. A single song can be associated with multiple genres. This project will demonstrate how to create the edit functionality when a many-to-many relationship resides in the backend.

Step-by-Step

1. We need to change two pages to accomplish our intended functionality. The first is the update page: Songu.cfm. The second is the processing page: Songp.cfm. We start by looking at the update page, which is from our original template in Project 9-2.

```
<!---
Description: Page to update Song Data

Entering: N/A
Exiting: Songp.cfm

Dependencies: N/A
Expecting: SongID

Modification History
Date    Modifier         Modification
****************************************************
```

13

```
10/23/2001 Jeff Houser, DotComIt    Created
11/19/2001 Jeff Houser, DotComIt Modified to use
                cfloop inside cfoutput
                and check the default
             values for drop down lists
12/19/2001 Jeff Houser, DotComIt Modified to allow
                for selecting of Genres
--->

<!-- get the song info -->
<cfquery datasource="Chapter13" name="GetSongInfo">
 SELECT Song.*
 FROM Song
 WHERE Song.SongID = #url.SongID#
</cfquery>

<!-- get all artists -->
<cfquery datasource="Chapter13" name="GetArtists">
 SELECT Artist.*
 FROM Artist
 ORDER BY Artist
</cfquery>

<!-- get all discs -->
<cfquery datasource="Chapter13" name="GetDiscs">
 SELECT Discs.*
 FROM Discs
 ORDER BY Disc
</cfquery>

<!-- the form -->
<cfoutput>
  <form action="Songp.cfm" method="post">
  <table>
   <!-- pass the hidden songID -->
   <input type="hidden" name="SongID"
      value="#GetSongInfo.SongID#">

   <!-- The Song Name -->
    <tr>
    <td>Song Name: </td>
    <td>
     <input type="Text" name="Song"
        value="#GetSongInfo.Song#">
   </td>
```

```
    </tr>

    <!-- Select the Artist -->
    <tr>
     <td>Artist:</td>
     <td>
      <select name="ArtistID">
      <cfloop query="GetArtists">
       <option value="#GetArtists.ArtistID#"
        <cfif GetArtists.ArtistID IS
           GetSongInfo.ArtistID>selected
        </cfif>
        >
       #GetArtists.Artist#
      </cfloop>
      </select>
     </td>
    </tr>

    <!-- Select the Disc -->
    <tr>
     <td>Disc:</td>
     <td>
      <select name="DiscID">
      <cfloop query="GetDiscs">
       <option value="#GetDiscs.DiscID#"
        <cfif GetDiscs.discID IS GetSongInfo.DiscID>
         selected
        </cfif>
        >
       #GetDiscs.Disc#
      </cfloop>
      </select><br>
     </td>
    </tr>

    <tr>
     <td colspan="2"><input type="Submit"></td>
    </tr>

   </table>

  </form>
</cfoutput>
```

13

We made one change to the template, which was adding an entry into our modification history. As discussed, we're going to modify the template to allow for the selection of multiple genres.

2. The original template didn't contain any genre information at all. We'll add two queries to this template: one to get all the genres and a second to get all the genres already associated with this specific song:

```
<!---
Description: Page to update Song Data

Entering: N/A
Exiting: Songp.cfm

Dependencies: N/A
Expecting: SongID

Modification History
Date     Modifier           Modification
*********************************************************
10/23/2001 Jeff Houser, DotComIt    Created
11/19/2001 Jeff Houser, DotComIt Modified to use
              cfloop inside cfoutput
              and check the default
              values for drop down lists
12/19/2001 Jeff Houser, DotComIt Modified to allow
              for selecting of Genres
--->

<!-- get the song info -->
<cfquery datasource="Chapter13" name="GetSongInfo">
 SELECT Song.*
 FROM Song
 WHERE Song.SongID = #url.SongID#
</cfquery>

<!-- get all artists -->
<cfquery datasource="Chapter13" name="GetArtists">
 SELECT Artist.*
 FROM Artist
 ORDER BY Artist
</cfquery>
```

```
<!-- get all discs -->
<cfquery datasource="Chapter13" name="GetDiscs">
 SELECT Discs.*
 FROM Discs
 ORDER BY Disc
</cfquery>

<!-- get all Genres -->
<cfquery datasource="Chapter13" name="GetGenre">
 SELECT Genre.*
 FROM Genre
 ORDER BY Genre
</cfquery>

<!-- get Genres associated with this product -->
<cfquery datasource="Chapter13"
     name="GetThisDiscGenre">
 SELECT Genre.GenreID
 FROM Genre, SongGenre
 WHERE SongGenre.songID = #url.songID# AND
  SongGenre.GenreID = Genre.GenreID
 ORDER BY Genre
</cfquery>

<!-- the form -->
<cfoutput>
 <form action="Songp.cfm" method="post">
  <table>
   <!-- pass the hidden songID -->
   <input type="Hidden" name="SongID"
      value="#GetSongInfo.SongID#">

   <!-- The Song Name -->
   <tr>
    <td>Song Name: </td>
    <td>
     <input type="Text" name="Song"
        value="#GetSongInfo.Song#">
    </td>
   </tr>

   <!-- Select the Artist -->
   <tr>
```

New queries

13

```
    <td>Artist:</td>
    <td>
     <select name="ArtistID">
     <cfloop query="GetArtists">
      <option value="#GetArtists.ArtistID#"
       <cfif GetArtists.ArtistID IS
          GetSongInfo.ArtistID>selected
       </cfif>
       >
      #GetArtists.Artist#
     </cfloop>
     </select>
    </td>
   </tr>

   <!-- Select the Disc -->
   <tr>
    <td>Disc:</td>
    <td>
     <select name="DiscID">
     <cfloop query="GetDiscs">
      <option value="#GetDiscs.DiscID#"
       <cfif GetDiscs.discID IS getSongInfo.DiscID>
        selected
       </cfif>
       >
      #GetDiscs.Disc#
     </cfloop>
     </select><br>
    </td>
   </tr>

   <tr>
    <td colspan="2"><input type="Submit"></td>
   </tr>

  </table>

 </form>
<cfoutput>
```

New queries

The two queries perform our intended actions. GetGenre performs a select on everything in the Genres table. GetThisDiscGenre limits itself using a WHERE clause, based on the SongID.

3. The next step is to create the code to output the list of genres. The code can be seen in the following:

```
<!---
Description: Page to update Song Data

Entering: N/A
Exiting: Songp.cfm

Dependencies: N/A
Expecting: SongID

Modification History
Date    Modifier            Modification
**********************************************************
10/23/2001 Jeff Houser, DotComIt    Created
11/19/2001 Jeff Houser, DotComIt Modified to use
                cfloop inside cfoutput
                and check the default
                values for drop down lists
12/19/2001 Jeff Houser, DotComIt Modified to allow
                for selecting of Genres
--->

<!-- get the song info -->
<cfquery datasource="Chapter13" name="GetSongInfo">
 SELECT Song.*
 FROM Song
 WHERE Song.SongID = #url.SongID#
</cfquery>

<!-- get all artists -->
<cfquery datasource="Chapter13" name="GetArtists">
 SELECT Artist.*
 FROM Artist
 ORDER BY Artist
</cfquery>

<!-- get all discs -->
<cfquery datasource="Chapter13" name="GetDiscs">
 SELECT Discs.*
 FROM Discs
 ORDER BY Disc
</cfquery>
```

13

```
<!-- get all Genres -->
<cfquery datasource="Chapter13" name="GetGenre">
 SELECT Genre.*
 FROM Genre
 ORDER BY Genre
</cfquery>

<!-- get Genres associated with this product -->
<cfquery datasource="Chapter13"
     name="GetThisDiscGenre">
 SELECT Genre.GenreID
 FROM Genre, SongGenre
 WHERE SongGenre.SongID = #url.SongID# AND
  SongGenre.GenreID = Genre.GenreID
 ORDER BY Genre
</cfquery>

<!-- the form -->
<cfoutput>
 <form action="Songp.cfm" method="post">
  <table>
   <!-- pass the hidden songID -->
   <input type="Hidden" name="SongID"
      value="#GetSongInfo.SongID#">

   <!-- The Song Name -->
    <tr>
     <td>Song Name: </td>
     <td>
      <input type="Text" name="Song"
         value="#GetSongInfo.Song#">
     </td>
    </tr>

   <!-- Select the Artist -->
   <tr>
   <td>Artist:</td>
   <td>
    <select name="ArtistID">
    <cfloop query="GetArtists">
     <option value="#GetArtists.ArtistID#"
      <cfif GetArtists.ArtistID IS
         GetSongInfo.ArtistID>selected
      </cfif>
```

```
      >
        #GetArtists.Artist#
    </cfloop>
    </select>
  </td>
</tr>

<!-- Select the Disc -->
<tr>
  <td>Disc:</td>
  <td>
    <select name="DiscID">
    <cfloop query="GetDiscs">
      <option value="#GetDiscs.DiscID#"
        <cfif GetDiscs.DiscID IS GetSongInfo.DiscID>
          selected
        </cfif>
      >
        #GetDiscs.Disc#
    </cfloop>
    </select><br>
  </td>
</tr>

<tr>
  <td>Genres:</td>
  <td></td>
</tr>

<!-- code to output over the genre list -->
<cfloop query="GetGenre">
  <tr>
    <td></td>
    <td>
    <input name="GenreID" type="Checkbox"
        value="#GetGenre.GenreID#">
    #GetGenre.Genre#
    </td>
  </tr>
</cfloop>

<tr>
  <td colspan="2"><input type="Submit"></td>
</tr>
```

Loop over
GetGenre
query

13

```
</table>

</form>
<cfoutput>
```

We enter into a loop that cycles over the GetGenre query. In each loop, we create a form check box (see Figure 13-2), with the value of the check box being the GenreID and the identifier text being the genre.

4. The final step in modifying the update page is using some of our knowledge from the lists. We want to check the check boxes already associated automatically with the current song. The first thing we need is a list of all

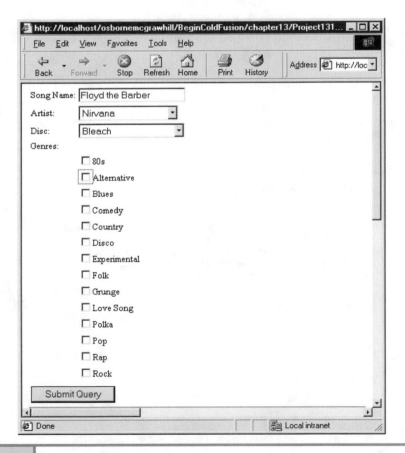

Figure 13-2   Form check box page

GenreIDs associated with the current song. Our GetThisDiscGenre query contains that information. We can turn the query results into a list using ColdFusion's ValueList function. The *ValueList* function creates a list that contains all the query data from a specific query column. This is your updated code:

```
<!---
Description: Page to update Song Data

Entering: N/A
Exiting: Songp.cfm

Dependencies: N/A
Expecting: SongID

Modification History
Date     Modifier             Modification
********************************************************
10/23/2001 Jeff Houser, DotComIt     Created
11/19/2001 Jeff Houser, DotComIt Modified to use
              cfloop inside cfoutput
              and check the default
              values for drop down lists
12/19/2001 Jeff Houser, DotComIt Modified to allow
              for selecting of Genres
--->

<!-- get the song info -->
<cfquery datasource="Chapter13" name="GetSongInfo">
 SELECT Song.*
 FROM Song
 WHERE Song.SongID = #url.SongID#
</cfquery>

<!-- get all artists -->
<cfquery datasource="Chapter13" name="GetArtists">
 SELECT Artist.*
 FROM Artist
 ORDER BY Artist
</cfquery>

<!-- get all discs -->
<cfquery datasource="Chapter13" name="GetDiscs">
```

13

```
 SELECT Discs.*
 FROM Discs
 ORDER BY Disc
</cfquery>

<!-- get all Genres -->
<cfquery datasource="Chapter13" name="GetGenre">
 SELECT Genre.*
 FROM Genre
 ORDER BY Genre
</cfquery>

<!-- get Genres associated with this product -->
<cfquery datasource="Chapter13"
     name="GetThisDiscGenre">
 SELECT Genre.GenreID
 FROM Genre, SongGenre
 WHERE SongGenre.SongID = #url.SongID# AND
  SongGenre.GenreID = Genre.GenreID
 ORDER BY Genre
</cfquery>

<!-- the form -->
<cfoutput>
 <form action="Songp.cfm" method="post">
  <table>
   <!-- pass the hidden songID -->
   <input type="Hidden" name="SongID"
     value="#GetSongInfo.SongID#">

   <!-- The Song Name -->
   <tr>
    <td>Song Name: </td>
    <td>
     <input type="Text" name="Song"
       value="#GetSongInfo.Song#">
    </td>
   </tr>

   <!-- Select the Artist -->
   <tr>
    <td>Artist:</td>
    <td>
     <select name="ArtistID">
```

```
  <cfloop query="GetArtists">
  <option value="#GetArtists.ArtistID#"
   <cfif GetArtists.ArtistID IS
      GetSongInfo.ArtistID>selected
   </cfif>
  >
  #GetArtists.Artist#
  </cfloop>
  </select>
 </td>
</tr>

<!-- Select the Disc -->
<tr>
 <td>Disc:</td>
 <td>
  <select name="DiscID">
  <cfloop query="GetDiscs">
  <option value="#GetDiscs.DiscID#"
   <cfif GetDiscs.DiscID IS GetSongInfo.DiscID>
    selected
   </cfif>
  >
  #GetDiscs.Disc#
  </cfloop>
  </select><br>
 </td>
</tr>

<tr>
 <td>Genres:</td>
 <td></td>
</tr>

<!-- code to output over the genre list -->
<cfset GenreIDList =
      ValueList(GetThisDiscGenre.GenreID)>
 <cfloop query="GetGenre">
 <tr>
  <td></td>
  <td>
  <input name="GenreID" type="Checkbox"
      value="#GetGenre.GenreID#"
```

ValueList function

13

```
      <cfif ListContains(GenreIDList,
             #GetGenre.GenreID#)>
   Checked
   </cfif>>#GetGenre.Genre#
   </td>
  </tr>
 </cfloop>

 <tr>
  <td colspan="2"><input type="Submit"></td>
 </tr>

</table>

</form>
<cfoutput>
```

Conditional statement

After using the ValueList function, the final modification to this template is to add the conditional. Is the current GenreID in the list of GenreIDs associated with this song? If so, we check the check box using the checked function. Otherwise, we do nothing. We use the ListContains to perform the condition and our resulting template looks like Figure 13-3.

5. Now we have to modify the processing page for song update process. This is our original template:

```
<!---
Description: Page to update Song Data

Entering: Songp.cfm
Exiting: N/A

Dependencies: N/A
Expecting: form.SongID
   form.Song
  form.ArtistID
  form.DiscID
  form.GenreID

Modification History
Date    Modifier    Modification
***********************************************************
10/23/2001 Jeff Houser, DotComIt  Created
12/19/2001 Jeff Houser, DotComIt  Modified to allow
            for inserting of GenreIDs
--->
```

```
<cfquery datasource="Chapter13" name="GetDiscs">
 UPDATE song
 SET Song = '#form.Song#',
 DiscID = #form.DiscID#,
 ArtistID = #form.ArtistID#
 WHERE Song.SongID = #form.SongID#
</cfquery>

<cfoutput>
 <a href="Songu.cfm?SongID=#form.SongID#">
 Back to the Song
  </a>
</cfoutput>
```

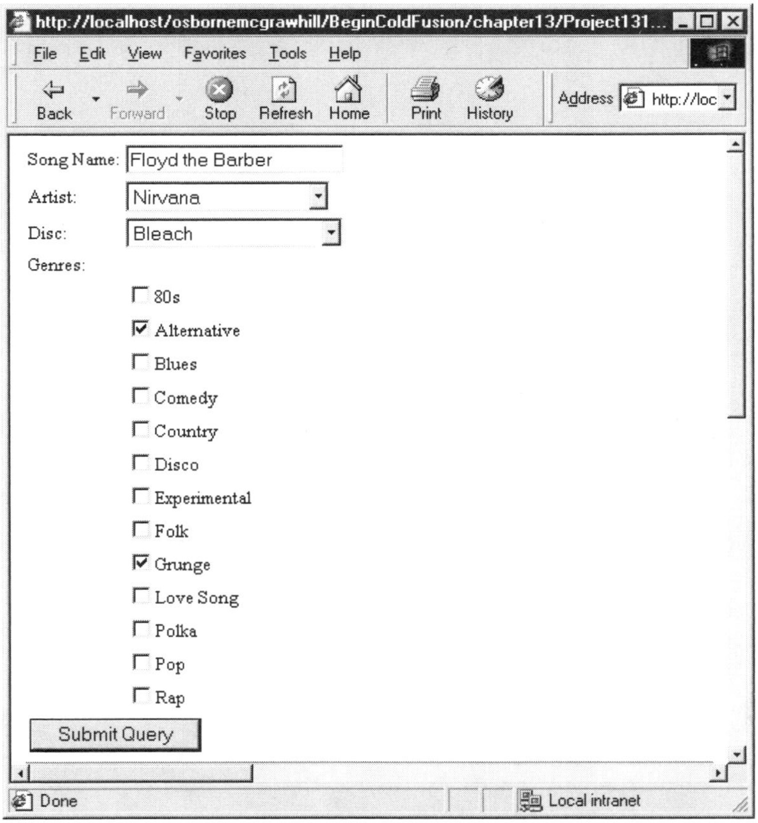

Figure 13-3   Template after performing ListContains

In this step, we added our modification history and that we're now expecting a GenreID list when we enter this page.

6. Two things could happen on the update page. A user could select a new genre and the user could remove an existing genre. Our code must allow for all potential possibilities. The first thing we want to do is remove all associations from the SongGenre table where the SongID is equal to the CurrentID and the GenreID isn't in the form GenreID variable. This is our code:

```
<!---
Description: Page to update Song Data

Entering: Songp.cfm
Exiting: N/A

Dependencies: N/A
Expecting: form.SongID
    form.Song
  form.ArtistID
  form.DiscID
  form.GenreID

Modification History
Date      Modifier    Modification
**********************************************************
10/23/2001 Jeff Houser, DotComIt  Created
12/19/2001 Jeff Houser, DotComIt  Modified to allow
              for inserting of GenreIDs
--->

<cfquery datasource="Chapter13" name="GetDiscs">
 UPDATE song
 SET Song = '#form.Song#',
 DiscID = #form.DiscID#,
 ArtistID = #form.ArtistID#
 WHERE Song.SongID = #form.SongID#
</cfquery>

<!-- Delete all GenreIDs that were removed -->
<cfquery datasource="Chapter13" name="DeleteGenres">
 DELETE FROM SongGenre
 WHERE SongGenre.SongID = #form.SongID# AND
  songGenre.GenreID NOT IN (#form.GenreID#)
</cfquery>
```

DeleteGenre query

```
</cfloop>


<cfoutput>
 <a href="Songu.cfm?SongID=#form.SongID#">
 Back to the Song
  </a>
</cfoutput>
```

7. The next step is to loop over the list of GenreIDs and insert each association into the database:

```
<!---
Description: Page to update Song Data

Entering: Songp.cfm
Exiting: N/A

Dependencies: N/A
Expecting: form.SongID
   form.Song
  form.ArtistID
  form.DiscID
  form.GenreID

Modification History
Date    Modifier   Modification
************************************************************
10/23/2001 Jeff Houser, DotComIt  Created
12/19/2001 Jeff Houser, DotComIt  Modified to allow
               for inserting of GenreIDs
--->

<cfquery datasource="Chapter13" name="GetDiscs">
 UPDATE Song
 SET Song = '#form.Song#',
 DiscID = #form.DiscID#,
 ArtistID = #form.ArtistID#
 WHERE Song.SongID = #form.SongID#
</cfquery>

<!-- Delete all GenreIDs that were removed -->
<cfquery datasource="Chapter13" name="DeleteGenres">
 DELETE FROM SongGenre
```

13

```
 WHERE SongGenre.SongID = #form.SongID# AND
   SongGenre.GenreID NOT IN (#form.GenreID#)
 </cfquery>

 <!--- insert the GenreID --->
 <cfloop index="TempGenreID" list="#form.GenreID#">

   <cfquery datasource="Chapter13"
       name="InsertSongGenre">
    INSERT INTO SongGenre (SongID, GenreID )
    VALUES (#form.SongID#, #TempGenreID# )
   </cfquery>

 </cfloop>

 <cfoutput>
  <a href="Songu.cfm?SongID=#form.SongID#">
   Back to the Song
  </a>
 </cfoutput>
```

InsertSongGenre query

We loop over the check box value, GenreID. This is a loop over a list. Inside the loop, we perform our query.

8. If you're looking at the code and wondering what happens if we try to insert an entry into the SongGenre table that already exists, then I need to congratulate you. Because this is an intersection table, the primary key is the sum of both the SongID and the GenreID. We can't have duplicate primary key entries. This is a great place to try out some of the error-catching capabilities discovered in Module 11.

```
<!---
Description: Page to update Song Data

Entering: Songp.cfm
Exiting: N/A

Dependencies: N/A
Expecting: form.SongID
   form.Song
  form.ArtistID
  form.DiscID
  form.GenreID
```

```
Modification History
Date     Modifier    Modification
************************************************************
10/23/2001 Jeff Houser, DotComIt   Created
12/19/2001 Jeff Houser, DotComIt   Modified to allow
            for inserting of GenreIDs
--->

<cfquery datasource="Chapter13" name="GetDiscs">
 UPDATE Song
 SET Song = '#form.Song#',
 DiscID = #form.DiscID#,
 ArtistID = #form.ArtistID#
 WHERE song.SongID = #form.SongID#
</cfquery>

<!-- Delete all GenreIDs that were removed -->
<cfquery datasource="Chapter13" name="DeleteGenres">
 DELETE FROM SongGenre
 WHERE SongGenre.SongID = #form.SongID# AND
  SongGenre.GenreID NOT IN(#form.GenreID#)
</cfquery>

<!--- insert the GenreID --->
<cfloop index="TempGenreID" list="#form.GenreID#">
 <cftry>

  <cfquery datasource="Chapter13"
      name="InsertSongGenre">
   INSERT INTO SongGenre (SongID, GenreID )
   VALUES (#form.SongID#, #TempGenreID# )
  </cfquery>

  <cfcatch type="Database">
   <!-- if it gets here, it just tried to insert
    an already existing item into the DB -->
  </cfcatch>
  </cftry>

</cfloop>

<cfoutput>
 <a href="Songu.cfm?SongID=#form.SongID#">
 Back to the Song
 </a>
</cfoutput>
```

Error checking

13

We surround our insert statement with a cftry statement. Inside the cftry statement, we use a cfcatch block to catch all database errors. Notice we don't do anything to resolve the error. This is a perfectly acceptable solution to handling an error and it simply makes the error go away. For example, if you think about the Windows operating system (OS), what happens if you click a mouse when the mouse click isn't being expected? Nothing happens! The mouse click is ignored and vanishes. It would make the OS extremely frustrating and unusable if you saw an error every time you clicked the mouse in an unexpected spot. The same sort of theory applies here.

Project Summary

We must deal with two pieces of data that form a one-to-one relationship in many situations in the real world. This project shows you how you can update the information in a database. You can also apply the concepts demonstrated here to more complex examples.

Module Summary

This module explored lists in ColdFusion. Lists are a good way to bridge the gap between simple data types and complex data types. The next modules go into more detail on structures and arrays, some of ColdFusion's true complex data types.

☑ *Mastery Check*

1. The character that separates two elements in a list is called a _____.

2. To find the number of values in a list, which function would you use?

   A. ListToArray

   B. ListValueCount

   C. ListChangeDelim

   D. ListCount

3. To find out the number of elements in a list, what function would you use?

   _____

   _____

4. It's possible to have a list with more than one delimiter. True/False

5. How do list functions handle empty elements?

   _____

   _____

6. What is the value for an empty list in ColdFusion?

   A.   " "

   B.   Null

   C.   Empty

   D.   None of the above

   E.   All of the above

7. To insert a character in the middle of a list, what function would you use?

   _____

   _____

13

☑ Mastery Check

8. What is the difference between ListValueCount and
ListValueCountNoCase?

_____

_____

9. What will be returned by this expression: ListLast(ListFirst("And They All
Laughed. At Night. Together",".")), " ")

_____

_____

Module 14

Complex Variable Types

The Goals of This Module

- Examine complex data types in ColdFusion
- Learn about arrays and structures
- Deal with queries as a complex data type

A simple data type, discussed in Module 2, is one that contains a single piece of data. Some examples of simple data types are integers, strings, and Boolean values. Complex data types are data types that can contain multiple pieces of data and, often, these are a collection of simple data types. This module discusses advanced data types and how to use them in ColdFusion.

Arrays

This section introduces you to arrays. Arrays are the first true complex data type discussed in this module. We learn what arrays are and how to use them, and then we're introduced to some advanced array functionality.

What Is an Array?

An *array* is a group of elements you can reference under a single variable name. Arrays are referenced by a number that corresponds to the location of the item in the array. This number is known as the *index* of the array item.

The simplest type of array is like a single row or column in a table. This is called a *one-dimensional array*. The following is an example:

Index	Data
1	First
2	Second
3	Third
4	Fourth

In a situation like this, you would reference the text First by the index 1. ColdFusion enables us to reference variables in an array using the syntax:

```
ArrayName[Index]
```

The index follows the name of the array variable, surrounded by brackets. In ColdFusion, when the element of an array is deleted, all the indexes move up one. So, if the second element is deleted, then the third element becomes the second element, and the fourth element will become the third. This would be the resulting array:

Index	Data
1	First
2	Third
3	Fourth

This function of arrays might be contrary to what you have dealt with in other languages, which is why I draw specific attention to it. This is a way to conserve memory by automatically resizing arrays as elements are removed.

Arrays can have multiple dimensions. A one-dimensional array, as previously discussed, is like a single database row or column. A two-dimensional array is similar to a database table and might look like this:

	1	**2**
1	FirstFirst	FirstSecond
2	SecondFirst	SecondSecond
3	ThirdFirst	ThirdSecond
4	FourthFirst	FourthSecond

A two-dimensional array is similar to an array of arrays. That is to say that each element of a one dimensional array is a one dimensional array itself.When accessing an array, you use the syntax:

```
Arrayname[index1][index2]
```

The first index is the vertical index and the second index is the horizontal index. To get the element SecondFirst, we would reference ArrayName[2][1]. When an element is deleted, the array is automatically shrunk, as in a one-dimensional array. Because we're dealing with an array of arrays, only the array where the element was removed is affected. If you were to remove the SecondFirst item, the resulting array would be

	1	**2**
1	FirstFirst	FirstSecond
2	SecondSecond	
3	ThirdFirst	ThirdSecond
4	FourthFirst	FourthSecond

The second array minimizes itself and no item is at arrayname[2][2].

Arrays can also be created in three, or more, dimensions. A three-dimensional array is like a cube, like that in Figure 14-1.

14

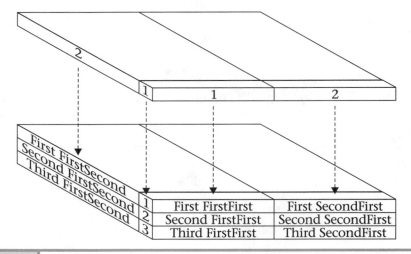

Figure 14-1   Three-dimensional array

Three-dimensional arrays can be created easily in ColdFusion, just like one or two-dimensional arrays. Arrays that are bigger can be created, although they become hard to visualize and are rarely used. For example, to create a four-dimensional array in ColdFusion, you must first create two variables: a one-dimensional array and a three-dimensional array. Set one of the three-dimensional elements equal to the one-dimensional array: This creates a four-dimensional array. I've never needed a three-dimensional array, so I've never needed anything larger.

Array Creation

The first thing we need to look at is array creation and population. This section demonstrates how to create arrays of varying dimensions. Then, we learn some different methods to fill an array with data. All the functions we'll discuss are in Table 14-1.

We first need to create an array. Unlike lists, you can't create an array using a simple cfset; instead, you must use a special function called ArrayNew inside the cfset. ArrayNew accepts a single value, which is the dimension of the array you're creating. Let's create a simple one-dimensional array:

```
<cfset MyArray = ArrayNew(1)>
```

Function Name	Parameters	Usage
ArrayNew	**Dimension**: The dimension of the array you're creating	Used to create an array.
ArraySet	**Array**: The array **StartPos**: The first position in the array you want to set to the value. **EndPos**: The final position in the array you want to set to the value **Value**: The value you're setting the range to	Used to set all values in the range to a specific value.
ArrayResize	**Array**: The array **MinimumSize**: Set the size of an array	Sets the size of an array. This function can achieve performance gains if you set the array to its expected maximum size.
ArrayAppend	**Array**: The array **Value**: The value you're adding to the array	Used to add an element to the end of an array.
ArrayPrepend	**Array**: The array **Value**: The value you're adding to the array	Used to add an element to the beginning of an array.
ArrayInsertAt	**Array**: The array **Position**: The position of the array element you want to insert **Value**: The value you're inserting into the array	Inserts an item at the specific position. Array indexes are recalculated to compensate for the added index.
ArrayDeleteAt	**Array**: The array **Position**: The position of the array element you want to delete	Deletes data at the specific array position. When this is done, array indexes are recalculated to compensate for the deleted index.
ArrayClear	**Array**: The array	Deletes all data in an array.

Table 14-1   Functions to Create and Populate an Array

We now have our array—MyArray—but, at this point, it's an empty array with no elements in it. The next step is to populate the array.

We can populate an array with data in a number of ways. The first is to populate each element separately by using cfset:

```
<cfset MyArray[1] = "Test">
<cfset MyArray[2] = "Test2">
```

The two previous statements populate the array with two elements. We can insert a value into position two without adding a value to position one.

Hint

In ColdFusion, arrays can't have an index of zero.

Another way to fill an array with initial values is to use the *ArraySet* function, which populates the items in an array under the range you specify, with default values. Say you want to populate the first six elements of your array with the word "populate":

```
<cfset DidPopulate =
    ArraySet(MyArray, 1, 6, "populate")>
```

The first argument in the function is the array. The second argument is the first index we want to populate with our default value, and the third argument is the last index we want to populate with your value. The final argument to the array is the value with which we want to populate the array.

The previous statement takes our empty array, adds six elements to it, and sets each element to the text value populate. If the array already had items in it, within those first six elements we specify, the value for those items would be reset to populate. The value returned by this function is a Boolean value, indicating whether the function was successful.

We could also use an index loop to populate an array. You'll remember from Module 9 that index loops are used to increment a specific number of times. This is our loop:

```
<cfloop index="Temp" from="1" to="6">

  <cfset MyArray[Temp] = Temp>

</cfloop>
```

This loop creates six elements in your array and initializes each one to the current number.

When dealing with large arrays, you might gain some performance improvements by using the *ArrayResize* function, which we can do immediately after creating an array to specify the minimum size of the array. If we don't know the size your array will be, then this action might not be feasible. Say you were going to create an array that will hold, in any given time, at least 100 items. After creating it, you could use the ArrayResize function:

```
<cfset MyArray = ArrayNew(1)>
<cfset ArrayResized = ArrayResize(MyArray, 100)>
```

The ArrayResize function will create the array in memory with elements that haven't yet been initialized.

We won't be able to access the values in the array until those elements are populated. This function simply reserves memory space for the elements. The strong recommendation is that you use this function for arrays that will have at least 500 elements.

Now, pretend we have a populated array. What happens when we want to add a value to the beginning or the end of the array? When we were dealing with lists, we had two functions: ListPrepend and ListAppend, to add values to the beginning or the end of a list, respectively. ColdFusion provides parallel functions for operating on arrays: an ArrayPrepend function and an ArrayAppend function. Both have the same attributes—the first is the array and the second is the value you're inserting. An example follows.

Let's use the array you populated with the loop. So, now we have an array that's six elements in length and the values number from 1 to 6, incrementally. This is our array:

Index	Element
1	1
2	2
3	3
4	4
5	5
6	6

Suppose we want to add a 0 value to the beginning of the list. We would use this statement:

```
<cfset WasPrepended = ArrayPrepend(MyList, 0)>
```

Our list now has seven values, starting at 0, and incrementing up to 6, like this:

Index	Element
1	0
2	1
3	2
4	3
5	4

14

Index	Element
6	5
7	6

We can follow along to add a 7 to the end of the array with ArrayAppend:

```
<cfset WasPrepended = ArrayAppend(MyList, 7)>
```

We now have an array with eight values in it, counting from 0 to 8, like this:

Index	Element
1	0
2	1
3	2
4	3
5	4
6	5
7	6
8	7

The value returned by these functions is a Boolean value indicating whether the operation was successful. You'll remember that list functions return a modified list without affecting the original value. Arrays in this context operate differently.

ArrayAppend and ArrayPrepend were compared to the similar list functions. If we want to insert an item into the middle of an array, we'd have an ArrrayInsertAt function. If we want to add the number 3.5 in between 3 and 4, we could use this statement:

```
<cfset Temp = ArrayInsertAt(MyArray, 5, 3.5)>
```

The resulting array is

Index	Element
1	0
2	1
3	2
4	3
5	3.5
6	4
7	5
8	6
9	7

If we want to change an item in the middle of an array, we could use cfset, so there's no need for a function to change elements in the middle of an array:

```
<cfset MyArray[5] = 3.8>
```

The benefit of the insert function over the use of the cfset is that the cfset changes the value of the array, without changing the size of the array. The ArrayInsertAt function inserts an item into the middle of the array without modifying any other values in the array.

Just as you can insert items into an array, you might need to remove an item from an array. ColdFusion provides the ArrayDeleteAt function to accomplish this task. The ArrayDeleteAt function has the opposite affect of the ArrayInsertAt function:

```
<cfset Deleted = ArrayDeleteAt(MyArray, 5>
```

This function has two attributes—the array and the item we want to delete. As we delete the item, the index values are recalculated.

Index	Element
1	0
2	1
3	2
4	3
5	4
6	5
7	6
8	7

Finally, if we want to delete all elements from an array, we can use the ArrayClear function. This function removes all data, while still keeping the variable as an array. If we were to use cfset to set the variable name to a blank value, that variable would no longer be recognized as an array. Let's clear out this array using the ArrayClear function:

```
<cfset ArrayDeleted = ArrayClear(MyArray)>
```

That wipes out this array.

14

Using Mathematical Functions on Arrays

Arrays are often used to keep track of a group of numbers. Because of this, some functions are included in ColdFusion that can enable you to process those numbers. This section examines those functions, as shown in Table 14-2.

The first function to look at is one to take the *sum*—the result of all the numbers added together—of all array elements. Let's continue using the array from the previous section. This array has eight elements, numbering from 0 to 8. The ArraySum function accepts one parameter, the array. This is how we use it:

```
<cfset MyArraySum = ArraySum(MyArray)>
```

This function computes the sum, like this, $0 + 1 + 2 + 3 + 4 + 5 + 6 + 7$, and returns 28 as the result.

The next function to look at is *ArrayAvg*, which computes the average of all the numbers in an array. The average of a group of numbers is computed by taking the sum of all the numbers, and then dividing the result by the number of items that were added together. The average can be taken like this:

```
<cfset MyArrayAverage = ArrayAvg(MyArray)>
```

We already know the sum of the array is 28 because 28 divided by 8 is 3.5. That's our average, as returned by the function.

ColdFusion provides functions to find the largest, and the smallest, number in an array. These functions are ArrayMax and ArrayMin, respectively. Both functions accept an array as the value. We use them like this:

```
<cfset MyArrayMax = ArrayMax(MyArray)>
<cfset MyArrayMin = ArrayMin(MyArray)>
```

After this code is executed, the MyArrayMax variable will be set to 7 because this is the largest number in the array. The MyArrayMin variable will be set to 0.

Function Name	Parameters	Usage
ArraySum	**Array**: The array	Returns the sum of all elements in the array.
ArrayAvg	**Array**: The array	Computes the average of all array values.
ArrayMax	**Array**: The array	Finds the largest value in an array.
ArrayMin	**Array**: The array	Finds the smallest value in an array.

Table 14-2 Mathematical Array Functions

Miscellaneous Array Functions

You should also know about some other important functions regarding arrays. These functions provide a variety of functionality that's important to using arrays. You can see the list of functions in Table 14-3.

The first two functions to look at are used to check an array's status. The first function is the *IsArray* function, which tells whether the variable name we pass it is an array. The second function is the *ArrayIsEmpty* function, which tells us whether the array is empty. You can use these functions to prevent errors from trying to access variables as arrays that aren't arrays.

The IsArray function enables you to check for an array of a specified dimension. It accepts two parameters: the variable name and the dimension of

Function Name	Parameters	Usage
IsArray	**Variablename**: The name of the variable **Dimension**: The dimension of the array you're checking	Returns true if the variable contains an array of the given dimension.
ArrayIsEmpty	**Array**: The array	Returns true if the array contains no data.
ArrayLen	**Array**: The array	Returns the number of elements in an array.
ArraySort	**Array**: The array **SortType**: Defines how you want to sort the array. Valid values are numeric, text, and textnocase **SortOrder**: How you want to results to be ordered. Valid values are asc or desc	Returns true if the array was sorted and false otherwise.
ArraySwap	**Array**: The array **Position1**: Position of the first element you want to swap **Position2**: Position of the second element you want to swap	Swaps two elements of an array. Returns true if the two elements are correctly swapped and false otherwise.
ArrayToList	**Array**: The array **Delimiter**: Optional attribute that specifies the delimiter of the resulting list. Default is a comma.	Returns your array into a list. The opposite of ListToArray.

Table 14-3   Other Array Functions

14

the array you're checking. If we want to see if our array is a one-dimensional array, we would use this:

```
<cfif IsArray("MyArray",1)>
  <!--- insert array processing here --->
</cfif>
```

The ArrayIsEmpty function checks to see if the array is empty. We don't want to process an empty array. We can expand the previous example, like this:

```
<cfif IsArray("MyArray",1)>
  <cfif NOT ArrayIsEmpty(MyArray)>
  <!--- insert array processing here --->
  </cfif>
</cfif>
```

These functions enable you to avoid errors before they happen and can be important when dealing with arrays in ColdFusion.

Another useful function is the ArrayLen function. The *ArrayLen* function accepts one parameter, which is the array, and returns the number of elements in the array. This function is most useful if you want to loop over the array's elements:

```
<cfloop index="Temp" from="1" to="#ArrayLen(MyArray)#">
  <!--- insert array processing here --->
</cfloop>
```

The previous code processes each element of the array.

If you need to sort your array values, ColdFusion also provides a way to do that with the ArraySort function, which has three parameters: the first is the array; the second is the *SortType,* which can be numeric, text, or textnocase; and the third is the sortorder. The *sortorder* parameter accepts the value of *asc,* for an ascending sort, or *desc,* for a descending sort. You'll recognize asc and desc as the same type of sorts we can use in SQL. To use the function:

```
<cfset ArraySorted =
       ArraySort(MyArray, "numeric", "desc")>
```

The value returned from the array is a Boolean value, indicating whether the array was sorted.

Our original array, sorted in descending order, now looks like this:

Index	Element
1	7
2	6
3	5
4	4
5	3
6	2
7	1
8	0

As discussed with lists, we can convert a list to an array using the ListToArray function. And, there's also a way to convert in the opposite direction, using the ArrayToList function. The *ArrayToList* function accepts two parameters: the array and an optional parameter defining the delimiter of the list. To change the sorted array into a list, we could do this:

```
<cfset MyArrayList = ArrayToList(MyArray)>
```

The MyArrayList variable is set to 7,6,5,4,3,2,1,0.

The final function to examine is the *ArraySwap* function, which enables us to switch the locations of two elements easily in an array. The ArraySwap function accepts three parameters: the array, the first position, and the second position:

```
<cfset MyArraySwapped = ArraySwap(MyArray,5,3)>
```

The previous function swaps the fifth and third elements of our array. It returns a Boolean value stating whether the two values were swapped.

After running the previous code, this would be your array:

Index	Element
1	7
2	6
3	3
4	4
5	5
6	2
7	1
8	0

The third value in the array was swapped with the fifth.

14

1-Minute Drill

- What is an array?
- A two-dimensional array is like what?

Structures

This section discusses structures, the final complex data type in ColdFusion. We learn what structures are, and discuss how to create and use them in ColdFusion.

What Are Structures?

Structures are similar to arrays, in that they're a group of elements stored under a single variable name. In arrays, we use a number to access the specific value. With a structure, we use a string. Structures are known as associative arrays because we're associating a name with a specific value. The elements that make up a structure are known as *key value pairs* because the index of a value is called a *key*.

Let's look at how a structure is stored in memory. Say this is a structure, called Person, that contains specific information about a person:

Key	Value
Name	Jeff Houser
Email	jeff@farcryfly.com
ZIP code	12345
Phone	123-4567

To access the values of this structure in ColdFusion, we would use the syntax:

```
StructureName.StructureKey
```

So, to find the person's name, we would use `Person.Name`.

To find the E-mail address, we would use `Person.Email`. This is known as the *object property notation* because the StructureName is the object and the property would be the key, such as Name or Email.

- An array is a grouping of simple data types, indexed by a number.
- A two-dimensional array is like a single database table or a spreadsheet.

You can also access the individual elements of a structure using a notation similar to an array:

```
StructureName["StructureKey"]
```

Using this notation, we would access the person's name by `Person["Name"]` and his e-mail by `Person["Email"]`. This is known as the *associative array notation*.

Before we can access a structure, though, we need to create it. The next section shows you how.

Creating and Populating Structures

This section discusses some of the ways to create and access a new structure. You can see the list of functions and their arguments in Table 14-4. Let's begin by examining how you can create a structure.

Function Name	Parameters	Usage
StructNew	N/A	Returns a new structure.
StructInsert	**Structure**: The Structure **Key**: The Key **Value**: The Value **AllowOverWrite**: A Boolean value that tells the function whether to overwrite an already existing value	Inserts an item into a structure. An error is thrown if the structure doesn't exist or if the structure exists and AllowOverWrite is false.
StructUpdate	**Structure**: The Structure **Key**: The Key **Value**: The Value	Updates the structure key with the specified value. An error is thrown if the structure doesn't exist.
StructFind	**Structure**: The Structure **Key**: The key whose value to return	Returns the value associated with the specified key.
StructClear	**Structure**: The Structure	Removes all elements from a structure and always returns yes.
StructDelete	**Structure**: The Structure **Key**: The key of the item you want to remove **IndicateNonexisting**: A Boolean value that indicates whether the function will return false if the key doesn't exist.	Deletes an item from a structure. If IndicateNonexisting is set to true and the key doesn't exist in the structure, then the function returns false. Otherwise, it returns true.

Table 14-4   Functions to Create and Populate a Structure

14

Function Name	Parameters	Usage
StructCopy	**Structure**: The Structure	Returns a new structure with the keys and values of the old structure.
Duplicate	**Variable**: The variable you want to copy	Performs a copy, so no reference exists to the original variable.

Table 14-4   Functions to Create and Populate a Structure (*continued*)

A structure is created using the *StructNew* function, which has no parameters; it merely returns an empty structure. We can create a structure like this, using cfset:

```
<cfset MyStructure = StructNew()>
```

This creates an empty structure without anything in it.

Once we create our structure, we need to know how to add things to it and we can do this in two different ways. First, ColdFusion provides a function— StructInsert—that creates a new key value pair in the structure. StructInsert accepts four parameters: the structure, the name of the key you want to add, the value you want to add, and an overwrite parameter. The *overwrite* parameter is a Boolean value that accepts a value whether or not you want to overwrite the value in the key if it already exists. Let's add a few items to our structure:

```
<cfset InsertName =
    StructInsert(MyStructure, "Name", "Jeff Houser")>
<cfset InsertEmail = StructInsert(MyStructure,
            "Email", "jeff@farcryfly.com")>
```

The value returned by the function is a Boolean, indicating whether the insert operation was successful. We now have a structure with two items in it: Name and Email.

The structure looks like this:

Index	Value
Name	Jeff Houser
E-mail	jeff@farcryfly.com

ColdFusion also provides an alternate way to add items to a structure. We can use the notation discussed earlier in this module with a cfset block:

```
<cfset MyStructure["ZipCode"] = "12345">
<cfset MyStructure["Phone"] = "123-4567">
```

This successfully adds the final two items to our structure:

Index	Value
Name	Jeff Houser
E-mail	jeff@farcryfly.com
ZIP Code	12345
Phone	123-4567

Now that we know how to put an element into our structure, what happens when we want to update an item? The powers that be at Macromedia have thought of a solution to this.

We can update the value to an existing key in two ways: use a function, StructUpdate, or use the associative array notation. Let's use the function first:

```
<cfset MyStructUpdate =
   StructUpdate(MyStructure,"Name","Jeffry Houser")>
```

The StructUpdate function has three arguments: the structure, the key, and the value. The value returned from the function is a Boolean value indicating whether we were able to update the value successfully.

We can achieve the same result as the previous ones with this syntax:

```
<cfset MyStructure["Name"] = "Jeffry Houser">
```

This is using the associative array notation, just as if we were setting the variable for the first time.

Our updated structure is this:

Index	Value
Name	Jeffry Houser
E-mail	jeff@farcryfly.com
ZIP Code	12345
Phone	123-4567

Only one value has changed based on our previous actions.

We already know how to get the value of a structure's key using the associative array notation. ColdFusion provides a function to accomplish the same task, *StructFind*, which accepts two attributes: the structure and the key you want to find. The StructFind function returns the value of the given key. To display the current user's name, do this:

```
<cfoutput>
 #StructFind(MyStructure, "Name")#
</cfoutput>
```

14

The text Jeffry Houser displays on the screen.

As there are always ways to add and update the data in a structure, ways also exist to remove a specific item or to clear the whole structure. To remove an item from a structure, we can use the StructDelete function, which contains three different arguments: the structure, the key we want to delete, and a flag. The flag is used to tell the function to return false if the specified key doesn't exist. If you set this flag to true, the function returns true if the key exists and it returns false otherwise. If we don't specify this flag or we set it to false, then the function will return true. If you were to remove the phone number from our structure:

```
<cfset MyStructDeleted = StructDelete(MyStructure, "Phone")>
```

the results from our structure would be

Index	Value
Name	Jeffry Houser
E-mail	jeff@farcryfly.com
ZIP Code	12345

Instead of four values, we now have three. There's no trace of the Phone key.

If we want to delete a structure completely, we can use the StructClear function. The one parameter this function accepts is the structure. After execution of the function, the variable still exists in memory, but it won't have any values associated with it:

```
<cfset MyStructureGone = StructClear(MyStructure)>
```

This effectively removes all the remaining elements from our structure.

The last thing to discuss before moving on is a way to make a copy of a structure. ColdFusion provides two functions to accomplish this. The first function is *StructCopy,* which accepts one argument, a structure. StructCopy returns a copy of the structure. When using StructCopy, all top-level elements are copied by value. This means the value is copied over completely. If you have a structure inside a structure, however, it's copied by reference. This means a pointer to the variable is copied, but the actual variable isn't copied. To create a separate copy, you can use the Duplicate function on the structure.

Looping Over the Elements in a Structure

This section shows us how you can use the cfloop tag to loop over a structure. The cfloop tag was originally introduced, along with looping concepts, in Module 9.

One of the topics we weren't prepared to discuss yet was looping over a structure. This section shows you how.

The cfloop tag has two attributes that enable us to loop over a structure:

- **Collection**   The *collection* attribute accepts the name of the structure.

- **Item**   The *item* attribute defines a temporary name for the current item we're examining.

To loop over the MyStructure variable from the previous section, we can use this code:

```
<cfloop collection=#MyStructure# Item="Temp">
 #MyStructure[Temp]#<br>
</cfloop>
```

The output we get from this will look like this:

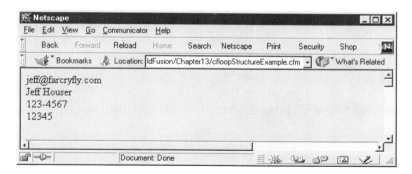

You will use this technique many times when we process structures.

Ask the Expert

Question: I've heard you can process the session scope as a structure. Is this true? How can I do that?

Answer: Yes, this is true and we can not only process the session scope as a structure, but we can also process the application, form, server, request, and URL variable scopes. You can process any of these scopes with little knowledge of what resides in them. The following is

14

some code I commonly use when debugging my applications. It prints all the variables and their values in the session scope:

```
<cfloop collection=#session# item="TempKey">
  <cfoutput>
  #TempKey# #structfind(session, TempKey)#
  </cfoutput><br>
</cfloop>
```

We use a cfloop tag to loop over a structure.

In the loop, we output the name of the current key and the value of that key. This lets me keep track of what's happening in the session scope to see if I'm getting the desired results. The same code could be modified easily for any of the other structure scopes.

Structure Functions

This final section examines some of the miscellaneous structure functions available for our use within ColdFusion. We won't discuss some more advanced functions, but you'll have a good understanding of how to use structures and you can research the outstanding functions on your own. You can see the list of functions we'll look at in Table 14-5.

Function Name	Parameters	Usage
IsStruct	**VariableName**: name of structure	Returns true if the given variable name is a structure. Otherwise, returns false.
StructIsEmpty	**Structure**: The Structure	Returns true if the structure is empty. Otherwise, returns false.
StructKeyExists	**Structure**: The Structure **Key**: The key to test	Returns true if the specified key exists in the given structure. Otherwise, returns false.
StructKeyArray	**Structure**: The Structure	Returns an array of all the keys in the structure.
StructKeyList	**Structure**: The Structure **Delimiter**: The delimiter for the list, default is a comma	Returns a list that contains all the keys in the structure.

Table 14-5 Miscellaneous Structure Functions

Function Name	Parameters	Usage
StructCount	**Structure**: The Structure	Returns the number of keys in a structure.
StructAppend	**Structure1**: The first structure **Structure2**: The second structure **OverwriteFlag**: A Boolean value if you want values in Structure2 to overwrite values in Structure1	Adds all the keys and values from Structure2 into Structure1. This function always returns yes.

Table 14-5   Miscellaneous Structure Functions (*continued*)

The first group of functions to examine are some Boolean functions that enable us to check our structure variable for certain characteristics. The first function is the *IsStruct* function, which accepts a string as the parameter and checks to see if the given variable is a structure. This is a useful error-prevention maneuver. We can check to see if the structure exists before we try to access that variable as a structure:

```
<cfif IsStruct(MyStructure)>
 The function is a Structure
 <!-- other structure processing -->
</cfif>
```

The function returns a Boolean value, indicating whether the variable is a structure.

The next function to examine—*StructIsEmpty*—tells us whether any elements are in the structure. The structure is its only argument. We can expand the previous example like this:

```
<cfif IsStruct(MyStructure) AND
   NOT StructIsEmpty(MyStructure)>
 The function is a Structure
 <!-- other structure processing -->
</cfif>
```

This checks to be certain the variable is a structure, and then checks to make sure the structure isn't empty. If both of these conditions are true, the processing continues.

Finally, ColdFusion provides a way to check for the existence of a specific key in a structure. If you try to access a structure with a nonexistent or invalid key, this causes errors. If you're unsure if a specific key exists, always check its

14

existence using the StructKeyExists function. This function has two arguments: the structure and the key. This is how we use it:

```
<cfif StructKeyExists(MyStructure, "Name")>
 <cfoutput>#MyStructure.Name#</cfoutput>
</cfif>
```

The previous three functions enable us to prevent errors from being shown to a user.

What if we want to get a listing of all the keys in a structure? ColdFusion gives us two ways to do this. One function gives us all the keys in a list. Another gives us an array of all the keys. First, to get an array of all the keys, we use the *StructKeyArray* function. Its single argument is the structure and we can use it like this:

```
<cfset MyStructKeyArray = StructKeyArray(MyStructure)>
```

The MyStructKeyArray variable now contains an array with four elements: Name, E-mail, ZIP, and Phone.

To get the same list of keys as a list, ColdFusion provides the *StructKeyList* function, which has two arguments: the structure and the list delimiter. The list delimiter, as always, defaults to a comma:

```
<cfset MyStructKeyList = StructKeyList(MyStructure)>
```

The MyStructKeyList variable now contains `Name,Email,Zip,Phone`.

The next function to examine is the StructCount function. The single argument for the *StructCount* function is the structure, which returns the number of keys in a structure. You can use it like this:

```
<cfset MyStructKeyNum = StructCount(MyStructure)>
```

Using the person structure as the example, the MyStructKeyNum variable now contains four because four unique keys are in the structure.

1-Minute Drill

● A structure can also be called _____ array.

● A structure is made up of name and _____ pairs.

● What can be used for the index of a structure?

● A structure can also be called an associative array.
● A structure is made up of name and value pairs.
● Any valid ColdFusion variable name can be used to create the index of a structure.

The last function to discuss is one that appends two structures together and this function is *StructAppend.* Its first argument is the first structure and the second argument is the second structure. The final argument to StructAppend is one that specifies whether duplicate keys from Structure2 will be overwritten in Structure1. If the final argument is set to true, then Structure2 takes precedence. If the final argument is set to false, Structure1 takes precedence. The default is true.

Note

When using the StructAppend function, Structure2 isn't modified.

Pretend we have two structures. This is MyStructure:

Index	Value
Name	Jeffry Houser
Email	jeff@farcryfly.com
ZIP Code	12345
Phone	123-4567

And this is MyStructure2:

Index	Value
Address	15 North Salem Rd
City	Blue Haven
State	Nowhere
Phone	456-7890

Execute this function:

```
<cfset MyStructsAppended =
    StructAppend(MyStructure,MyStructure2, True)>
```

The function tells us to add the information in MyStructure2 to MyStructure. MyStructure2 values take priority if a key is equal.
This is the updated MyStructure:

Index	Value
Name	Jeffry Houser
Email	jeff@farcryfly.com
ZIP Code	12345
Phone	456-7890
Address	15 North Salem Rd

14

Index	Value
City	Blue Haven
State	Nowhere

However, MyStructure2 remains unchanged:

Index	Value
Address	15 North Salem Rd
City	Blue Haven
State	Nowhere
Phone	456-7890

SongList.cfm

Project 14-1: Creating Next and Previous Links

When we were learning about structures, you might have noticed the object property notation looked similar to our access of queries. You would be correct: A query is stored in memory as a structure of arrays. Each key in the structure is a column, and each row is stored as a separate entity in the array. This project shows you how to access a query as an array of structures, instead of directly as a query object. We'll create forward and next buttons, so you only display a limited number of elements on a single page.

Step-by-Step

1. This project shows you how to process a query as a structure of arrays. We edit our SongList.cfm template, which follows.

```
<!---
Description: Page to Display a list of all songs and
        show links to edit the songs

Entering: N/A
Exiting: N/A

Dependencies: N/A
Expecting: N/A

Modification History
Date    Modifier         Modification
*****************************************************
10/23/2001 Jeff Houser, DotComIt Created
```

```
12/20/2001 Jeff Houser, DotComIt  Added forward /next
                   buttons
--->

<cfquery datasource="Chapter13" name="GetSongs">
 SELECT Song.*
 FROM Song
 ORDER BY Song.Song
</cfquery>

<cfoutput query="GetSongs">
 <a HREF="Songu.cfm?SongID=#GetSongs.SongID#">
  #GetSongs.Song#
 </a><br>
</cfoutput>
```

I added an entry into our modification history. Now, let's make the changes.

2. The next thing we need to do is add some variables to keep track of what items we're displaying. We use a variable called Start and we begin displaying entries from the query, based on the value of Start.

```
<!---
Description: Page to Display a list of all songs and
        show links to edit the songs

Entering: N/A
Exiting: N/A

Dependencies: N/A
Expecting: N/A

Modification History
Date    Modifier        Modification
**********************************************************
10/23/2001 Jeff Houser, DotComIt Created
12/20/2001 Jeff Houser, DotComIt  Added forward /next
                   buttons
--->

<cfquery datasource="Chapter13" name="GetSongs">
 SELECT Song.*
 FROM Song
 ORDER BY Song.Song
</cfquery>
```

14

```
<!-- set a default for the start parameter -->
<cfparam name="Start" default="1">          ◄─────┐
<cfset Last = Start+19>                            │
                                                   │   Initialize Start and
<cfif GetSongs.RecordCount LT Last>                │   Last variables
 <cfset Last = GetSongs.RecordCount>               │
</cfif>                                      ◄──────┘

<cfoutput query="GetSongs">
 <a HREF="Songu.cfm?SongID=#GetSongs.SongID#">
  #GetSongs.Song#
 </a><br>
</cfoutput>
```

In addition to setting the start variable, we also set up a last variable. This code will display 20 items on each page, so our last variable will be set to start+19. We need to perform one last check in this step. If the number of items in the query is less than the Last variable, we receive errors because we're trying to access elements that aren't in the query. We can fix this by setting the Last variable to the largest number in the query, GetSongs.RecordCount. GetSongs.RecordCount is a special variable that can tell us the number of rows returned by the query.

3. Now that we have the Start and Last variables defined, we need to modify the query output to limit its output to 20 items. This is how we do it:

```
<!---
Description: Page to Display a list of all songs and
        show links to edit the songs

Entering: N/A
Exiting: N/A


Dependencies: N/A
Expecting: N/A


Modification History
Date     Modifier        Modification
*************************************************************
10/23/2001 Jeff Houser, DotComIt Created
12/20/2001 Jeff Houser, DotComIt  Added forward /next
                buttons
--->

<cfquery datasource="Chapter13" name="GetSongs">
 SELECT Song.*
```

```
FROM Song
ORDER BY Song.Song
</cfquery>

<!-- set a default for the start parameter -->
<cfparam name="Start" default="1">
<cfset Last = Start+19>

<cfif GetSongs.RecordCount LT Last>
 <cfset Last = GetSongs.RecordCount>
</cfif>

<cfoutput>
                                              ┌─────────────────┐
                                              │ Modified cfloop │
                                              └─────────────────┘
 <cfloop from="#Start#" to="#Last#" index="Row"> ◄────────┘

  <a HREF="Songu.cfm?SongID=#GetSongs.SongID[Row]#">
   #GetSongs.Song[Row]#
  </a><br>

 </cfloop>
</cfoutput>
```

To loop over the query information, we use an index loop, going from the start to the Last variable. The name of our temporary index variable is Row. When we access our query variables, we specify the row number at the end of our query.

4. The final step is to add our Previous and Next buttons into the query. The code is shown in the following:

```
<!---
Description: Page to Display a list of all songs and
       show links to edit the songs

Entering: N/A
Exiting: N/A

Dependencies: N/A
Expecting: N/A

Modification History
Date    Modifier        Modification
***************************************************************
10/23/2001 Jeff Houser, DotComIt Created
12/20/2001 Jeff Houser, DotComIt  Added forward /next
                   buttons
```

14

```
--->

<cfquery datasource="Chapter13" name="GetSongs">
 SELECT Song.*
 FROM Song
 ORDER BY Song.Song
</cfquery>

<!-- set a default for the start parameter -->
<cfparam name="Start" default="1">
<cfset Last = Start+19>

<cfif GetSongs.RecordCount LT Last>
 <cfset Last = GetSongs.RecordCount>
</cfif>

<cfoutput>
 <cfloop from="#Start#" to="#Last#" index="Row">
  <a HREF="Songu.cfm?SongID=#GetSongs.SongID[Row]#">
   #GetSongs.Song[Row]#
  </a><br>
 </cfloop>

 <br>
 <cfif Start GT 1>
 <cfset Start = Start - 20>
  <a HREF="SongList.cfm?Start=#Start#">Previous</a>
  </cfif>
 <cfif GetSongs.RecordCount GT Last>
 <cfset Start = Last + 1>
  <a HREF="SongList.cfm?Start=#Start#">Next</a>
  </cfif>

</cfoutput>
```

Previous button

Next button

The variable we want to pass in the URL is the start variable. To display the previous button, we need to make sure the start number is greater than one or else we'd have nothing to go back to. If we do want to display the previous link, we must first compute our new start value. To go backward, we're subtracting 20 from the current start value.

The final thing we need to add is our next link. We only want to display this if the number of records returned is greater than the Last variable. The new value for our start variable is Last + 1. This way, the next page begins one item after final entry we display on the current page.

Project Summary

Just as every carpenter has many different tools in his toolbox, every web developer should know different methods to accomplish the same task. This project showed you an alternate way to process the results from a query, while creating Next and Previous buttons to cycle through a query's result set.

Module Summary

This final module explored ColdFusion's complex data types. These concepts are important. You now have a broad base from which you can build your development tasks at hand. Thanks for reading this book and please let me know what you think: jeff@instantcoldfusion.com.

14

✓ Mastery Check

1. The two types of notations for accessing structure variables are

    A. Associative array notation

    B. Structure notation

    C. Object property notation

    D. Display notation

2. cfloop will inherently support looping over a structure or list. What type of loop can be used to loop over an array?

    _____

    _____

3. Arrays are indexed by a _____. Structures are indexed by a _____.

4. To get a list of all keys in a structure, you would use

    A. StructKeyArray

    B. StructKeyList

    C. StructAllKey

    D. StructListKey

5. What's the difference between StructCopy and Duplicate functions?

    _____

    _____

6. What function would you use to determine the number of elements in an array?

    _____

    _____

☑ *Mastery Check*

7. Which of these scopes are stored internally as structures in ColdFusion?

   A. Form

   B. Session

   C. Variables

   D. Caller

   E. URL

8. Pick one of the structure scopes from Question 7 and write some code to loop over the scope, printing all the variable names and values.

9. A query object is a structure of _____.

Part 3

Appendixes

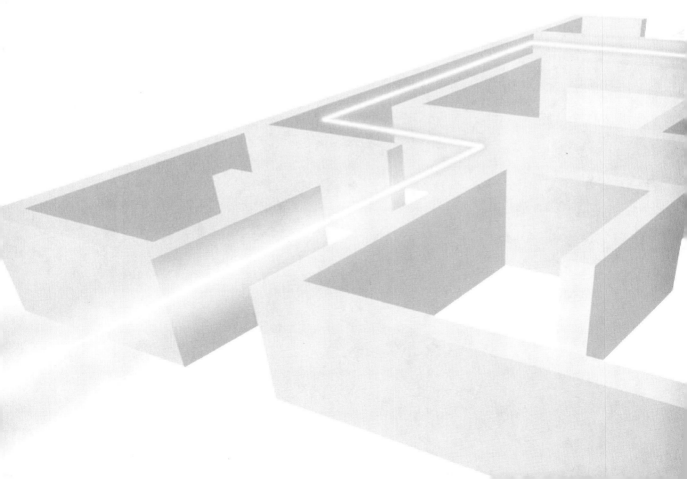

Appendix A

Answers to Mastery Checks

Module 1: The Web and ColdFusion

1. The Internet grew out of research from a government-funded project called _____.

ARPNET

2. The World Wide Web was created by Tim Berners-Lee based on the concept of many decentralized _____ of unrelated information being able to connect to each other.

nodes

3. HTML stands for

C. HyperText Markup Language

4. Both HTML and CFML are _____-based languages.

tag

5. Create an HTML page that links to Macromedia's Home Page.

```
<html>
<head>
 <title>Sample HTML Document </title>
</head>
<body>
<a href="http://www.macromedia.com">
 Macromedia
</a>

</body>
</html>
```

6. What types of links can you make between documents (select two)?

A. Absolute   and   **C.** Relative

7. The language of ColdFusion is called _____.

ColdFusion Markup Language (CFML)

8. ColdFusion is an _____ server.

application

9. Two directories you might include in your web site are the _____ directory and the _____ directory.

image; include

10. The home page of a web site is called the _____ page.

index

11. Name some important documentation to put in your templates.

Important documentation pieces to put in your template are the description, the data, the creator's name and company, the modification description, where the template came from, where the template is going, file dependencies and expected variables.

Module 2: All about Variables

1. A variable can also be referred to as a _____ pair.

name value

2. Choose which are valid variable scopes:

A. URL and **C.** Application

3. A variable's _____ defines the extent of its availability.

scope

4. What two tags can be used to create a variable?

cfset and cfparam

5. What are the differences between cfset and cfparam?

cfparam can perform type checking and will check to see if the variable is already defined; cfset will not.

6. The cfoutput tag is used to _____ a variable.

output

7. Which of these choices would be a valid variable name?

B. TheBVariable and **C.** TheBVariable02

A

8. What is the prefix for the local variable scope?

variables

9. Which cfset tag is in the correct format?

C. <cfset samplec = 1> and **D.** <cfset sampled = "My Sample">

10. Which attributes are valid cfparam attributes?

B. Name and **C.** Default

Module 3: Database Design Theory

1. What are some characteristics of a database table?

Some characteristics of a database table are that it consists of rows and columns, all rows must be unique, and all columns must contain a single piece of data.

2. What is a primary key? What is a foreign key?

A primary key is a way to uniquely define the row in a database table. A foreign key is the primary key from a separate table and is used to associate two separate tables together.

3. When accessing databases through ColdFusion, you use ODBC. What does ODBC stands for?

A. Open Database Connectivity

4. Upon examination of our Account table in the section of one-to-many relationships, you may notice that the table is not completely normalized. What must be done to further normalize the table?

The AccountType field has a one-to-many relationship with Accounts. We can normalize it by creating a new AccountType table, and adding an AccountTypeID column to the Accounts table. This is the new AccountType table:

AccountTypeID	AccountType
1	Savings
2	Checking
3	COD

Add the AccountTypeID as a foreign key in the Accounts table.

AccountID	CustomerID	Account Number	Bank	Account TypeID
1	1	12345	Bank 1	1
2	2	22-3334	Random Bank 2	2
3	2	BBN250034	1st Bank of Nowhere	3
4	4	4567109	Bank 1	2

5. When you normalize a database you are _____ data anomalies.

removing

6. An Insertion anomaly occurs when:

A.   You cannot create one piece of data without creating a second type of unrelated data.

7. What is wrong with this table? How would you fix it?

ID	Student	Grade	Teacher
1	Jeff	1	Mr Smith
2	Mary	1	Mr Smith
3	Angela	3	Ms Teeker
4	Jude	4	Ms Tilly

This table has insertion and deletion anomalies. You cannot insert a teacher without also inserting a student. It needs to be split into two tables: one for teachers:

GradeID	Grade	Teacher
1	1	Mr Smith
2	3	Ms Teeker
3	4	Ms Tilly

and one for students:

ID	Student Name	GradeID
1	Jeff	1
2	Mary	1
3	Angela	2
4	Jude	3

A

8. What are some characteristics of a one-to-one relationship?

A one to one relationship has one piece of data X for every piece of data Y and one piece of data Y for every piece of data X.

9. Pick the two main types of databases:

A. file-based databases   and   **D.**   Client/Server databases

Module 4: Parameter Passing and Forms

1. What are the differences between variables and parameters?

There is no difference between variables and parameters. They are the same thing.

2. Variables are passed in a URL via the _____

query string

3. If you have multiple variables in a URL, what character would you use to separate them?

C.   &

4. Take the site that we created in Project 2-1, and modify the pages so that they will work with the new page we created in Project 4-1. The finished files are located on the web site for this book, **www.instantcoldfusion.com**.

5. Name three attributes to the form tag.

action, method, and enctype

6. HTML forms usually have an _____ page and a _____ page.

input; processing

7. Select the two types of form elements you can create with the HTML input tag:

C.   Hidden   and   **A.**   Radio

8. What are the fallbacks of specialized ColdFusion form tags and cfform?

The fallbacks of the specialized ColdFusion form tags and cfform is that they are less efficient than straight HTML code because the ColdFusion server has to do extraneous processing that could be avoided.

9. The select tag and the _____ tag are usually used together.

option

10. Why are form fields named?

Form fields are named so that we can access them on the action page.

Module 5: SQL: The Language of the Database

1. What is a Query?

A query is a group of SQL commands that are executed together. You can also use the term query to refer to the results of those SQL commands.

2. What is the only required portion of a SELECT query?

A. Select Portion

3. When performing a join the _____ of two tables is taken. What is the difference between an Inner and Outer join?

intersection; Inner Joins only return rows with common elements, Outer Joins return all rows from one table, but only common elements from the second table.

4. What are the required attributes of a cfquery tag? Select two:

A. Name and **D.** Datasource

5. What are the four main types of SQL Queries that you can execute?

select, update, insert, and delete

6. ColdFusion provides its own versions of two important SQL Statements. What are the tags?

cfinsert and cfupdate

7. The _____ command can involve multiple tables.

multiple

8. Why would you not want to give your end users the ability to delete data?

You would not want to give your end users the ability to delete data because you want to prevent them from making mistakes and mistakenly deleting data. Setting a database column to keep track of what should be deleted and what should be kept gives you, as the programmer, some padding in case your users change their minds.

9. The group attribute of the cfoutput is used to _____.

control the display of a query's result set where one of the columns has the same value for many other records

10. The concepts demonstrated in Project 5-2 are important; however, the project is a bit limited. Based on the pages we created, you must explicitly define the SongID in the URL. This is not as user friendly as it could be. Create a page, SongList.cfm, that will display a list of songs. Make the song name clickable so that it goes to the edit song page.

```
<cfquery datasource="chapter5" name="GetSongs">
 SELECt Song.*
 FROM Song
 ORDER BY Song.Song
</cfquery>

<cfoutput query="GetSongs">
 <a href="songu.cfm?songID=#GetSongs.songID#">
  #GetSongs.song#
 </a><br>
</cfoutput>
```

Module 6: Getting Things Done in ColdFusion

1. What is an expression?

An expression is a way to process data.

2. What are elements of an expression?

A. Variables and **C.** Strings

3. What is the difference between a simple and a complex expression?

The difference is that complex expressions are made up of simple expressions.

4. What are the different types of operators that can be used to build complex expressions out of simple ones?

E. All of the above

5. In addition to tags, ColdFusion provides an extensive library of _____ to help in your development needs.

functions

6. What will the value of myvar1 be after these statements are executed:

```
<cfset MyVar1 = 10*((5*2)-4)/(5*(2-4))>
```

The value of MyVar1 will be 6 after the statement is executed.

7. To get the number of records returned in a query, we can use what property of the query object?

queryname.recordcount

8. Why are Boolean values different from other variables?

Boolean values can only have two values, 1 or 0 / True of False / Yes or No.

9. If a date is created without a time, ColdFusion creates a default time and associates it to that date. What is the time?

   A. 12:00 a.m.

10. Which statement(s) has the correct usage of pound signs:

   D. <cfset myvar1 = myvar2 + 1>

Module 7: ColdFusion's Application Framework

1. The session, application, and client scopes are called _____ scopes

persistent

2. What are the differences between the application variables and session variables?

Application variables exist once no matter how many users are on the site, while session variables exist once for every user on the site.

3. What is the only required attribute to the cfapplication tag?

   C. Name attribute

4. What file is the opposite of the Application.cfm?

The OnRequestEnd.cfm file

A

5. ColdFusion automatically creates two cookie values to help handle session management. What are these values?

B. CFID   and   **D.**   CFTOKEN

6. The cflock tag provides locking for ColdFusion variables located in shared scopes. The two types of locking that it provides are _____ and _____.

exclusive; read-only

7. Where does ColdFusion look for the Application.cfm file? Where does it look for the OnRequestEnd.cfm file?

ColdFusion looks for the Application.cfm file in the current directory. If it does not find it, ColdFusion will look in the parent directory, and continue looking in parent directories until it either finds it or finds the root directory of the current domain. It looks for the OnRequestEnd.cfm in the same directory where it found the Application.cfm file.

8. How do we use the CreateTimeSpan function?

We use the createtimespan function in the cfapplication tag to define the default timeout lengths for our Application:

```
<cfapplication name="SampApp"
applicationtimeout=#createtimespan(1,0,0,0)#
sessiontimeout=#createtimespan(0,1,0,0)#>
```

9. The three potential methods for storing client variables are?

Cookies, Registry, and datasource

10. When you implement _____ management on your web site you are providing a way to manage a user's preferences as they surf from one page to another.

state

Module 8: Making Decisions with ColdFusion

1. A function that is used to check for the existence of a variable is ___ ?

IsDefined

2. Create the truth table for this statement: `((NOT A) and (((X and Y) or Z) EQV ((X or Y) and Z)))`

(NOT A)	X	Y	Z	X and Y	X or Y	((X and Y) or Z)	((X or Y) and Z))	(((X and Y) or Z) EQV ((X or Y) and Z))	((NOT A) and (((X and Y) or Z) EQV ((X or Y) and Z)))
True	True	True	True	True	True	True	True	True	True
True	True	True	False	True	True	True	False	False	False
True	True	False	True	False	True	True	True	True	True
True	True	False	False	False	True	False	False	True	True
True	False	True	True	False	True	True	True	True	True
True	False	True	False	False	True	False	False	True	True
True	False	False	True	False	False	True	False	False	False
True	False	False	False	False	False	False	False	True	True
False	True	True	True	True	True	True	True	True	False
False	True	True	False	True	True	True	False	False	False
False	True	False	True	False	True	True	True	False	False
False	True	False	False	False	True	False	False	True	False
False	False	True	True	False	True	True	True	True	False
False	False	True	False	False	True	False	False	True	False
False	False	False	True	False	False	True	False	False	False
False	False	False	False	False	False	False	False	True	False

3. Based on Project 8-3, expand our code to include additional genre layouts. You can design the layouts in any way you choose.

There are numerous ways to approach this. The important parts in regards to ColdFusion development are setting up the cfcase and outputting the variables. This would be the simplest form:

```
<cfcase value="x">
 Album: #getDisc.disc#
 <cfoutput>
  #GetDisc.Song# #GetDisc.Artist# <br>
 </cfoutput>
</cfcase>
```

4. What are the primary tags that are used in conjunction with the cfif statement?

B. cfif, **C.** cfelse, and **D.** cfelseif

5. A Boolean variable is one that can have only _____ values.

two

6. What is the tag used to create a default condition in a cfswitch statement?

   C. cfdefaultcase

7. Which are boolean operators and which are decision operators?

   Boolean operators are **A.** Not, **C.** And, and **D.** EQV
   Decision operators are **B.** Equal, **E.** GT, and **F.** (IT)

8. What is used to list all possible answers to a Boolean expression?

   A truth table

9. The AND operator returns a _____ value if both the conditions are true.

   true

10. The OR operator will return a _____ value if the two conditions are opposites of each other?

   true

Module 9: How To Loop in ColdFusion

1. A loop is designed to _____ a certain section of code.

   repeat

2. Another name for an index loop is:

   B. For Loop

3. In an index loop, what is a step?

   The step in an index loop is the value that the index will increment during each iteration.

4. Conditional Loops in ColdFusion are created with one attribute, the condition attribute. What is the value for this attribute?

   The value of a condition attribute to a conditional loop is a ColdFusion expression.

5. The cfoutput tag can use the _____ and _____ attributes to process only part of a query.

   startrows; maxrows

6. What will the output be for this code?

```
<cfloop index="temp" from="1" to="100" step="5">
 <cfoutput>#temp#, </cfoutput>
</cfloop>
```

The output will be: 1, 6, 11, 16, 21, 26, 31, 36, 41, 46, 51, 56, 61, 66, 71, 76, 81, 86, 91, 96

7. The cfoutput tag can be used to loop over a _____ .

database query

8. When looping over a query what are the differences between cfoutput and cfloop?

    C. Cfoutput can be used to group query output, cfloop can't.

9. cfloop can be used to create all types of loops, except _____.

    D. Repeat Loops

10. Conditional loop execution is controlled by a ColdFusion expression. The execution of the loop will cease when the expression result is _____.

true

Module 10: Reusing Your Code

1. The two forms of code modularization in ColdFusion are _____ and _____ .

includes; custom tags

2. How are CFML custom tags different than normal ColdFusion templates?

CFML custom tags are not any different than normal ColdFusion templates. Custom tags have the full range of CFML functions. The main difference is in the way that the template is called.

3. What are some of the benefits of code modularization?

    A. Quicker Coding   and   **D.** Parallel Development

4. What is the one parameter to the cfinclude tag?

The single parameter for the cfinclude tag is the template parameter.

5. Why does code modularization make for less debugging?

Code modularization allows for less debugging because you code and debug your module once, yet can use it in many places. You do not have to go through the debugging process again each time you use the code module.

6. Custom tags can be called using:

B. cfmodule and **C.** The syntax cf_*tagname*

7. In Project 10-1 we showed the code only for the include that displayed the default template. Create the includes for the other genres with special display types.

These are the files. FolkTemplate.cfm:

```
<!---
Description: The default disc folk display template

Entering: N/A
Exiting: N/A

Dependencies: N/A
Expecting: getdisc query

Modification History
Date        Modifier                 Modification
************************************************************
11/26/2001 Jeff Houser, DotComIt    Created
--->

<!-- cfoutput over the query -->
<cfoutput query="GetDisc" group="Disc">

  <!-- if the genre is Folk -->
  <tr>
   <td colspan="2" bgcolor="##00ffff">
    <font color="##000000">Album: #getDisc.disc#</font>
   </td>
  </tr>
  <tr>
   <td bgcolor="##00ffff">
    <font color="##000000">Song</font>
```

```
   </td>
   <td bgcolor="##00ffff">
    <font color="##000000">Artist</font>
   </td>
  </tr>

  <cfoutput>
   <tr>
    <td bgcolor="##00ffff">
     <font color="##000000">#GetDisc.Song#</font>
    </td>
    <td bgcolor="##00ffff">
     <font color="##000000">#GetDisc.Artist#</font>
    </td>
   </tr>
  </cfoutput>
</cfoutput>
```

RapTemplate.cfm:

```
<!---
Description: The default disc rap template

Entering: N/A
Exiting: N/A

Dependencies: N/A
Expecting: getdisc query

Modification History
Date       Modifier                Modification
*********************************************************
11/26/2001 Jeff Houser, DotComIt   Created
--->
<!-- cfoutput over the query -->
<cfoutput query="GetDisc" group="Disc">


  <!-- if the genre is rap -->
  <tr>
   <td colspan="2" bgcolor="##000000">
    <font color="##ffffff">Album: #getDisc.disc#</font>
   </td>
  </tr>
  <tr>
   <td bgcolor="##000000">
```

```
   <font color="##ffffff">Song</font>
  </td>
  <td bgcolor="##000000">
   <font color="##ffffff">Artist</font>
  </td>
 </tr>

 <cfoutput>
  <tr>
   <td bgcolor="##000000">
    <font color="##ffffff">#GetDisc.Song#</font>
   </td>
   <td bgcolor="##000000">
    <font color="##ffffff">#GetDisc.Artist#</font>
   </td>
  </tr>
 </cfoutput>
</cfoutput>
```

TVTemplate.cfm:

```
<!---
Description: The default disc TV display template

Entering: N/A
Exiting: N/A

Dependencies: N/A
Expecting: getdisc query

Modification History
Date       Modifier                Modification
*********************************************************
11/26/2001 Jeff Houser, DotComIt   Created
--->

<!-- cfoutput over the query -->
<cfoutput query="GetDisc" group="Disc">
 <!-- if the genre is TV -->
 <tr>
  <td>Album: </td>
  <td>Song</td>
  <td>Artist</td>
 </tr>
```

```
<cfoutput>
 <tr>
  <td>#getDisc.disc#</td>
  <td>#GetDisc.Song#</td>
  <td>#GetDisc.Artist# </td>
 </tr>
 </cfoutput>
</cfoutput>
```

8. Where can custom tags reside?

A. The customtag directory of your ColdFusion server,
C. The current directory, and **D.** Your web site's parent directory

9. What is Parallel Development?

Parallel development is when two separate pieces of an application can be developed at the same time, by two different developers and pieced together later.

10. In what languages can custom tags be written?

CFML Custom tags can be written in CFML. CFX tags can be written in either Java, C++, or Delphi.

Module 11: Handling Errors in ColdFusion

1. When an error occurs, the program is known to _____ an error. The error handle that tries to address the error is said to be _____ the error.

throw; catching

2. What are some common types of errors that you may come across in web development?

A. Database Errors, **B.** Data Input Errors, and **E.** File Errors

3. Generic error handlers are usually defined with the _____ tag in the _____ file

cferror; application.cfm

4. What are the types of generic error handlers you can create?

B. Monitor and **C.** Exception

5. When an error occurs ColdFusion creates a special variable object called
____. This variable is available to the template called by the cferror tag.

error

6. If you think that some code might throw an error, what might you
surround the code in?

If you think that some code might throw an error, you might surround your
code in a cftry block.

7. If a cfcatch error handler is unable to handle a specific error you can use
_____ to throw the error again.

cfrethrow

8. If you are creating a custom tag and need to create your own error type,
what tag would you use?

the cfthrow tag

9. What tag can be used to send an e-mail message?

B. Cfmail

10. Take the example from the text, shown below, and rewrite it so that
the extendedinfo attribute of the cfthrow tag will tell you what variables
are undefined:

```
<cfif not isDefined("firstname") and
      not isdefined("lastname") and
      not isdefined("username") and
      not isdefined("password")>
 <cfthrow type="UndefinedError"
         Message="required variables were undefined"
         errorCode = "711">
</cfif>
```

There are numerous ways to accomplish this. This is one:

```
<cfset Message= "">
<cfset iserror = false>

<cfif not isDefined("firstname")>
 <cfset Message= Message & "No FirstName<BR>">
 <cfset iserror = true>
</cfif>
```

```
<cfif not isDefined("lastname")>
 <cfset Message= Message & "No lastname<BR>">
 <cfset iserror = true>
</cfif>

<cfif not isDefined("username")>
 <cfset Message= Message & "No username<BR>">
 <cfset iserror = true>
</cfif>

<cfif not isDefined("password")>
 <cfset Message= Message & "No password<BR>">
 <cfset iserror = true>
</cfif>

<cfif IsError is true>
 <cfthrow type="UndefinedError"
          Message="#message#"
          errorCode = "711">
</cfif>
```

Module 12: CFScript

1. As with index loops in CFML, for loops in CFScript can also be used to count down. Write a for loop that will execute from 5 to 1.

```
<cfscript>
 for (LoopControl = 5;
      LoopControl GTE 1 ;
      LoopControl = LoopControl - 1) {
  WriteOutput(LoopControl);
 }

</cfscript>
```

2. What is the difference between a while loop and a do-while loop.

The while loop will check the condition before you enter the loop; the do-while loop will only check the condition after the loop is executed. The do-while loop will always execute at least once.

3. Groups of code in CFScript are enclosed between what two characters?

A. {}

A

4. What can you use to output the result of an expression in CFSCript?

The WriteOutput function

5. If you want to stop the execution of a switch-case statement, what command would you use:

C. Break

6. How are local variables created in a User Defined Function?

By using the var keyword. Local variables must be defined at the top of the function before any code.

7. Write some CFScript to create a variable named Chapter12. Give it a default value of "Question 7."

```
<cfscript>
 variables.Chapter12 = "Question 7";
</cfscript>
```

8. You can define the default case in a switch-case statement by using which keyword?

A. Default

9. If you want to check for the existence of a variable, you would use what type of statement?

An if statement

10. CFScript has access to the full range of CFML. True or false?

False. CFScript can access all the functions, but cannot access any CFML tags.

Module 13: Lists

1. The character that separates two elements in a list is called a _____.

delimiter

2. To find the number of values in a list, which function would you use?

B. ListValueCount function

3. To find out the number of elements in a list, what function would you use?

The ListLen function

4. It is possible to have a list with more than one delimiter. True or False?

True

5. How do list functions handle empty elements?

List functions will ignore empty elements.

6. What is the value for an empty list?

A.   ""

7. To insert a character in the middle of a list, what function would you use?

The ListInsertAt function

8. What is the difference between ListValueCount and ListValueCountNoCase?

ListValueCount will perform a case sensitive search, while ListValueCountNoCase will perform a noncase sensitive search.

9. What will be returned by this expression: ListLast(ListFirst("And They All Laughed. At Night. Together","."), " ")

The result of this expression will be: Laughed

Module 14: Complex Variable Types

1. The two types of notations for accessing structure variables are:

A.   Associative Array Notation   and   **C.**   Object Property Notation

2. cfloop will inherently support looping over a structure or list. What type of loop can be used to loop over an array?

An index loop can be used to loop over an array, going from 1 to ArrayLen(MyArray).

3. Arrays are indexed by _____; structures are indexed by _____ .

an integer; a string

4. To get a list of all keys in a structure you would use:

B.   StructKeyList

A

5. What is the difference between the StructCopy and Duplicate functions?

StructCopy will only copy the top level structure variables, but will copy references for complex structure-in-a-structure variables. Duplicate will make a deep copy of a variable.

6. To find out the number of elements in an array, what function would you use?

The ArrayLen function

7. Which of these scopes are stored internally as structures in ColdFusion?

   A. form,
   B. session, and
   E. URL

8. Pick one of the structure scopes from question 7 and write some code to loop over the scope, printing out all the variable names and values.

```
<cfloop collection=#form# item="TempKey">

 <cfoutput>
  #TempKey# #structfind(session,  TempKey)#
 </cfoutput><br>
</cfloop>
```

9. A Query object is actually a structure of _____.

arrays

Appendix B

What Is the
Next Step?

Now that you have read this book, you should have a good understanding of ColdFusion. Since there are too many features and applications of the ColdFusion language to present in a single book, you may be asking yourself "What's the next step?"

You could check out some of the web references listed in Appendix C. Sign up on ColdFusion e-mail lists; you'll find that some of the industry's top ColdFusion developers are happy to answer your questions.

I strongly suggest you check out other ColdFusion offerings published by McGraw-Hill/Osborne: my own book, *Instant ColdFusion* (2001); *Optimizing ColdFusion* by Chris Cortes (2001); and *ColdFusion5: Developer's Guide* by Michael Buffington (2001). The documentation provided by Macromedia is also a good resource to find out more about ColdFusion development. A search of most bookstores' shelves will uncover a wide array of ColdFusion reference and tutorial materials for you to choose from.

The next generation of ColdFusion, code-named Neo, has been in development for quite some time, and is a complete rework of the ColdFusion engine based on Java technology. Neo will provide the ability to distribute compiled ColdFusion applications, native support for double byte languages, broader deployment options, and seamless interoperability with Java Server Pages (JSP) tag libraries. Learning about Java and Object Oriented Design methodologies will serve you well as we move into the next version of ColdFusion.

Good luck! Drop me an e-mail to let me know how this book helped you become a top notch ColdFusion developer: jeff@instantcoldfusion.com.

Appendix C
Web References

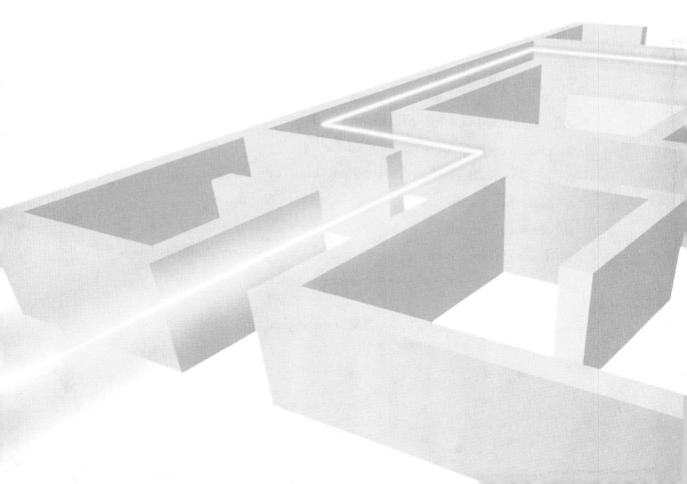

ColdFusion Reference Sites

- **www.macromedia.com**   Macromedia is the company that owns and develops ColdFusion

- **www.allaire.com**   Allaire, the company that originally built ColdFusion, has since merged with Macromedia

- **www.instantcoldfusion.com**   The web site for this book

- **www.optimizingcoldfusion.com**   The web site for *Optimizing ColdFusion* by Chris Cortes (McGraw-Hill/Osborne, 2001)

- **www.thenetprofits.co.uk/coldfusion/faq/**   Frequently Asked Questions on ColdFusion

- **www.sys-con.com/coldfusion/**   ColdFusion Developer's Journal home page

- **www.cfcomet.com**   Using ColdFusion and COM

- **www.cflib.org**   The ColdFusion Common Function library project; a source for user-defined functions

- **www.defusion.com**   Articles on ColdFusion

- **cfhub.com**   ColdFusion information

- **www.teratech.com/coldcuts**   ColdFusion code samples

- **www.fusioncube.net**   Information site on ColdFusion

- **www.ctcfug.com**   The author's ColdFusion User Group web site

- **www.cfnewbie.com**   Resources for developers new to ColdFusion

- **www.cfbughunt.org**   A site dedicated to identifying bugs in ColdFusion 5

- **livedocs.macromedia.com/cf50docs/dochome.jsp**   ColdFusion 5 documentation on-line

ColdFusion Development Methodologies

- **www.fuesbox.org** Fusebox is the most widely accepted development methodology

- **www.cfobjects.comcf** Objects is a framework for developing Applications in ColdFusion, with a hint of object oriented programming

- **www.black-box.org** Site for Black Box, a ColdFusion development methodology

- **www.switch-box.org** Site for Switch Box, a ColdFusion development methodology

- **www.smart-objects.com** Another methodology aligning ColdFusion and Object Oriented Development

- **www.iiframework.com** Framework for developing ColdFusion applications

ColdFusion Hosting

- **cf-developer.net** Free ColdFusion hosting

- **www.cfm-resources.com** More free ColdFusion hosting

Mailing Lists and Publications

- **www.houseoffusion.com** The best source for ColdFusion e-mail discussion lists

- **www.sys-con.com/coldfusion/list.cfm** The ColdFusion Developer's Journal Mailing List

C

- **www.sys-con.com/coldfusion**   The ColdFusion Developer's Journal
- **www.tallylist.com**   Mailing list archives
- **www.bromby.com/cfwireless**   Mailing list for developing wireless applications with ColdFusion
- **www.fusionauthority.com**   Fusion Authority, a weekly ColdFusion zine
- **www.cfadvisor.com/api-shl/engine.cfm**   CF Advisor

Training and Certification

- **www.vue.com**   Home page for the company that administers Macromedia Certification tests
- **cfcertification.com**   Online study guides for Macromedia certification
- **www.centrasoft.com**   Home of CF_Buster, a program designed to help in preparing for ColdFusion certification
- **www.brainbench.com**   Independent third party certification company
- **www.Brainbuzz.com**   Independent third part certification company
- **www.ecertifications.com**   Another third part certification company
- **www.smartplanet.com**   Online courses in a variety of topics

Other Technologies

- **www.flashcfm.com**   Developing with Flash and ColdFusion
- **www.openwddx.org**   The WDDX home page
- **www.sswug.org**   SQL Server Worldwide User's Group
- **www.mssqlserver.com**   SQL Server Resource
- **www.swynk.com**   Biggest resource for Microsoft BackOffice products, such as SQL Server, Exchange, IIS, and Windows 2000

- **www.sqlmag.com** SQL Server Magazine home page
- **www.apache.org** Free web server

Other References

- **www.cf-community.com** Place for ColdFusion developers to get away from it all
- **www.tagservlet.com** Java-based interpreter for ColdFusion Markup Language
- **www.irt.org** Information on a number of languages, including ColdFusion
- **forta.com** Home page for ColdFusion's technical evangelists
- **www.cfconf.org** Iinformation site on ColdFusion Conferences
- **hshelp.com** Reference site for VTML, the customizing language of HomeSite and ColdFusion Studio
- **w3.org** The World Wide Web Consortium

Index